Armin Blass · Wolf Friederich

Englischer Wortschatz

IN SACHGRUPPEN

Max Hueber Verlag

Das Werk und seine Teile sind urheberrechtlich geschützt. Jede Verwertung in anderen als den gesetzlich zugelassenen Fällen bedarf deshalb der vorherigen schriftlichen Einwilligung des Verlages.

4.	3.	2.		Die letzten Ziffern bezeichnen
1998	97	96	95	94	Zahl und Jahr des Druckes.

Alle Drucke dieser Auflage können, da unverändert, nebeneinander benutzt werden.
12. Auflage 1990
© 1956 Max Hueber Verlag, D-85737 Ismaning
Satz: Hartmann + Heenemann KG, Berlin
Druck: Ludwig Auer GmbH, Donauwörth
Printed in Germany
ISBN 3-19-002077-9

Vorwort zur ersten Auflage

Aus dem ungeheuren, auch für den Kundigen kaum übersehbaren Wortschatz des Englischen sind hier etwa 10 000 Wörter und Ausdrücke als breite Grundlage ausgewählt worden. Die Neubildungen der jüngsten Vergangenheit und der Gegenwart wurden ebenso wie der amerikanische Sprachgebrauch gebührend berücksichtigt. So kann dieser systematische Wortschatz ein Hilfsmittel sein zum Lernen, Wiederholen und Nachschlagen. Dem Lernenden kann es viel zeitraubendes Sammeln und Aufzeichnen ersparen; aber auch dem Lehrenden dürfte es erwünscht sein.

Neben dem Hauptwort, das im Vordergrund steht, wurde auch dem Zeitwort und dem Eigenschaftswort ein breiter Raum gewährt. Die übrigen Wortarten (samt Eigennamen) blieben im wesentlichen unberücksichtigt.

Die Auswahl erfolgte nach dem Gesichtspunkt der Häufigkeit und Wichtigkeit; dabei wurde kein enger Maßstab angelegt. Die Wörter erscheinen mindestens in ihrer wichtigsten Bedeutung. Die von Michael West (A General Service List of English Words, 1953) gebrachten Wörter wurden, soweit sie den obengenannten Wortarten angehören, fast sämtlich aufgenommen. Die vorliegende Auswahl, in der auch der Wortschatz des Progressive English Dictionary (ed. by A. S. Hornby and E. C. Parnwell, London 1952) größtenteils wiederzufinden ist, geht jedoch beträchtlich über die General Service List hinaus; denn jedes Kapitel soll ja eine nicht zu schmale Grundlage für den Wortschatz des betreffenden Stoffgebietes darstellen.

Die Einreihung der Wörter war ebenso wie die Abgrenzung der einzelnen Gruppen nicht immer leicht; überdies wurden um der Raumersparnis willen Wiederholungen auf ein Mindestmaß beschränkt. Der Benutzer wird des öfteren Wörter, die er in einer Abteilung vermißt, in einer ähnlichen finden; öfters sind entsprechende Hinweise gegeben.

Natürlich kann und soll diese nach Sachgruppen geordnete Auswahl das umfassende alphabetische Wörterbuch nicht ersetzen. Daher — und weil diese Auswahl sich nicht an Anfänger im engeren Sinn wendet – konnte auf die durchgehende Angabe der Aussprache verzichtet werden. Der Anhang enthält jedoch die Aussprachebezeichnung (einschließlich der amerikanischen Abweichungen) von rund 430 weniger häufigen oder oft falsch ausgesprochenen Wörtern; auf sie ist im Text durch (*) hingewiesen.

Eine notwendige Ergänzung ist das Auswahlverzeichnis sinnverwandter englischer Wörter (Synonyme) (rund 650 Wörter in 200 Gruppen) mit reichem Beispielmaterial (aus dem Concise Oxford Dictionary, Reum u. a.); im Hauptteil — in den übrigens auch manches Synonymische hineingearbeitet wurde — ist fortwährend darauf verwiesen.

Armin Blass

Vorwort zur fünften Auflage

In der gründlich revidierten und ergänzten fünften Auflage wurde verschiedenen Wünschen der zahlreichen Benutzer Rechnung getragen. Einmal sind die deutschen und englischen Wörter jetzt in Spalten getrennt, wodurch sich eine wesentlich größere Übersichtlichkeit und Einprägsamkeit des Wortschatzes ergibt. Auf ein ruhiges Druckbild wurde hierbei besonders Wert gelegt. Die schon in die erste Auflage eingearbeiteten bewährten Grundsätze der Worthäufigkeit und Wichtigkeit blieben weiterhin maßgebend; darüber hinaus wurde eine weitgehende Differenzierung der zahlreichen Synonyma des Englischen angestrebt, wobei der Synonymenanhang jetzt in den Hauptteil des Buches eingearbeitet wurde. Die Hinweise zum Gebrauch der Wörter, vor allem zur Rektion, wurden stark vermehrt. Sehr viel zahlreicher sind jetzt auch die Hinweise zur Aussprache. Da das Einschalten der Lautschrift die Les- und Lernbarkeit des Stoffes beeinträchtigt und da die Angabe der Lautschrift für einzelne Wortteile wenig zweckdienlich erschien, wurde die Angabe der Aussprache weiterhin in einem Anhang belassen, auf den durch Sternchen verwiesen wird. Ein weiterer neuer Anhang enthält alle unregelmäßigen Plurale der Substantive, die im Englischen erfahrungsgemäß Schwierigkeiten bieten.
Auf die Unterscheidung des britischen und des amerikanischen Englisch wurde bei Wortwahl, Rechtschreibung und Aussprache große Sorgfalt verwendet; neueste Quellen bedingten nicht wenige Änderungen und Ergänzungen. Hierbei ist zu beachten, daß die Hinweise BE und US jeweils nur für das unmittelbar folgende Wort gelten und auch nur bedeuten, daß das betreffende Wort im britischen (oder amerikanischen) Bereich Gültigkeit hat, *nicht* aber daß es dort allein verwendet oder bevorzugt wird. Solche Ausschließlichkeit ist nur gegeben, wenn bei zwei Wörtern das eine mit BE, das andere mit US gekennzeichnet ist.

Wolf Friederich

Vorwort zur elften Auflage

In dieser revidierten und ergänzten Auflage wurden einige überholte Ausdrücke getilgt, eine größere Zahl neuer Wörter aufgenommen und in nicht wenigen Fällen die Angaben über britisches und amerikanisches Englisch geändert, so daß das Buch jetzt wieder auf dem neuesten Stand ist. An den bewährten Prinzipien des Buches wurde nichts geändert.
Für Verbesserungen und Ergänzungen bin ich stets dankbar.

Wolf Friederich

Vorwort zur zwölften Auflage

Für diese Auflage wurde der gesamte Wortschatz gründlich überprüft, Angaben zum britischen und amerikanischen Wortgebrauch korrigiert, soweit erforderlich, und eine ganze Reihe von Zusätzen gemacht, insbesondere in den Bereichen Computer und Umwelt. Es wurden auch nicht wenige Streichungen vorgenommen bei Ausdrücken, die sich als für die Praxis wenig relevant erwiesen haben. Die damit gegebene Straffung dürfte allen Lernenden willkommen sein.

Wolf Friederich

Inhalt

1.	**Der Mensch**	7
1.1.	Allgemeines	7
1.2.	Der Körper	7
1.3.	Sinnestätigkeiten und -eindrücke	9
1.4.	Geist und Seele	10
1.5.	Leben und Tod	10
2.	**Die Vielgestaltigkeit des menschlichen Lebens**	11
3.	**Äußerungen des menschlichen Lebens**	19
3.1.	Tätigkeit allgemeiner Art und Zustand	19
3.2.	Fühlen und Ausdruck der Gefühle	25
3.3.	Denken	26
3.4.	Willensäußerung	27
3.5.	Sprechen, mitteilen	28
3.6.	Sprache	29
4.	**Menschliche Eigenschaften, Gefühle und Fähigkeiten**	30
4.1.	Substantive	30
4.2.	Adjektive	35
5.	**Gesundheit und Krankheit**	41
6.	**Nahrung**	45
7.	**Kleidung**	48
8.	**Haus und Wohnung**	51
8.1.	Haus	51
8.2.	Hausrat	53
9.	**Name, Familie, Verwandtschaft**	56
10.	**Berufsleben**	57
10.1.	Allgemeines	57
10.2.	Berufe und Gewerbe	58
11.	**Wirtschaftsleben**	60
11.1.	Handwerk und Industrie	60
11.2.	Handel	61
11.3.	Geldwesen	65
12.	**Naturwissenschaft und Technik, Elektrizität**	66
13.	**Verkehr**	68
13.1.	Eisenbahn	68
13.2.	Kraftfahrzeug	69
13.3.	Schiffahrt	71
13.4.	Flugwesen	73
14.	**Nachrichtenwesen**	73
14.1.	Zeitung	73
14.2.	Post- und Fernmeldewesen	74
15.	**Die Stadt**	76
16.	**Dorf und Landwirtschaft**	78
17.	**Erholung, Spiel, Sport**	79
18.	**Bildung, Wissenschaft und Kunst**	84
18.1.	Schule	84
18.2.	Wissenschaft	87
18.3.	Buch	89
18.4.	Literatur	90
18.5.	Bildende Künste, Musik	91

18.6.	Theater, Film, Photographie	93
18.7.	Rundfunk, Fernsehen	94
19.	Der Staat (Verwaltung, Regierung, Politik)	95
20.	Die Gemeinde	99
21.	**Rechtswesen**	99
22.	**Heer, Flotte, Luftwaffe; Krieg**	102
23.	**Weltanschauung, Religion, Kirche**	105
24.	**Weltall und Erde**	107
25.	**Wetter und Klima**	110
26.	**Tiere und Pflanzen**	111
26.1.	Tiere	111
26.2.	Pflanzen	115
27.	**Die anorganische Natur**	117
28.	**Raum und Form; Beschaffenheit**	118
29.	**Mengenangaben und Maße**	120
30.	**Die Zeit**	122

Anhang

1.	Aussprache	124
2.	Unregelmäßige Plurale	128
Schlußbemerkung		130
Literaturangaben		132

Verzeichnis der Abkürzungen

BE = British English
US = American English

{ Beide Hinweise gelten nur für das jeweils folgende Wort und bedeuten, daß das betreffende Wort jeweils im anderen Land nicht üblich ist.

a. = auch
bes. = besonders
coll. = colloquial, umgangssprachlich
e-m, e-n = einem, einen
e-r, e-s = einer, eines
fig. = figürlich
j-m, j-n = jemandem, jemanden
Kap. = Kapitel
mst. = meistens
o.s. = oneself
s-o = someone
s-th = something
* = siehe Anhang „Aussprache", Seite 124
+ = siehe Anhang „Unregelmäßige Plurale", Seite 128

Abweichungen der amerikanischen Rechtschreibung sind angegeben, außer: -or für -our, -er für -re, -l- für -ll- (z. B. color, theater, traveling) und der Schreibung ohne Bindestrich (z. B. blood vessel).

1. Der Mensch

1.1. Allgemeines

Lebewesen	living being
Mensch	man, human being
Menschheit	mankind*, humanity, the human race
Rasse	race
Volk	people, race
Volksstamm	tribe
Einzelwesen, Individuum	individual
Person	person
persönlich	personal
Leute	people
Geschlecht	sex
männlich	male
weiblich	female
Mann	man+
Frau	woman+

1.2. Der Körper

Körper	body
Körperbau	physique*
Körperhaltung	carriage, posture
Gestalt	figure
äußere Erscheinung, Äußeres	outward appearance
Riese	giant*
Zwerg	dwarf
Ader	vein
Schlagader	artery
Arm	arm (upper arm; forearm)
Auge	eye
Augenbraue	eyebrow
Augenlid	eyelid
Augenwimper	eyelash
Backe, Wange	cheek
Backenknochen	cheek-bone
Backenzahn	back tooth, molar
Bart	beard
Backenbart	whiskers
Schnurrbart	moustache* (US mustache)
Becken	pelvis+
Bein	leg
Oberschenkel	thigh
Unterschenkel	lower leg
Blinddarm	blind gut, caecum*+, *mst.* appendix
Blut	blood
Blutgefäß	(blood-)vessel
Blutkreislauf	circulation (of the blood)
Puls	pulse
Brust	chest, *(weibl.)* breast
Brustbein	breast-bone
Brustkorb	chest, thorax+
Darm	bowels, intestines*
Drüse	gland
Magendrüse	gastric gland
Schilddrüse	thyroid* gland
Ellbogen	elbow
Finger	finger
Fingerspitze	finger-tip
Daumen	thumb
Zeigefinger	forefinger, index+ finger
Mittelfinger	middle finger
Ringfinger	ring-finger, fourth finger
kleiner Finger	little finger
Fleisch	flesh
Fuß	foot
Fußgelenk	ankle
Fußknöchel	ankle-bone
Ferse	heel
Sohle	sole
Galle	bile
Gallenblase	gall-bladder
Gaumen	palate*
Gehirn	brain, *(bes. fig.)* brains
Gelenk	joint
Gesicht	face
Gesichtsfarbe, Teint	complexion
frisch	fresh
rosig	rosy
bleich	pale
Gesichtszug	feature

Gesichtsausdruck, Miene	(facial) expression, air (an innocent ~, an ~ of superiority), countenance	**Lunge**	lung
		Atmung	respiration
		Atem(zug)	breath
		atmen	to breathe (in, out)
eine ernste Miene bewahren	to keep a straight face, to keep one's countenance	keuchen	to pant, to gasp
		Magen	stomach*
		Mandeln	tonsils
Gewebe	tissue*	**Milz**	spleen
Glieder	limbs	**Mund**	mouth
Haar(e)	hair	**Muskel**	muscle*
blond	fair	**Nabel**	navel*
dunkel	dark	**Nagel**	nail
Locke	curl	**Nase**	nose
Strähne	lock	Nasenloch	nostril
Zopf	plait*	Nebenhöhle	sinus+
Hals	neck; throat *(vgl. Kehle)*	**Nerv**	nerve
		Nervensystem	nervous system
Hand	hand	**Niere**	kidney
Handfläche	palm (of the hand)	**Ohr**	ear
Handgelenk	wrist	Ohrläppchen	lobe of the ear
Faust	fist	Ohrmuschel	auricle, external ear
Haut	skin	**Rippe**	rib
Herz	heart	**Rücken**	back
Herzschlag	heart-beat	Rückgrat, Wirbelsäule	vertebral column, spine, *(bes. fig.)* backbone
Hirn	brain		
Hirnschale	skull, cranium		
Hüfte	hip		
Hüftgelenk	hip joint	Rückenmark	spinal cord
Kehle	throat	**Rumpf**	trunk
Kehlkopf	larynx+	**Schädel**	skull
Kiefer	jaw (upper ~, lower ~)	**Schienbein**	shinbone, tibia+
		Schläfe	temple
Kinn	chin	**Schulter**	shoulder
Knie	knee	Schulterblatt	shoulder-blade
Kniegelenk	knee-joint	**Sehne**	sinew, tendon
Knöchel (Finger ~)	knuckle	**Skelett**	skeleton
Knochen	bone	**Speiseröhre**	gullet, oesophagus*+ (US eso-)
Mark	marrow		
Kopf	head	**Stimmbänder**	vocal cords*
Kopfhaut	scalp	Stimme	voice
Leber	liver	**Stirn**	forehead*
Leiste	groin	Stirnhöhle	sinus+
Lippe	lip (upper ~, lower ~)	**Taille**	waist
		Unterleib	abdomen*
Luftröhre	windpipe, trachea*+	Bauch	belly

8

Wade	calf+	**Farbe**	colour
Zahn	tooth+	Farbton	hue
Zahnfleisch	gums	heller Farbton	tint
Zehe	toe (big *or* great ~, little ~)	dunkler Farbton	shade
		blau	blue (dark ~, light ~, a delicate ~)
auf den Zehenspitzen	on tiptoe	rot	red
Zunge	tongue	karmesinrot	crimson
groß, hochgewachsen	tall (How tall are you? What's your height?)	violettrot, purpurrot	purple
		weiß	white
		reines Weiß	pure white
klein (v. Wuchs)	short, small	heitere, lebhafte Farben	gay colours
beleibt	corpulent, stout	düster	gloomy
Beleibtheit	corpulence	matt, glanzlos	dull
rundlich, vollschlank	plump (she is getting rather ~)	trüb, glanzlos	dim
		hell, leuchtend	bright
hager	gaunt, skinny	bunt	(multi)coloured, (of birds, insects) variegated
mager	lean, thin, meagre		
schlank	slender, slim		
stämmig	sturdy	einfarbig, uni	of one colour, one-coloured, (dress) plain

1.3. Sinnestätigkeiten und -eindrücke

		Licht	light
Sinn	sense	(auf)blitzen	to flash
Sinnesorgan	sense-organ	funkeln	to sparkle
scharf	acute, keen	glühen	to glow
schwach	blunt, dull	leuchten	to gleam
Sehvermögen	(eye-)sight, vision	schimmern	to shimmer
sehen	to see	scheinen, leuchten, glänzen	to shine
sichtbar	visible		
bemerken, wahrnehmen	to notice, to observe, to perceive	strahlen	to beam
		blendend	dazzling (~ sunshine)
(an-)schauen	to look (at)		
anstarren	to stare at, to gaze at	grell leuchtend, blendend (hell)	glaring (the ~ sun)
beobachten	to watch, to observe		
betrachten	to look at	durchsichtig	transparent
schwache (scharfe) Augen	weak (sharp) eyes	undurchsichtig	opaque*
		Gehör	hearing
Blick	look (a kind ~; a keen ~)	hören	to hear
		zuhören	to listen
durchdringender Blick	a penetrating look	Geräusch	noise
		Laut, Klang	sound
flüchtiger Blick	glance	Schallwellen	sound waves
durchbohrend	piercing	(er)tönen, klingen	to sound (it ~s very strange)
verständnisvoll	knowing		
e-n flüchtigen Blick von etw. erhaschen	to catch a glimpse of s-th	die Glocke ertönte	the bell rang
		Lärm	noise, din
		betäubend	deafening

geräuschvoll, lärmend	noisy (crowd, street)
Getöse	roar
Widerhall, Echo	echo+
Stille, Schweigen	silence (deep ~, to keep ~)
schweigsam, still	silent
Geruch(ssinn)	smell
riechen	to smell
Geruch	smell, odour
Geschmack(ssinn)	taste
kosten, versuchen, schmecken	to taste
lecken	to lick
süß	sweet
bitter	bitter
sauer	sour
Tastsinn	touch
berühren	to touch
fühlen	to feel
tasten(d suchen) nach	to grope for

1.4. Geist und Seele

Charakter, Wesen(sart)	character
stark	strong
schwach	weak
labil	unstable
Geist	mind; spirit (the ~ is willing, but the flesh is weak); genius
~ und Materie	mind and matter
Geistes-, Gemütsverfassung	frame of mind
geistig	mental (faculties); spiritual (forces)
Gedächtnis	memory (to slip one's ~)
Gefühl	feeling, sentiment, emotion (love, joy and fear are ~ s)
~sbewegung, Rührung	emotion
Gemüt	mind; feeling; heart
Gewissen	conscience
reines (schlechtes) Gewissen	clear (guilty) conscience
Neigung	inclination (for s-th)
Phantasie, Einbildungskraft	imagination (creative ~); fancy
Seele	soul
Stimmung	mood, frame of mind, temper, humour (good ~, bad ~, ill ~)
Temperament, Gemüt(sart)	temper, temperament, disposition
ein heiteres (sanftes) Gemüt	a serene, cheerful (gentle) temper
Vernunft	reason
vernunftgemäß	reasonable; rational
Verstand, Denkfähigkeit	intelligence, intellect; brains; faculty of thought
Intelligenzprüfung	intelligence test
gesunder Menschenverstand	common sense
Urteil(svermögen)	judgment
Wille	will
fest	firm
stark	strong
schwach	feeble

1.5. Leben und Tod

Leben	life
leben	to live
Geburt	birth
Kindheit	childhood
Jugend	youth
junger Mann	young man, a youth (of 18)
aufwachsen	to grow up
auf dem Höhepunkt des Lebens stehen	to be in the prime of life
altern	to grow old
Greis	old man
ein runzliges Gesicht	a wrinkled face
Greisenalter	old age
Tod	death
freiwillig	voluntary
sterben	to die, to pass away
sterblich	mortal

tot	dead
Selbstmord begehen	to commit suicide*
der (die) Verstorbene	the deceased
mein verstorbener Vater	my late father
Leiche	corpse
Sarg	coffin
Begräbnis	burial*, funeral
bestatten	to bury*
Friedhof	graveyard, cemetery
Grab	grave, tomb*
Grabstein	gravestone, tombstone
Inschrift	inscription
Kranz	wreath+
Einäscherung	cremation
Urne	urn
trauern (um)	to mourn (for)

2. Die Vielgestaltigkeit des menschlichen Lebens

das Wesen e-r Sache	essence; character
Kern	gist*, core
Hauptsache	main thing
wesentlich	essential (features, an ~ characteristic)
Charakter	character
charakteristisch, kennzeichnend (für)	characteristic (of)
Ursache	cause
Grund	cause
Vernunftgrund	reason
Beweggrund	motive
Wirkung	effect
wirkungsvoll, wirksam	effective (measures); efficacious* (cure)
Ausgang	conclusion, outcome
Ergebnis	result
dürftig	poor
befriedigend	satisfactory
glänzend	brilliant
sich ergeben aus, entstehen aus, herrühren von	to result from
Folge	consequence
Zustand	state, condition
Lage	situation
mißlich, peinlich	awkward
ernst	serious
ausweg-, hoffnungslos	hopeless
Gelegenheit, Anlaß	occasion
günstige Gelegenheit	opportunity
gelegentlich	occasional (visits)
Umstand	circumstance
Einfluß	influence
heilsam, wohltätig	beneficial, salutary
verderblich	pernicious
beeinflussen	to influence, (negativ) to affect (strong coffee ~s the heart)
Vergleich	comparison
Verhältnis, Beziehung	relation (the ~ of height to weight)
verhältnismäßig	comparatively (late)
in jeder Beziehung (Hinsicht)	in all respects (perfect in ~ ~)
Ähnlichkeit	resemblance
auffallend	striking
ähnlich	similar (~ methods; in ~ cases; on a ~ occasion)
entsprechend	corresponding (to) (find the ~ expression in German)
Gleichheit	equality*
gleich	equal
gleichwertig	equivalent
er ist ihr nicht gewachsen	he is no match for her
Unterschied	difference; distinction (to make exact ~s between all these words)
verschieden	different
mannigfach	various, diverse
alle Arten von...	all kinds (or sorts) of...
Mannigfaltigkeit	variety
Nachahmung	imitation
Einförmigkeit	uniformity
eintönig	monotonous*

Gegensatz	contrast	**Kultur, Gesittung, Zivilisation**	civilization
merkwürdig	curious, strange		
das Gegenteil zu...	the contrary, the opposite of...	Kulturgeschichte	history of civilization
Regel	rule	geistige, künstler. Kultur, Bildung	culture (Greek ~ ; a man of high ~)
Beispiel	example		
regelmäßig	regular	Verfeinerung	refinement
Ausnahme	exception (the ~ proves the rule)	zivilisieren	to civilize
		Kulturvolk	civilized nation
Wert	value	zurückgebliebene, unterentwickelte Völker	backward, underdeveloped nations
innerer Wert	worth		
wertvoll	valuable		
es ist (nicht) der Mühe wert	it is (not) worth the trouble	ein Wilder	a savage
		Einzelwesen und Gemeinschaft	the individual and the community
wertlos	worthless		
Entwicklung	development; evolution (the ~ of a plant from a seed)	Gesellschaft	society
		gesellschaftlich, sozial	social (position, rank, life, evils, problems)
Entwicklungsabschnitt, Stadium	stage (the final ~)		
		gemeinsam	common (interests, views; it's ~ to all; to make ~ cause with s-o)
Ursprung	origin		
ursprünglich	original*		
Anfang	beginning		
Wechsel, Veränderung	change	öffentlich	public (meeting, opinion)
		privat, persönlich	private (life, affairs)
allmählich	gradual	**Vereinigung, Verbindung**	
plötzlich	sudden		
Verbesserung	improvement	(v. Personen od. Dingen)	union; combination
Bewegung	motion		
einzelne ~	movement		
Wachstum	growth	Einheit (innere ~), Einigkeit	unity (to give ~ to a work of art; national ~, to live together in ~)
Fortschritt(e)	progress (slow, rapid, astonishing ~)		
vorrücken, fortschreiten	to advance	Ordnung	order
		stabil, dauerhaft	stable
Unterbrechung	interruption	**Trennung**	separation
Aufschub, Verzögerung	delay	Uneinigkeit, Zwietracht	disharmony, discord
kritischer (entscheidender) Augenblick	crucial moment	Unordnung, Verwirrung, Durcheinander	disorder, confusion
Wendepunkt	turning-point		
Niedergang, Verfall	decline, decay	**Schicksal**	fate *(negativ)*, destiny *(positiv); (Zufall)* lot, *(Katastrophe)* doom
verfallen	to decay		
Untergang	fall, ruin		
Zerstörung	destruction		
Ende	end	Zufall	chance, accident
endlos	endless	ein reiner Zufall	a mere chance
		verhängnisvoll	fatal

unvermeidlich, unausweichlich	unavoidable, inevitable
Notwendigkeit	necessity, need (there was no ~ for him to do so)
notwendigenfalls	in case of need
notwendig	necessary
die Lebensbedürfnisse	the necessities of life
unentbehrlich	indispensable
Glück	fortune, good luck
glücklich	lucky, fortunate
Erfolg	success
vollständig	complete, total
beispiellos	unprecedented
offensichtlich	evident, obvious, apparent
unbestreitbar	indisputable
unleugbar	undeniable
zweifelhaft	doubtful
d. Geheimnis des Erfolgs	the secret of success
erfolgreich	successful
Gewinn	gain, profit
Gunst	favour
günstig	favourable
passend, geeignet	fit (for), suitable, appropriate*
e-e glänzende Laufbahn	a brilliant career
Höhepunkt, Gipfel	climax
Unglück	misfortune, bad luck, disaster
unglücklich	unfortunate, unlucky
Elend	misery
elend	miserable
armselig, erbärmlich	wretched*
Un(glücks)fall	accident
tödlich	fatal
Mißerfolg, Fehlschlag	failure
die Opfer e-r Katastrophe	the victims of a disaster (catastrophe*)
Not(lage), Bedrängnis	distress
plötzlich auftauchender Notfall	emergency
im Notfall	in case of emergency
Krise	crisis+
Last, Bürde	burden
Zeitverschwendung	waste of time
Verdruß, Unannehmlichkeit, Ärger	trouble, annoyance, worry (I had much tr., a lot of w.)
ärgern	to annoy, to worry; to make angry, to anger
wie ärgerlich (unangenehm)!	what a nuisance!
mach dir keine Sorge, es wird schon recht werden	don't worry, it'll be all right
lästig	troublesome (a ~ visitor)
ein Grund zur Klage	a cause of complaint
ein Opfer bringen	to make a sacrifice
ein furchtbarer Schreck	a terrible shock
Verlust	loss
unbedeutend	insignificant
geringfügig	slight
schwer	heavy
beklagenswert	deplorable
schmerzlich	painful
unersetzlich	irreparable*
Trost	consolation, comfort
Erleichterung	relief
erleichtern	to relieve (I felt much ~ d), to ease (a burden, one's mind)
Nutzen, Vorteil	profit, benefit, advantage
Verwendbarkeit	use
es nützt nichts	it is (of) no use
Wohltat	blessing, boon
nützlich	useful, profitable
angenehm	agreeable, pleasant
unschädlich	harmless
Schaden	damage
Unheil anrichten	to do damage
schädlich	harmful, injurious
nutzlos	useless, unprofitable, futile
unangenehm	disagreeable, unpleasant

Nachteil	disadvantage, drawback (bad health is a great ~ in life)	es fehlt ihm an Mut	he lacks courage
		Fehler	mistake, *(grober)* blunder, *(leichter)* slip; error; *(Schuld)* fault; defect
Lebenshaltung	standard of living		
die Lebenshaltungskosten sind sehr hoch	the cost of living is very high	eine Lücke ausfüllen	to fill a gap
Reichtum	wealth, riches	**Freundschaft**	friendship (*enge* close)
Reichtum anhäufen	to heap up, accumulate* wealth	das Band der Freundschaft	the bond of friendship
reich	rich, wealthy	Freund	friend
wohlhabend	well-off, well-to-do	teuer, lieb	dear
in Wohlstand leben	to live in prosperity	treu	faithful
sich etwas leisten, die Mittel haben zu etwas	to afford s-th (I can't afford a car)	freundschaftliche Beziehungen, fr. Verkehr	friendly relations, ~ intercourse
Eigentum	property	freundlicher Gruß	friendly greeting
eigen	own (this house is my ~ ; it was her ~ idea; with my ~ eyes)	vertraut	intimate (an ~ friend of mine)
		vertraut mit	familiar with
Vermögen	fortune	Vertrautheit	intimacy*
Überfluß	abundance	zusammenhalten	to stick together
Luxus	luxury	Kamerad	comrade*
Luxusartikel	luxuries	Bekanntschaft, Bekannte(r)	(an) acquaintance
es ist reine Verschwendung	it is sheer waste	e-e zufällige, flüchtige Bekanntschaft	a casual* acquaintance
Vorrat	supply (a good ~ of coal), store	ich möchte ihn kennenlernen	I should like to meet him, to make his acquaintance
Schatz	treasure		
Wertsachen	valuables	besuchen	to (pay a) visit; *(kurz)* to go (*or* come) to see, to call on s-o; to attend (a school)
sein kostbarster Besitz	his most precious possession		
Armut	poverty		
arm	poor, penniless	Besuch	visit
e-e bescheidene Lebensweise	a modest way of life	Geschenk	present (a birthday ~), gift
Elend	misery, distress	ein prachtvolles Geschenk	a splendid (*or* gorgeous) gift
e. elendes Leben	a miserable life	Schenkung	donation
Not leiden	to suffer want	Andenken	souvenir*, *(an j-n)* keepsake from s-o
Mangel an etw., Knappheit	shortage (of food; paper ~)		
knapp	scarce* (food was very ~)	**Hilfe**	help
		erste Hilfe	first aid
Bettler	beggar	Beistand	assistance
Mangel(haftigkeit), Unzulänglichkeit	deficiency, shortcoming	Unterstützung	support
		gegenseitig	mutual
aus Mangel an (Zeit, Geld usw.)	for want (*or* lack) of (time, money, etc.)	gemeinsames Handeln	joint action

wertvolle (hervorragende) Dienste	valuable (eminent) services	Gefahr laufen zu verlieren	to be in danger (or to run the risk) of losing
Mit-, Zusammenarbeit	collaboration, cooperation	der Gefahr aussetzen	to expose to danger
Schutz	protection	e-r Gefahr ins Auge sehen	to face a danger
seine Zuflucht nehmen zu	to have recourse (or to resort) to	auf eigene Gefahr	at one's own risk
Hilfsquellen	resources	trotzen, Trotz bieten	to brave, to defy (death, the storm, public opinion)
Erlaubnis	permission		
Ermutigung	encouragement		
ermutigen	to encourage	Wagnis, gewagtes Unternehmen	venture, risky undertaking, hazardous enterprise
Rat(schläge)	advice		
Angebot	offer		
verlockend	tempting	Abenteuer	adventure
unannehmbar	unacceptable	mit knapper Not davonkommen	to have a narrow escape
annehmen	to accept		
ablehnen	to decline, to reject	in Sicherheit sein	to be in safety
vielen Dank!	many thanks!, thanks a lot!	sicher	safe, (geborgen) secure

Feindschaft enmity
aggressive ~ hostility
Feind enemy
Gegner opponent, (aktiv) adversary

		Schwierigkeit	difficulty
		entstehen	to arise
		stoßen auf	to meet with
		meistern überwinden	to master to overcome, to surmount, to get over
Widerstand, Gegnerschaft	resistance, opposition		
Rivale, Nebenbuhler	rival	schwierig	hard, difficult
		heikel	delicate (affair, subject)
Rivalität	rivalry		
Haß	hatred, hate	leicht	easy; simple; (ganz mühelos) facile*
Streit	quarrel		
erbittert	fierce	einfach	simple (it's really quite ~)
schlichten	to settle		
Auseinandersetzung	dispute, argument	schlicht, allen verständlich	plain (~ food; a book for the ~ man; he said it in a few ~ words)
Drohung	threat		
Bluff	bluff		
Widerspruch	contradiction	Hindernis	obstacle
e-e glatte Weigerung (Absage)	a flat refusal	auf Hindernisse stoßen	to run into obstacles (or difficulties)
Rache	revenge, vengeance (to take r., v. on s-o for s-th)	beseitigen	to remove
		Fall(grub)e	pitfall (to avoid a ~), trap (to set a ~ for s-o; he walked straight into the ~)
Versöhnung	reconciliation*		
versöhnen	to reconcile*		
Gefahr	danger	**Tätigkeit**	activity
drohende ~	peril	Beschäftigung	occupation
große ~	jeopardy*; risk	Arbeit	work; job; (anstrengend) labour, toil
gefährlich	dangerous, perilous, jeopardous; risky	ermüdend	tiring

er ist gerade beschäftigt, hat zu tun	he is busy	**Benehmen, Verhalten**	behaviour, *(bewußt)* conduct, *(anerzogenes)* deportment, *(gesellschaftlich)* manners
Bemühung, Anstrengung	effort		
starke ~	exertion	Sitte, Brauch	custom, usage
heftig	violent	(pers.) Gewohnheit	habit
vergeblich	vain, futile	gewöhnt an	accustomed to, used to (doing) s-th
Versuch	attempt		
gelingen	to succeed	**Ehre**	honour
mißlingen, scheitern	to fail	Ruf (guter, schlechter ~, in dem man steht)	reputation, repute
große (od. viel) Mühe	great pains (to take ~ ~ to please s-o), much trouble (did the work give you ~ ~?)	Weltruf	world-wide renown
		Ansehen	prestige*
		Ruhm	glory, fame
		berühmt	famous
eifrige Bemühung	endeavour	gefeiert	celebrated
fortgesetzt	continual	**Lob**	praise
der Kampf ums Dasein	the struggle for existence	hoch	high
		Lob verdienen	to deserve praise
Mühsal, Strapazen	strain, hardships	Billigung	approval
Fleiß	industry, *(Sorgfalt)* diligence	Zustimmung	consent, agreement
		Bewunderung	admiration
Anspannung	strain	bewundernswert	admirable*
Pflicht	duty	Verdienst	merit
seine Pflicht tun	to do one's duty	Belohnung, Lohn	reward, recompense* (in ~ for your help)
seine Pflichten erfüllen	to perform one's duties		
e-e ungeheure Aufgabe	a gigantic task	belohnen	to reward, to recompense*
e-e ungeheure Verantwortung	a tremendous responsibility	**Tadel, Vorwurf**	blame, reproach
Leistung (bes. Technik, Sport)	performance	scharfer Tadel	sharp reproof, rebuke
e-e ausgezeichnete Leistung	an excellent piece of work	Einwand	objection
		Makel	blemish; a blot (*or* a stain) on s-o's character
bedeutende Leistung	achievement		
Untätigkeit	inactivity	Strafe	punishment
Müßiggang	idleness, laziness	hart, streng	severe
Muße(stunden), Freizeit	leisure* (hours), spare time	mild	mild
		Gedanke	thought, idea
Ruhe, Rast	rest	Begriff, Vorstellung v. etw.	idea (*or* notion) of s-th
Ruhe und Behaglichkeit	ease and comfort		
		ich will Ihnen e-e ungefähre Vorstellung geben	I'd like to give you a rough idea
		Eindruck	impression
		Meinung, Ansicht	opinion

(bestimmte) Ansicht	conviction
persönliche Ansicht	view
Haltung, Einstellung	attitude
Standpunkt	point of view, viewpoint, standpoint; *(einseitig)* angle
Überzeugung	conviction, (firm) belief
Glaube	belief
Lebens- (od. Welt)anschauung	view (*or* philosophy) of life (s. Kap. 23)
gesunde Grundsätze	sound principles
nach sorgfältiger Überlegung	after careful consideration
Behauptung	assertion, affirmation
noch zu beweisende ~	allegation
Feststellung, Erklärung (Aussage)	statement, declaration
Erläuterung	explanation
Beschreibung	description
Frage	question
Antwort	answer
ausweichend	evasive
Erwiderung	reply, retort
Anspielung	allusion
Wink, Andeutung	hint, suggestion
Vorschlag	proposal
Anregung	suggestion
unklar, verschwommen	vague*
Versprechen	promise (to keep, break one's ~)
Bruch e-s Versprechens	breach of (a) promise
Entschuldigung	excuse, apology
e-e faule Ausrede	a poor (*or* lame) excuse
Wahrheit	truth+
die reine, ungeschminkte Wahrheit	the plain truth, *(jurist.)* the truth and nothing but the truth
Binsenwahrheit	truism
Gemeinplatz	commonplace, platitude
wahr	true
echt	genuine
Beweis	proof, evidence
Unwahrheit	falsehood, untruth
falsch	false (friend, name, teeth); *(unrichtig)* wrong
unecht, unwirklich, fingiert	fictitious (name)
Lüge	lie
Lügner	liar
reine Erfindung	pure invention
Täuschung	deception
täuschen	to deceive
Betrug, Schwindel	fraud, cheat
List, Kniff	trick
überlisten	to outwit
Vorwand	pretext, pretence, US -nse
dürftig, nichtig, fadenscheinig	flimsy
reiner (glatter) Unsinn	pure (sheer, downright) nonsense
unsinnig	absurd, nonsensical
Neuigkeit, Nachricht	(a piece of) news
beruhigend	reassuring
beunruhigend	alarming
traurig	sad
unglaublich	incredible
verbürgt	authentic
überbrachte Nachricht, Botschaft	message
Bote	messenger
Auskunft	information
Bericht	account, report
eingehender Bericht	detailed account
Einzelheiten	details
alle ~	full details, full particulars
geheim, Geheimnis	secret
Gerücht	rumour
unbegründet	unfounded
(sich) verbreiten	to spread
müßiges Gerede, Geschwätz	idle talk
Wirklichkeit	reality
wirklich	real
eingebildet, Phantasie-	imaginary

17

Gewißheit	certainty	Entschlossenheit	determination
sicher, gewiß	certain, *(subjektiv)* sure, *(nachdrücklich)* positive	Plan	plan, scheme*
		skizzenhafter Entwurf	project, sketch
Tatsache	fact	Vorhaben	design, intention
die nackten Tatsachen	the bare facts	grobe Umrisse	rough outlines
		e-n Plan ausführen	to carry out a plan
nüchterner Tatsachenmensch	matter-of-fact man	fallenlassen	to abandon
		durchkreuzen, vereiteln	to upset, to thwart, to frustrate
Angelegenheit	affair, matter		
Sache	thing; matter; business (mind your own ~!)	Wunsch	wish
		Begehren	desire
		Bitte, Gesuch (um)	request (for)
e-e Selbstverständlichkeit	a matter of course	Forderung	demand
		bescheiden	modest
Wichtigkeit, Bedeutung	importance	**Beweggrund**	motive
		einleuchtend	plausible
v. hervorragender Bedeutung	of outstanding importance	Antrieb	impulse
		Ansporn	stimulus+
v. äußerst großer Bedeutung	of the utmost importance	er tat es um... willen	he did it for the sake of (honour, for his family's s., for my s.)
wichtig	important		
lebenswichtig	vital	freiwillig	voluntary (service)
Kleinigkeit	trifle	spontan	spontaneous (offer, reply)
Möglichkeit	possibility (unlimited ~ies), chance (there is not the least ~ of doing it)		
		Ziel	aim (to reach, to attain one's ~), *(fern, schwierig)* goal (one's ~ in life)
(un)möglich	(im)possible		
e-e glatte (reine) Unmöglichkeit	a sheer impossibility*	d. gleiche Ziel verfolgen	to pursue the same object
Wahrscheinlichkeit	probability, likelihood	Zweck	purpose, *(Endziel)* end (to what ~?)
wahrscheinlich	probable, likely		
er kommt wahrscheinlich nicht	he is not likely to come	Tendenz, Neigung	tendency
		e-e Tendenz zeigen (zu)	to tend (to do)
Problem	problem, question	der Zug zur (das Streben nach) Vereinheitlichung	the trend towards unification
verwickelt	complicated, intricate, involved		
		Unternehmen	undertaking, *(schwierig)* enterprise
anpacken, in Angriff nehmen	to tackle		
		Vorbereitung	preparation
mit e-m Problem ringen	to wrestle with a problem	Versuch	attempt
		vergeblich	vain, futile
lösen	to solve	hoffnungslos	hopeless
Lösung	solution	es war alles vergeblich	it was all in vain
Entscheidung	decision		
Absicht, Vorsatz	intention, purpose	Schritte tun, Maßnahmen ergreifen	to take steps, measures
Entschluß	decision		

Verfahren, Methode	method	
fragwürdig	questionable	
wirksam	effective	
Mittel	means (this ~, these ~), (zweckmäßig) expedient	
Notbehelf	makeshift; expedient	
Zweckdienlichkeit	expediency	
Tat	act, (das Tun) action	
hervorragende ~	deed	
e-e Theorie in die Praxis umsetzen	to put a theory into practice	
Ereignis	event	
aufregend	stirring	
ungewöhnlich	unusual, remarkable	
denkwürdig	memorable	
wichtig	important	
gewichtig, bedeutsam	momentous	
Begebenheit	occurrence*	
Vorfall, Zwischenfall	incident	
s. ereignen, geschehen, vorkommen	to happen, to occur	
Erlebnis	experience	
schrecklich	terrible	
sonderbar	strange	
traurig	sad	
Überraschung	surprise	
Freiheit	freedom (Fehlen jeden Zwanges); liberty (Möglichkeit der persönl. Entscheidung)	
frei	free	
Unabhängigkeit	independence	
unabhängig	independent (of)	
Unfreiheit, Knechtschaft	bondage; servitude	
Abhängigkeit	dependence	
abhängig (von)	dependent (on)	
Sklave	slave	
Sklaverei	slavery	
abschaffen	to abolish	
Tyrannei	tyranny*	
Tyrann	tyrant*	

3. Äußerungen des menschlichen Lebens

(Weitere Verben sind bei den Sachgruppen eingereiht.)

3.1. Tätigkeit allgemeiner Art und Zustand

abhängen von, abhängig sein	to depend on (our success ~s on certain circumstances; he ~s on his relatives)
ändern, sich ~	to change, (ab ~) to alter, (berichtigen) to modify, to vary
anfangen, beginnen	to begin, (energisch) to start (work, a business, he ~ed with little money)
anhalten, zum Stehen bringen; aufhören mit	to stop (a train, a car, a machine; ~ thief! ~ the work, ~ working; here I must ~)
annehmen (Angebot, Geschenk)	to accept (an offer, a present)
anwachsen, zunehmen	to increase
anwenden	to employ, to apply, to use
arbeiten	to work; (mühselig) to labour, to toil
aufhören nicht fortsetzen	to stop, to cease* to discontinue
aufstehen, sich erheben	to get up, to rise
ausbreiten, sich ~	to spread
bedecken	to cover
beend(ig)en	to end, to finish; to conclude
beeinflussen	to influence
befestigen (an)	to fasten (to); to fix (to), to affix
befreien	to free, to deliver (s-o from prison, from anxiety)

befriedigen	to satisfy	binden	to bind
begegnen	to meet	festbinden	to tie
begleiten	to accompany	bleiben	to remain
begrenzen	to limit (the expense)	dableiben	to stay
begünstigen	to favour	brauchen, benötigen	to want, to need
behalten	to keep (old letters)	Zeit ~	to take (I won't ~ a minute; it will ~ me two hours)
behandeln j-n od. etw.	to treat	brechen	to break
beherrschen	to control; to govern, to rule; to master (the saxophone); to have a good command of (English)	bringen (herbringen)	to bring (~ him here; ~ me the book)
		fortbringen	to take (~ it to the post office)
bekommen, erhalten	to get, to receive	dienen	to serve
mit Bemühung ~	to obtain	drehen	to turn, to revolve; to roll, to wind
sich bemühen, sich bestreben	to endeavour (to do s-th)	zusammendrehen, verdrehen	to twist (several threads; to ~ s-o's words)
sich große Mühe geben	to take great pains		
keine Mühe scheuen	to spare no trouble	drohen	to threaten, to menace
benehmen, sich (gut) ~	to behave (well)	dulden, erdulden, leiden, erleiden	to suffer (pain, wrong; to ~ without complaining)
benimm dich!	behave yourself!		
benutzen, verwenden	to use, to make use	eilen	to hurry
sich e-e Gelegenheit zunutze machen	to avail oneself of (an opportunity)	stürzen, stürmen	to rush, to dash
		beeile dich!	be quick! hurry up!
		sich einmischen	to interfere (with s-th)
berühren	to touch		
beschädigen	to damage	einschüchtern	to intimidate
beschaffen	to procure, to get; to obtain	eintreten	to enter
		eindringen	to penetrate (into)
beschmutzen	to soil, to dirty	entdecken	to discover; to detect (a crime, flaw)
beseitigen	to remove, to do away with		
wegfegen	to sweep away	entscheiden	to decide (a question)
ich konnte ihn (es) nicht loswerden	I could not get rid of him (it)	enttäuschen	to disappoint
		entwickeln, sich ~	to develop
Besitz nehmen von	to take possession of	erfordern	to require (great skill)
besitzen	to possess, to own		
bewegen, sich ~	to move	es erfordert viel Zeit	it takes much time (to do that)
sich regen, sich rühren	to stir (to sit for hours without stirring)		
		ergreifen, packen	to seize, to catch hold of, to grasp
biegen, beugen	to bend	erhalten, bewahren	to save, to preserve

erkennen	to recognize, to know; to realize
erlangen	to obtain
erregen	to excite, to stir up
erreichen	to reach, to attain; *(Ziel)* to achieve
erscheinen	to appear; *(Buch)* to come out
erschrecken	to frighten, to startle
ertragen, aushalten	to bear, to stand (can't ~ the hot weather; *(lange)* to endure)
erwarten	to expect, to await
erwerben	to acquire (knowledge)
kaufen	to buy
erzeugen	to produce; to manufacture
existieren, vorhanden sein	to exist, be available
fahren	to drive (a car); to ride (in a car, bus, train), to go (by train, by car, by bus); to run (trains ~ in every direction)
abfahren	to leave, depart
reisen	to travel
fallen	to fall, *(senkrecht)* to drop
fallenlassen	to drop
fangen	to catch
finden	to find
folgen	to follow
die Folge sein	to ensue
formen, gestalten	to shape
führen	to lead
den Weg zeigen	to guide
geleiten	to conduct, to escort
geben	to give
zurückgeben	to give back, to return
übergeben, ausliefern	to deliver
j-m etwas schenken (j-n mit etwas beschenken)	to present s-o with s-th
gedeihen	to thrive; to prosper, to do well
gehen	to go
zu Fuß ~	to walk
vorüber-, hindurchgehen	to pass (I saw him ~ing by the door; time ~ed (by); sad thoughts were ~ing through my mind)
gehorchen	to obey
gelingen	to succeed (the attempt ~ed)
es gelang ihm, seinen Plan auszuführen	he succeeded in carrying out his plan
genießen	to enjoy (fresh air and sunshine, one's holidays, good health)
Vergnügen finden an, sich e-r Sache erfreuen	
gewähren, bewilligen	to grant
gewinnen	to win; *(mit Bemühung)* to gain
gießen, schütten	to pour
sich ergießen, strömen	to pour* (the people ~ed out of the hall; ~ing rain)
grüßen, begrüßen	to greet, *(feierlich)* to salute
willkommen heißen	to welcome
halten	to hold; to keep
haltmachen, stehenbleiben	to stop
handeln, wirken	to act (wisely, promptly, generously)
handhaben, behandeln	to handle
hängen	to hang (a picture on the wall; a rock ~ing over the river; his life hung by a thread)
heben	to lift (a weight, a stone, one's eyes, face, hands; one's hat), to raise (one's head, eyes, arm, hand, hat; to ~ the curtain)

aufheben vom Boden	to pick up (a paper, a pin, etc.)	sorgfältig ~ liefern, beschaffen	to peruse to furnish, to provide, to supply
helfen beistehen	to help to aid, to assist	**liegen**	to lie; to be situated
heucheln	to feign (illness, attention)	**lösen, lockern** **machen**	to loosen (a screw) to make; to do; *(mit Adjektiv)* to render
hindern, j-n an etw.	to prevent s-o (from) doing s-th	**meiden**	to avoid
behindern (j-n, etwas)	to hamper, to hinder	**mischen**	to mix, *(teilweise)* to mingle, *(völlig)* to blend
hinzufügen	to add		
holen	to fetch, to go for (*or* to come for), to get (s-o s-th *or* s-th for s-o)	**nachahmen** **nachgeben** sich unterwerfen, sich fügen	to imitate to yield (to s-o) to submit (to)
holen lassen	to send for	**sich nähern**	to approach
sich irren	to make a mistake, to be mistaken, to be wrong	**necken**	to tease, to chaff s-o about s-th
		nehmen	to take, *(fest)* to grasp
kämpfen	to fight; to struggle (against difficulties, with death)	**öffnen** **opfern** **ordnen**	to open to sacrifice to put in order
kaufen	to buy, to purchase	alphabetisch ordnen	to put in alphabetical order
kennen	to know	zurechtmachen, -schneiden, put-	to trim (a hedge; a hat with ribbons)
kennzeichnen	to mark, to characterize	zen, schmücken	
sich klammern an	to cling to	**prüfen**	to examine
kommen	to come	erproben	to try, to test
ankommen	to arrive	etwas auf seine Richtigkeit nach-	to verify, to check (a list, these figures)
lassen, veranlassen	to make (the engine start), to have (one's shoes repaired); to order; to induce	prüfen **quälen, peinigen** foltern	to torment, to harass to torture
zulassen	to let, to allow	**rächen**	to revenge
gestatten	to permit	sich rächen	to revenge o. s., to take revenge (on s-o for s-th)
zurücklassen, hinterlassen, überlassen	to leave (he left her to pay the sum)		
lassen Sie mich allein!	leave me alone!	**raten (Rat geben)** **rechnen**	to advise to do arithmetic* (sums), to reckon
laufen, rennen	to run	rechnen mit	to reckon on (you may reckon, rely, count on his help)
legen	to put, to lay, to place		
leiden	s. dulden (S. 20)	berechnen	to compute, *(schwierig)* to calculate (the cost of a trip)
lernen	to learn, to study		
lesen	to read		

reinigen	to clean, *(gründlich)* to cleanse*	spalten	to split (a log with an axe, the atom)
retten	to save, to rescue	stärken, kräftigen	to strengthen, to invigorate
rollen	to roll (a barrel, one's eyes; the ball ~ed; the thunder ~ed)	stehen	to stand
		stellen	to put
		aufrecht hinstellen	to stand (it against the wall)
ruhen	to rest	stören	to disturb, to trouble, to inconvenience
sammeln	to gather, to collect		
sich ansammeln	to gather	stoßen, schieben	to push, to shove*, *(heftig)* to thrust
scheinen, den Anschein haben	to seem *(bezweifelt)*; to appear *(wahrscheinlich)*		
		(sich) strecken, (sich) dehnen	to stretch (a rubber band; he ~ed out his hand; he ~ed and yawned)
scheitern, Mißerfolg haben, nicht gelingen	to fail (he ~ed in the examination, to pass the exam; the attempt ~ed)		
		streiten	to quarrel
		suchen	to look for, to try to find, *(gründlich)* to search for
schicken, senden	to send		
schlagen, e-n Schlag versetzen	to strike, *(mit offener Hand)* to slap, *(mit Faust)* to punch, *(treffen)* to hit; *(mehrfach)* to beat; *(mit Stock etc.)* to thrash	auf der Suche nach	in search of
		teilen	to divide (s-th into parts; opinions are ~d on that point; 6 ~d by 2 is 3) to share (he ~d the room with his brother; he ~d his brother's fate, joy, sorrows)
		etwas mit j-m ~, teilhaben an	
schließen	to close, to shut, *(bes. mit Schlüssel, Riegel)* to lock, to bolt		
schmücken	to adorn, *(mst. äußerlich)* to decorate, to ornament; to deck	tragen	to carry (a parcel, s-th in one's pocket); to bear (arms, the cost, a name); to wear (a dress, a ring, a beard)
schneiden	to cut		
schreiben	to write		
abschreiben	to copy		
unterschreiben, unterzeichnen	to sign	treffen	to hit
		antreffen, begegnen	to meet, to find
notieren Sie es!	write it down!		
schütteln	to shake	treiben, an~	to drive, to push on
schützen (vor)	to protect (from)	trennen	to separate
schwächen	to weaken	tun	to do (what are you ~ing? I am ~ing my homework; what is to be done? to have to do with s-o; it's easier said than done); to put (into the bag)
schwingen	to swing (a club; a ~ing motion)		
sitzen	to sit; to be seated		
sich setzen	to sit down		
sorgen für	to take care of, to look after		

übereinstimmen	to agree, to correspond	vermissen	to miss (one's purse; we ~ you terribly)
nicht übereinstimmen	to disagree, to differ	versammeln	to assemble
überraschen	to surprise	sich versammeln	to meet, to assemble
übertreffen	to surpass	verschwenden	to waste
übertreiben	to exaggerate	verschwinden	to disappear, *(plötzl. spurlos)* to vanish, *(dahinschwinden)* to fade (away), *(Zeit)* to pass
umstürzen	to upset, to overturn		
unterbrechen	to interrupt		
unterdrücken	to oppress; *(etwas)* to suppress	versehen, versorgen mit	to furnish, to provide, to supply with
unterscheiden	to distinguish, to differentiate*	versuchen (zu tun)	to try, to attempt
		verteilen	to distribute
unterstützen	to support; to aid, to assist	verursachen	to cause, to bring about
verbergen, verstecken verheimlichen, verhehlen	to hide to conceal	verwechseln	to confuse, to confound, to mistake (s-o *or* s-th) for s-o (s-th)
verbessern besser machen, vervollkommnen	to correct to improve	verwirklichen	to put into reality, to realize (hopes, plans)
verbinden, vereinigen, sich ~	to join, to unite	verzichten (auf)	to renounce (a right, a claim); to forgo (a pleasure)
verknüpfen	to connect, to combine	auskommen ohne	to do without
verbreiten	to spread	vollbringen	to accomplish, to achieve
verbringen (Zeit)	to spend, to pass	vorbereiten	to prepare
verderben	to spoil, to ruin; to upset (one's stomach)	wachsen	to grow; to increase
		wagen	to dare
verfehlen, verpassen, versäumen	to miss (the train, the mark; one's chance); to let slip (an opportunity)	auf gut Glück wagen, aufs Spiel setzen	to risk (a battle, one's life)
		sich an etwas wagen	to venture on s-th (on a new task, on risky speculations)
vergessen	to forget		
vergleichen	to compare, *(prüfend)* to check	wählen	to choose, *(sorgfältig)* to select, *(durch Abstimmung)* to elect, *(aussuchen)* to pick out
verhindern	to prevent		
verlassen	to leave; *(im Stich lassen)* to abandon, to forsake (one's family); to desert		
		warten (auf)	to wait (for)
verlieren	to lose	wecken	to call (~ me at 6 tomorrow morning), to wake (don't ~ the baby); to arouse (suspicion)
vermehren	to increase		
vermindern, verringern, sich ~	to diminish, to decrease, to reduce		

wenden, sich ~	to turn (round)	zurückkehren	to return
sich wenden an	to turn to, to apply to, to see (see your dealer for more information)	Rückkehr	return
		zustandebringen	to bring about, to accomplish, to achieve
werden	to become, to get (hungry, tired); *(allmählich)* to grow; *(plötzlich, endgültig)* to turn; to fall ill (lame, silent); to go bad (blind, mad, red with anger)	zwingen, nötigen	to force, *(bes. j-n)* to compel, *(mit Gewalt)* to coerce*, *(Gewissen, Gesetz)* to oblige, *(beschränkend)* to constrain

3.2. Fühlen und Ausdruck der Gefühle

achten	to respect
hochschätzen	to esteem, to appreciate
werfen	to throw, to cast (anchor)
schleudern	to throw, to fling, to hurl
sich aufregen	to get excited, to work o-s up
sich widersetzen	to resist (s-o *or* s-th)
wiederholen	to repeat
bedauern	to be sorry (for s-o *or* about s-th), to regret (a mistake); to pity, to have pity on s-o
willkommen heißen	to welcome
zeigen	to show
deuten auf	to point to *or* at
entfalten	to display
beklagen	to deplore
enthüllen	to disclose
sich beklagen über	to complain of (*or* about)
offenbaren	to reveal (a secret)
zerdrücken, zusammendrücken, zermalmen	to crush
beneiden (j-n um etwas)	to envy (I ~ you; I envied him his trip to Paris)
zerreißen (in Stücke)	to tear (to pieces)
mißgönnen	to grudge (I don't ~ him his success)
zerstören	to destroy
ziehen	to draw, *(kräftig)* to pull, *(schleifend)* to drag, *(Schweres, Großes)* to haul, *(zerren)* to tug
bereuen	to regret, to repent (one's folly, of what one has done)
		bewundern	to admire
billigen	to approve of (s-o's marriage)
zielen (auf)	to aim (at); to take aim
ehren	to honour
zögern	to hesitate
erschrecken	to be frightened, to be alarmed; *(j-n)* to frighten, to startle, to alarm
zugrunde gehen	to perish; to be ruined
zugrunde richten, zerstören, ruinieren	to ruin (a ~ed city; you've ~ed my new hat; ~ed hopes, a ~ed life; I'm ~ed); to wreck (his hopes were ~ed; his career, health was ~ed)	fluchen	to curse, to swear
sich freuen (über)	to be glad (about), to be pleased (with)
sich freuen auf	to look forward to
frohlocken, jubeln	to exult (at), to rejoice (at a success)

fühlen	to feel, to sense	verfluchen, verwünschen	to curse
fürchten	to fear, *(sehr)* to dread (a visit to the dentist)	sich vergnügen	to enjoy o-s, to delight (in)
sich fürchten (vor)	to be afraid (of)	sich verlassen auf	to rely on, to depend on
hassen	to hate		
hoffen (auf)	to hope (for)	verspotten	to ridicule, *(verächtlich)* to deride, *(ironisch)* to mock
küssen	to kiss		
umarmen	to embrace, to hug		
lachen	to laugh (at)		
lächeln	to smile (at)	vertrauen	to trust, to have confidence (in);
vergnügt in sich hineinlachen	to chuckle	anvertrauen	to entrust s-th to s-o (s-o with s-th), to confide s-th to s-o
kichern	to giggle		
grinsen	to grin		
lieben	to love	verzeihen, vergeben	to forgive, to excuse, to pardon
gern haben	to like, to be fond of		
nicht mögen	to dislike	verzweifeln (an)	to despair (of)
loben	to praise, to speak highly of	wehklagen	to lament*, to wail
mißbilligen	to disapprove of	weinen	to cry, to weep
murren (über)	to grumble (at, about)	in Tränen ausbrechen	to burst into tears
die Stirn runzeln	to frown (on)	Tränen vergießen	to shed tears
sich schämen	to be (*or* feel) ashamed of	sich e-e Träne abwischen	to wipe away a tear
schluchzen	to sob	sich wundern (über)	to be astonished (*or* surprised) (at), to marvel (at), to wonder (at)
schmeicheln	to flatter		
sich sehnen nach	to long for, to yearn for		
seufzen	to sigh	zittern	to shake, *(Furcht)* to tremble, *(Kälte)* to shiver
stöhnen	to moan, *(tief)* to groan		
tadeln, kritisieren	to blame (s-o for s-th, s-th on s-o), to find fault with, to criticize (s-o's work, s-o for s-th); to reproach s-o with s-th (for doing s-th), to reprove, *(scharf)* to rebuke	zurückschrecken vor	to shrink from
		3.3. Denken	
		abschätzen	to estimate
		überschätzen	to overestimate, to overrate
		unterschätzen	to underestimate, to underrate
übelnehmen	to take amiss, to resent		
beleidigt sein	to be offended (at)	ahnen	to forebode (disaster), to have a presentiment of s-th
verabscheuen	to detest, to abhor		
verachten	to despise, *(tief, leidenschaftl.)* to scorn, *(herabsehen)* to disdain	annehmen, den Fall setzen, daß...	to suppose, *(als wahr ~)* to assume
		argwöhnen	to suspect

begreifen	to understand, *(als Vorgang)* to comprehend (he understood the instructions without comprehending their purpose), *(sich klar machen)* to realize	vermuten	to suppose; to suspect
		verstehen	to understand, to comprehend
		mißverstehen	to misunderstand
		vorhersehen	to foresee
		sich (etwas) vorstellen	to imagine (s-th), *(Unwirkliches)* to fancy, *(im einzelnen)* to envision
denken	to think, to reflect, *(logisch)* to reason		
einsehen	to see (I don't ~ why...), to understand, to realize	wissen, kennen	to know
		zweifeln (an)	to doubt s-th, to be in doubt about s-th
sich erinnern	to remember		
sich besinnen	to recollect*	**3.4. Willensäußerung**	
erwägen, bedenken	to consider (going to Egypt)	Anspruch erheben auf etwas	to claim s-th, to lay claim to s-th
folgern, schließen (aus)	to infer (from), to conclude; to deduce (from)	auffordern	to call upon (he was ~ed upon to speak), to invite (to do); *(Befehl)* to tell s-o (to do s-th)
glauben	to believe		
halten für	to think (I ~ it useful)		
ansehen, betrachten als	to regard as, to consider (as)	~ zu kommen	to summon
		beabsichtigen	to intend (to do, doing)
sich interessieren für	to be interested in		
meinen	to think, to suppose, to believe, *(grundlos)* to fancy (he ~ied he heard footsteps)	befehlen	to order, to command
		bereit sein	to be ready *or* prepared (to do)
		beschließen	to decide (to do), to determine (to do, on s-th), to resolve (to do, on doing)
merken	to notice		
sich merken	to remember, to memorize		
nachdenken (über)	to reflect (upon), to meditate (on), to ponder (over an incident)	entschlossen sein	to be determined (to do s-th)
		sich entschließen	to make up one's mind, to decide (to do)
ich will es mir überlegen	I'll think it over		
urteilen	to judge, to give one's opinion	bestehen auf	to insist on
		bitten	to ask, *(formell)* to request, *(inständig)* to implore, to entreat
beurteilen	to judge (a man; whether...), to assess (a speech); *(bewerten)* to value, *(fachlich)* to appraise, *(den eigentl. Wert)* to evaluate		
		drängen	to urge (I ~d him to be punctual; he needs no urging)
		einwilligen (in)	to agree (to), to consent (to)

erlauben	to allow	Glückwunsch	congratulation(s)
gestatten	to permit	behaupten	to state, to assert, *(nachdrückl., überzeugt)* to affirm, to maintain; *(Unbewiesenes)* to allege*; *(vorgeben)* to pretend
ermächtigen	to authorize, to empower		
ermahnen	to admonish, to exhort		
fordern (etw. v. j-m)	to demand (s-th from s-o), to require (s-th of s-o, s-o to do s-th)	bekennen	to confess, to admit
		benachrichtigen	to inform
lassen	s. Kap. 3.1. (S. 22)	beschreiben	to describe, to depict
planen	to plan (a journey); *(Böses)* to scheme*	besprechen, erörtern	to discuss, to talk over
streben, trachten (nach)	to strive (for *or* after); to aim (at); to aspire (to fame)	debattieren	to debate
		beweisen	to prove
erstreben		danken	to thank
verbieten	to forbid (s-o to do s-th), *(amtlich)* to prohibit (s-o from doing s-th)	drohen	to threaten *(strafend)*, to menace *(feindlich)*
vorziehen, lieber wollen	to prefer	Einspruch erheben (gegen)	to object (to), to protest (against)
wählen	s. Kap. 3.1. (S. 24)	empfehlen	to recommend*
sich weigern, nicht wollen	to refuse (to do)	entschuldigen sich ~	to excuse to apologize (to s-o for s-th)
wollen	s. beabsichtigen, wünschen (S. 27/8)	erinnern (j-n an etwas)	to remind (s-o of s-th)
ich will (es tun)	I will (do it)		
wollte gerade (war im Begriff)...	I was going *(or* about) to...	erklären, sagen	to state *(öffentl.)*, *(erläutern)* to explain, *(auslegen)* to interpret, *(den Grund angeben, der Grund sein)* to account for (his absence, his conduct)
wünschen	to wish (for s-th, s-o s-th); *(für sich begehren)* to desire; *(haben wollen)* to want		
zwingen	s. Kap. 3.1. (S. 25)		
		erwähnen	to mention
3.5. Sprechen, mitteilen		erzählen	to tell; to relate
		in Einzelheiten ~	to recount
anerkennen	to acknowledge, to recognize	mit Spannung ~	to narrate
		fragen	to ask, *(viel)* to question, *(offiziell)* to interrogate*, *(zweifelnd)* to query, *(um Auskunft)* to inquire (about s-th, of s-o, the reason for s-th), *(um Rat)* to consult
ankündigen	to announce		
anspielen (auf)	to allude (to), to hint (at)		
antworten	to answer, to reply		
beglückwünschen	to congratulate (s-o on s-th)		

e-e Frage stellen	to ask (s-o) a question	stammeln	to stammer
gestehen	to confess (a weakness, to being proud)	tadeln	to rebuke, *(zurechtweisen)* to reprove, *(streng, offiziell)* to reprimand
leugnen	to deny		
lügen	to lie, to tell a lie	überreden	to persuade
mitteilen	to inform (s-o of s-th), to let s-o know s-th; to communicate (s-th to s-o; to ~ with s-o)	überzeugen	to convince, to persuade
		versichern	to assure (s-o of s-th)
		versprechen	to promise
berichten, melden	to report	vorschlagen	to propose, to suggest* (doing s-th)
nennen	to call; to name (after his father; can you ~ all the plants?)	vorwerfen (j-m etw.)	to reproach s-o with s-th (for being late)
		warnen	to warn (of a danger, s-o against thieves)
plaudern, sich unterhalten	to talk, *(gemütlich)* to chat	~ zu tun	to warn not to do
		widersprechen	to contradict
raten, vermuten	to guess (can you ~ my height? You've ~ed wrong)	einwenden	to object
		ich habe nichts einzuwenden	I have no objection
rufen	to call	Einwand	objection
laut ~	to shout	zugeben	to admit (I ~ it to be true), to own (one's faults, up to a fault, to having told a lie)
ausrufen	to exclaim		
sich rühmen	to boast (of)		
sagen	to say (he said to me that...), to tell (~ me your name; ~ me where you live; I told you so; ~ him to wait)	zustimmen	to agree, to consent
		3.6. Sprache	
		Sprache	language (ancient ~s, modern ~s, one's native ~); *(Sprechen)* speech (cultivated, colloquial ~); tongue (one's mother ~)
vorher ~	to foretell, *(berechnend)* to predict, *(Wahrscheinliches)* to forecast, *(mystisch)* to prophesy		
sprechen	to speak		
flüstern	to whisper	Aussprache	pronunciation*
murmeln	to mutter, *(murrend)* to murmur	gepflegt	cultivated
		schlampig, nachlässig	slovenly*
schreien	to cry, to shout	aussprechen	to pronounce
e-n Schrei ausstoßen	to utter a cry	**Laut, Klang**	sound
		Selbstlaut	vowel
gellender Schrei	yell	Mitlaut	consonant
brüllen, laut (auf)schreien	to roar (with pain, with laughter)	**Betonung**	stress (word ~; sentence ~)
kreischen	to shriek, to scream		
schrille Stimme	shrill voice		

schwebende ~	level stress	übertragen, bildlich	figurative, metaphorical
betonen	to stress		
ein Wort hervorheben	to emphasize a word	**Wortschatz**	vocabulary
		dürftig	poor
Nachdruck, Hervorhebung	emphasis	reich	rich
		begrenzt	limited
Tonhöhe	pitch (of the voice)	erweitern	to enlarge
Tonfall, Intonation	intonation; accent (he speaks with a French accent)	**Wörterbuch**	dictionary
		nachschlagen	to look up
		Stichwort	headword
Silbe	syllable	**das vorbildliche Englisch, die Hochsprache**	standard English
Silbentrennung	syllabication, word division		
Wort	word	Umgangssprache	colloquial speech
häufig	frequent		
selten	rare	## 4. Menschliche Eigenschaften, Gefühle und Fähigkeiten	
altertümlich	archaic		
veraltet	obsolete		
Neubildung	neologism*	**Eigenschaft**	quality
Modewort	vogue word	**Gefühl**	feeling
zusammengesetztes Wort, Kompositum	compound (word)	**Fähigkeit**	ability (to do)
		potentielle ~	capacity (for s-th)
		Befähigtsein	capability
Schreibung	spelling		
buchstabieren	to spell	### 4.1. Substantive	
Buchstabe	letter		
Großbuchstabe	capital letter	**Aberglaube**	superstition
Grammatik	grammar	**Abneigung gegen**	aversion (to), dislike (of, for), antipathy (to), distaste (for)
Formenlehre	accidence		
Satzlehre	syntax		
Ausdruck	expression	**Angst, Besorgnis**	anxiety*
ausdrücken	to express (one's feelings; it is well ~ ed)	**Anmaßung**	arrogance, presumption
		Anmut	grace; charm
Sprechweise	way of speaking	**Ansehen**	prestige*, esteem, authority
Stil	style (s. Kap. 18.4, S. 91)		
		Anstand	decency
der heutige (Engl.) Sprachgebrauch	modern (English) usage	Gefühl für ~	sense of propriety
		Argwohn (gegen)	suspicion (of)
Spracheigentümlichkeit	idiomatic expression *or* phrase, idiom	**Aufdringlichkeit**	obtrusiveness
		Aufmerksamkeit	attention
Bedeutung	meaning, denotation	gespannte ~	close attention
Grundbedeutung	original meaning	**Aufrichtigkeit**	sincerity
Nebenbedeutung	connotation	**Ausdauer**	perseverance
das Wort ist abgeleitet von...	the word is derived from...	Fleiß	assiduity
Sinn	sense	**Barmherzigkeit**	mercifulness
wörtlich	literal		

Bedenken	scruple, doubt
Zögern	hesitation
Bedenkenlosigkeit, Hemmungslosigkeit	unscrupulousness
Befähigung für, Eignung, Tauglichkeit	qualification (for), capacity (for), fitness, competence
Befangenheit	self-consciousness, shyness, embarrassment
Befriedigung	satisfaction
Begabung	gift, talent (for)
~ u. Neigung	aptitude
hervorragende Befähigung	outstanding ability
seine starke Seite	his strong point
Begeisterung	enthusiasm
Begierde, heftiges Verlangen (nach)	earnest desire, longing, greed (for)
Beobachtungsgabe	(power of) observation
Beredsamkeit	eloquence
Bereitwilligkeit	readiness, willingness
Bescheidenheit	modesty
Besonnenheit, Umsicht	prudence, circumspection
Bestürzung Verwirrung	alarm, consternation confusion, bewilderment, perplexity
Bewunderung	admiration
Bosheit	malice, maliciousness
Charakter	character (a man of ~)
Dankbarkeit	gratitude (to)
Demut	humbleness, humility
Duldsamkeit	tolerance
Dummheit	stupidity
Dünkel, Einbildung	conceit*, presumption
Edelmut	generosity, magnanimity
Ehrfurcht, Scheu	awe
Ehrgefühl	sense of honour
Ehrgeiz	ambition
Ehrlichkeit	honesty
Eifer	zeal, eagerness
Eifersucht	jealousy
Eigensinn	stubbornness
Einfachheit	simplicity
Eintracht	concord, harmony
Eitelkeit	vanity
Ekel	disgust (at, for), loathing (of)
Empfindlichkeit	sensitiveness; touchiness, irritability
Empfänglichkeit für etwas	susceptibility (to s-th)
Empfindsamkeit (gefühlvolle ~)	sentimentality
Energie	energy
Engherzigkeit	narrow-mindedness
Enthaltsamkeit	abstinence
völlige ~	total ~
Entrüstung	indignation
Entschlossenheit	determination, resolution, resoluteness
Entsetzen	horror, terror
Enttäuschung	disappointment
Erfahrung	experience
Erfindungsgabe, Erfindergeist	inventiveness, ingenuity, inventive genius (the ~ ~ of our people); imagination
Ergebenheit (gegen), Hingabe (an)	devotion (to)
Ernst	seriousness, earnestness; gravity
Erregung	excitement; emotion; fury
Erstaunen, Verwunderung	astonishment (at), amazement
Fanatismus	fanaticism
Feigheit	cowardice
Feindschaft	hostility (to)
Fertigkeit	skill, art; proficiency (in)

31

Geläufigkeit	fluency
Festigkeit	firmness
Fleiß	industry
Sorgfalt	diligence
Frechheit	impertinence, impudence
Freigebigkeit	generosity
Freimut, Freimütigkeit	frankness, candour
Freude (innere ~)	joy, joyfulness, gladness
Vergnügen	pleasure
Entzücken, Wonne	delight
Freundschaft	friendship
Friedfertigkeit	peaceableness, peaceable disposition
Frohsinn, Fröhlichkeit	cheer, cheerfulness, gaiety
Frömmigkeit	piety, devotion
Furcht	fear, *(große)* dread
Furchtsamkeit, Ängstlichkeit	timidity, fearfulness
Furchtlosigkeit	fearlessness
Gastfreundschaft	hospitality
Geduld	patience
Gefühllosigkeit, Herzlosigkeit	heartlessness
Gehorsam	obedience (to)
Geistesgegenwart	presence of mind
Geiz	meanness
Gelehrsamkeit	learning, scholarship
Gemütsruhe, Gelassenheit	calmness, composure*; peace of mind
Genauigkeit	accuracy*, exactness
Geradheit, aufrechtes Wesen	uprightness, straightforwardness
Gerechtigkeit	justice, justness, fairness (to)
Geschick(lichkeit), Gewandtheit	skill, dexterity; cleverness
Geschmack	taste
Gewissen	conscience
Gewissenhaftigkeit	conscientiousness*
Gewissenlosigkeit	unscrupulousness
Gier	greed(iness)
Gleichgültigkeit	indifference
Gleichmut	equanimity
Glück(sgefühl)	happiness
Gnade	mercy (to have ~ on, to show ~ to)
Gram	grief, (great) sorrow
Grausamkeit	cruelty (to)
Groll	resentment, anger
Gründlichkeit	thoroughness*
Güte	kindness (to); kindliness
Habgier	greed(iness), avarice, covetousness
Haß (gegen)	hatred (of, for), hate (for)
Häßlichkeit	ugliness
Hast	haste, hurry
Heftigkeit	violence
Heimweh	homesickness (to be homesick)
Heiterkeit (des Gemüts)	serenity
Heldenmut	heroism
Herzlichkeit	cordiality, heartiness
Heuchelei	hypocrisy
Hochherzigkeit	generosity
Hochmut	haughtiness*, arrogance
Höflichkeit	politeness
rücksichtsvolle ~	courtesy*
Hoffnung (auf)	hope (of s-th)
Humor (Sinn für ~)	(sense of) humour
Interesse	interest (a man of wide ~s)
lebhaftes ~ an	keen interest in
Ironie	irony*
Jugendlichkeit	youthfulness
Klugheit	intelligence, cleverness
Vorsicht	prudence
Konsequenz, Folgerichtigkeit	consistency

Kühnheit	boldness, audacity	Oberflächlichkeit	superficiality*; shallowness
Kummer	grief, sorrow		
Kurzsichtigkeit	short-sightedness	Offenheit, Freimütigkeit	frankness, candour
Langsamkeit	slowness		
Stumpfheit	dullness	Optimismus	optimism
Lässigkeit, Trägheit	indolence	Parteilichkeit	partiality
Laster	vice	Pedanterie	pedantry
Laune (Einfall)	caprice*, whim	Pflichtgefühl	sense of duty
Stimmung	mood, humour	Plumpheit	clumsiness; (fig.) coarseness
Launenhaftigkeit	capriciousness*		
Leichtgläubigkeit	credulity	Prahlsucht	boastfulness
Leichtsinn	carelessness, thoughtlessness	Pünktlichkeit	punctuality
		Rachsucht	revengefulness, vindictiveness
Leidenschaft	passion (for s-th)		
Leistungsfähigkeit	efficiency	Rechtschaffenheit, Lauterkeit	honesty, integrity, righteousness*
Liebe	love		
Mäßigkeit	temperance	Reinlichkeit	cleanliness*
Mäßigung	moderation	Reiz	charm, attraction
Menschlichkeit	humanity, humaneness	Reue	repentance
		Roheit	brutality, rudeness (to)
Mißtrauen (gegen)	distrust (of)		
Mitgefühl, Teilnahme	sympathy	Rückständigkeit	backwardness
		Ruhelosigkeit	restlessness
Mitleid	pity, compassion	Sanftmut	gentleness, meekness
Müßiggang	idleness	Schamgefühl	(sense of) shame, modesty
Mut	courage, pluck		
Mutlosigkeit	discouragement, despondency	Scharfsinn	sagacity, ingenuity
		Schlagfertigkeit	ready wit, quickness at repartee*
Nachgiebigkeit	compliance, yielding character	Schlauheit, Verschlagenheit	cunning, artfulness
Nachlässigkeit	carelessness, negligence	Schlichtheit, Einfachheit	simplicity, plainness
Nachsicht	indulgence (in), leniency	Schönheit	beauty
		Schrecken	fright, terror
Nächstenliebe, Mildtätigkeit	love for one's fellowmen, charity	Schüchternheit	bashfulness; shyness
		Schwäche	weakness
Neid (auf)	envy (of)	e-e Schwäche (Vorliebe) haben für seine schwache Seite	to have a weakness for s-th his weak point
Nervosität	nervousness		
Neugier	curiosity, inquisitiveness		
		Schweigsamkeit	taciturnity
Niedergeschlagenheit	depression, low spirits	Schwerfälligkeit	clumsiness, heaviness
Nüchternheit	soberness, sobriety		

Schwermut	melancholy	Tugend	virtue
Seelenruhe, innere Ruhe	peace (or tranquility) of mind, calmness, composure*	Tugendhaftigkeit	virtuousness
		Überraschung	surprise (to my great ~ ; what a ~ !)
Selbstachtung	self-respect	Überspanntheit	eccentricity
Selbstbeherrschung	self-control	Unachtsamkeit	carelessness, inattention
Selbstlosigkeit	unselfishness		
Selbstsucht	selfishness, egotism	Unaufmerksamkeit	inattention, inattentiveness
Selbstvertrauen	self-confidence, self-reliance		
		Unaufrichtigkeit	insincerity
Selbstzufriedenheit	complacency, self-satisfaction	Unbeholfenheit	awkwardness
		Unbescholtenheit	integrity, blameless reputation
Skepsis	scepticism*, US skepticism		
		Unbesonnenheit	thoughtlessness, carelessness, rashness
Sorgfalt	carefulness; diligence		
Sparsamkeit	economy, thrift	Unbestechlichkeit	incorruptibility
Spitzfindigkeit	(over-)subtlety*, (piece of) hair-splitting	Unbeugsamkeit	inflexibility
		Undankbarkeit	ingratitude
		Unehrlichkeit	dishonesty
Standhaftigkeit	firmness, constancy, steadfastness	Uneigennützigkeit	unselfishness
		Unempfindlichkeit	insensibility, indifference
Starrsinn	obstinacy, stubbornness		
		Unentschlossenheit	indecision
Steifheit	stiffness, formality	Unerschrockenheit	intrepidity
Stolz	pride	Ungeduld	impatience
Streben nach Glück	pursuit of happiness	Ungehorsam	disobedience (to)
Streitsucht	quarrelsomeness	Ungerechtigkeit	injustice, unfairness
Strenge	severity (towards s-o), strictness	Unnachgiebigkeit	uncompromising attitude, inflexibility
Stumpfsinn	dullness; stupidity		
Taktgefühl	tact	Starrheit	rigidity
Taktlosigkeit	tactlessness	Eigensinn	stubbornness
Tapferkeit	bravery, valour	Unparteilichkeit	impartiality
Tatkraft	energy	Unternehmungsgeist, Entschlußkraft	(spirit of) enterprise, initiative
Teilnahmslosigkeit	apathy, indifference		
Torheit	foolishness, folly	Unverschämtheit	impertinence, impudence, insolence
Trägheit	laziness, idleness		
Traurigkeit	sadness		
Treue	faithfulness	Unwissenheit	ignorance
Ergebenheit	loyalty	Unzufriedenheit	discontent; dissatisfaction
Treulosigkeit	faithlessness, perfidy; disloyalty		
		Verachtung	contempt, (tiefe) scorn
Tüchtigkeit, Leistungsfähigkeit	efficiency; fitness, ability	Verantwortungsbewußtsein	sense of responsibility

Vergeßlichkeit	forgetfulness
Verlegenheit	embarrassment
Verschwendungssucht	extravagance, prodigality, lavishness
Verschwiegenheit	discretion
Vertrauen (auf)	trust (in)
festes Vertrauen, Zuversicht	confidence
Verzweiflung	despair
Volkstümlichkeit, Beliebtheit	popularity
Vollkommenheit	perfection
Vorliebe (für)	predilection (for)
Vorsicht	caution, carefulness
Klugheit	prudence
Vorurteil	prejudice, bias
vorgefaßte Meinung	preconceived idea
Wagemut	daring, boldness
Wankelmut	inconstancy, fickleness
Weichheit, Sanftheit	softness
Weisheit	wisdom
Weitblick, kluge Voraussicht	foresight, far-sightedness
Wichtigtuerei	self-importance, pomposity
Widerstandskraft, Ausdauer	resistance, endurance, stamina
Widerstreben	reluctance
Widerwille, Abneigung	dislike (of, for), aversion (to), repugnance, antipathy (to)
Wissen, Kenntnis(se)	knowledge*
Wohlwollen	benevolence
Würde	dignity
Wut	rage, fury
Zaghaftigkeit	timidity, faintheartedness
Zähigkeit	tenacity
Zartgefühl	delicacy of feeling
Zartheit	tenderness, delicacy
Zärtlichkeit	tenderness
Zerstreutheit, Geistesabwesenheit	absent-mindedness
Zögern	hesitation
Zorn	anger*, rage
Zufriedenheit	contentment
Befriedigung über etwas	satisfaction (at)
Zügellosigkeit	dissoluteness, licentiousness
Zuneigung	affection (friendly ~ ; mutual ~)
Zurückhaltung	reserve
Unaufdringlichkeit	unobtrusiveness
Zuverlässigkeit	reliability, trustworthiness
Zweifel	doubt*
Zwietracht	discord

4.2. Adjektive

abergläubisch	superstitious
altmodisch	old-fashioned
angesehen, achtbar	respectable (a ~ citizen)
ängstlich, besorgt, bang	anxious (about), uneasy
furchtsam	timid, faint-hearted
voll Bedenken	full of misgivings
anmaßend	arrogant, presumptuous
anmutig, graziös	graceful
anständig	respectable (man, girl, family), gentlemanlike (behaviour); proper, decent
anziehend	attractive, catching
ärgerlich	annoying, provoking; angry
argwöhnisch	suspicious (of)
aufdringlich	obtrusive
aufgeregt	excited, nervous; upset
aufmerksam	attentive, mindful (of)
aufrecht	upright
aufrichtig, offen, geradlinig	sincere, straightforward, candid, ingenuous*

35

ausgelassen mutwillig	unrestrained, wild wanton
ausgezeichnet	excellent
barmherzig	merciful (to)
bedacht auf, eifrig bestrebt	anxious (to do), intent (on doing s-th)
bedenkenlos, hemmungslos	unscrupulous
befangen, gehemmt	self-conscious, embarrassed
begabt	(highly) gifted, talented
begierig	eager (to do); avid (for, of)
bekümmert	sorrowful
beredt	eloquent
bescheiden unaufdringlich	modest unobtrusive
bezaubernd	charming, fascinating
bewährt	tried, proved
blödsinnig	nonsensical, idiotic
boshaft	malicious, spiteful
böse (verrucht)	wicked*, evil; *(zornig)* angry; naughty (child)
dankbar	grateful, thankful
demütig	humble, lowly
drollig	funny, droll
duldsam	tolerant (of), patient
dumm	stupid, dull
dünkelhaft, eingebildet	conceited*
edelmütig	noble-minded, generous, magnanimous
ehrerbietig	respectful (to)
ehrgeizig	ambitious
ehrenhaft, ehrenwert	honourable
ehrlich	honest, fair, sincere
ehrwürdig	venerable
eifersüchtig	jealous (of)
eifrig	eager, zealous*
eigennützig	selfish, self-seeking
eigensinnig	stubborn, wilful
einfach	plain (in ~ words), simple
einfältig	simple, foolish; naive*
eitel, eingebildet	vain, conceited*
empfänglich für	susceptible to (~ to flattery, kind treatment)
empfindlich (gegen etwas)	sensitive (to); *(reizbar)* irritable
empfindsam, rührselig	sentimental; *(sehr empfindlich, feinnervig)* sensitive
engherzig	narrow-minded; strait-laced
entgegenkommend	obliging, *(hilfsbereit)* helpful, *(nachgiebig)* indulgent
entschlossen	resolute (a ~ mind), determined
entzückt	delighted (with s-th)
erfahren	experienced
erfinderisch	inventive, ingenious*
erfolgreich	successful
ernst	serious; *(würdevoll; schwerwiegend)* grave; *(aufrichtig, ~ zu nehmen)* earnest
erstaunt, verwundert (über)	surprised (at), astonished (at)
fähig, befähigt	able (to do), capable (of doing); qualified, talented
fanatisch	fanatical
feierlich	solemn
feige Feigling	cowardly coward
feindselig	hostile
fest	firm (hand, step, voice)
flatterhaft	fickle, inconstant
fleißig	assiduous, *(rege)* industrious, *(sorgfältig)* diligent

flink	quick, *(geschickt)* nimble, *(flott)* brisk
fortschrittlich	progressive
frech (vgl. unverschämt)	impudent; saucy (girl)
freigebig	open-handed, liberal (a ~ offer), generous
freimütig, offen	frank, open-hearted, outspoken
freundlich	kind, friendly
friedlich, ruhig	peaceful (a ~ life)
friedliebend	peaceable, peaceloving
frivol	frivolous
froh	glad (about s-th)
(hoch-)erfreut	(highly) pleased
fröhlich, heiter gestimmt	merry, cheerful, gay
fromm	pious
furchtlos, unerschrocken	fearless, dauntless
furchtsam	timid, fearful
gastfreundlich	hospitable
gebildet	educated, well-bred
geduldig	patient
gefühlvoll, gefühlsselig	sentimental
gehorsam	obedient
geistesabwesend	absent-minded
geistreich	witty, brilliant; ingenious*
geizig	mean, stingy*
Geizhals	miser
gelehrt	learned*, scholarly
gemäßigt	moderate
gemein, niederträchtig	base (a ~ mind, ~ motives), mean (a ~ trick, a ~ rascal)
vulgär	vulgar
gerecht (gegen)	just (to)
geschäftig	busy*, active
geschickt	skilful, US skillful; clever
geschwätzig	garrulous, talkative
gesellig (Umgang liebend)	sociable
gesetzt, nicht impulsiv	sedate
gesprächig	talkative, communicative, chatty
gewandt	nimble; clever (diplomat); fluent (speaker)
gewandtes Auftreten	good manners
gewissenhaft	conscientious*
gewissenlos, skrupellos	unscrupulous
geziert	affected, minced
gierig	greedy (for s-th)
gleichgültig	indifferent (to)
gleichmäßig (im Wesen), stetig	steady (worker)
glücklich	happy; lucky, fortunate
grausam (gegen)	cruel (to)
griesgrämig, verdrießlich, mürrisch	sullen, morose
grimmig	grim (look, smile), fierce (enemy, hostility)
grob	coarse, rough, rude
grollend	resentful
großzügig	broad-minded; liberal, generous
gutmütig	good-natured
gütig	kind (father, heart), kind-hearted
habgierig	greedy, avaricious, covetous
hartherzig	hard-hearted
hartnäckig, halsstarrig	stubborn, obstinate
häßlich	ugly
heftig	violent (he is of a ~ temper)
heimtückisch verräterisch	insidious treacherous*

heldenhaft	heroic	leichtgläubig	credulous, gullible
hervorragend	eminent, excellent, outstanding	leichtsinnig	thoughtless; irresponsible
herzlos	heartless	leidenschaftlich	passionate
heuchlerisch	hypocritical	leistungsfähig	efficient; able
hilflos	helpless	liebenswürdig	amiable, kind
hilfsbereit	helpful (to s-o), ready to help	liebevoll	loving, affectionate
		lieblich	lovely (face), sweet (girl)
hochherzig	noble-minded, generous, magnanimous	lustig	gay, merry, jolly; cheerful
hochmütig	haughty*; arrogant	mächtig	powerful, mighty
höflich	polite (to); courteous	mäßig (im Essen und Trinken)	moderate, temperate
hoffnungsvoll	hopeful		
hübsch	pretty, nice	mildtätig	charitable (to), benevolent
human	humane		
humorvoll	humorous (a ~ writer)	mißmutig	ill-humoured, bad-tempered
ideal, vollkommen	ideal (an ~ housewife)	mißtrauisch (gegen)	suspicious (of), distrustful (of)
jugendlich	youthful	mitfühlend, teilnahmsvoll	sympathetic (a ~ heart, ~ looks, words)
kaltblütig	cold-blooded		
klarblickend	clear-sighted		
kleinlich	pedantic, narrow-minded, petty	mitleidlos	pitiless, ruthless
		mitleidsvoll	compassionate
klug, gescheit	intelligent	müde	tired, weary*
geschickt, gewandt, tüchtig	clever	mürrisch, verdrießlich	sullen, morose, sulky
geistig gewandt; geschäftsklug	smart	müßig	idle
vorsichtig	prudent	mutig	courageous*, plucky
knauserig	mean, niggardly, miserly	nachdenklich	thoughtful
		nachgiebig	compliant, yielding, indulgent
konsequent, folgerichtig	consistent	nachlässig	negligent, careless
		nachsichtig	indulgent, lenient
kühn	bold, daring, audacious	närrisch	foolish, crazy
		neidisch (auf)	envious (of)
lächerlich	ridiculous	nervös	nervous
langsam	slow, tardy	nett	nice (people; he was very ~ to me); kind; pretty
langweilig	boring, dull		
lasterhaft	vicious; wicked*		
launisch	capricious*, whimsical	neugierig	curious (I am ~ about it), inquisitive (an ~ person)
lebhaft	brisk, lively; spirited		

niedergedrückt, niedergeschlagen	depressed, downhearted
nörglerisch	grumbling
nüchtern, nicht betrunken, maßvoll, ruhig	sober
oberflächlich seicht	superficial (person), shallow (I find him ~)
offen, freimütig	frank, candid
aufrichtig	sincere
geradlinig	straightforward
pedantisch	pedantic
peinlich genau	scrupulous
es mit etwas p. genau nehmen	to be very particular about s-th
pflichttreu	dutiful
phlegmatisch	phlegmatic
plump	clumsy, awkward
prahlerisch	boastful, bragging
pünktlich	punctual
rachsüchtig	revengeful, vindictive
rastlos	restless (a ~ spirit), indefatigable
rechthaberisch	dogmatic; obstinate
rechtschaffen	righteous*, honest
rein	pure (heart, thoughts), clean (life), clear (conscience)
reizbar	irritable, sensitive
reizend	charming, fascinating
reuig, reuevoll	repentant
roh	brutal, rude
rückständig	backward (country)
ruhelos	restless
ruhig	quiet, *(gelassen)* calm, *(regungslos)* still, *(friedlich)* tranquil, *(schweigend)* silent
rührig, tätig	active, bustling, busy*
sachkundig	experienced, competent, expert
sanftmütig	gentle, meek, mild
scharfsinnig	sagacious, ingenious*, sharp-witted, keen (thinker, intellect)
schlagfertig	quick-witted, quick at repartee*
schlau	cunning; sly, crafty
schlicht	plain; modest, artless
schnell	fast, rapid; *(sofort, zeitl. kurz)* quick, speedy; *(sehr ~, leicht)* swift
schön	beautiful, lovely; *(wohlgestaltet)* handsome; *(rein)* fair; fine (weather, the ~ arts)
schöpferisch	creative, productive
schüchtern	bashful; shy, timid
schwach	weak; *(äußerst ~)* feeble; *(ungesund)* infirm; faint (smell, hope)
schweigsam	taciturn
schwerfällig	clumsy; *(schwer von Begriff)* dull (of comprehension)
schwermütig	melancholy, gloomy, dejected
selbstbewußt	self-confident; self-assertive
selbstgefällig, selbstzufrieden	complacent, self-satisfied
selbstlos, uneigennützig	unselfish, disinterested
selbstsicher, auf sich selbst vertrauend	self-assured, self-confident
selbstsüchtig	selfish, egotistic
seltsam, sonderbar	strange, curious, odd
skeptisch	sceptical*, US skeptical
sorgfältig	careful, painstaking

sparsam	thrifty, economical	unbarmherzig	merciless, pitiless, ruthless
spaßig, drollig	amusing, funny, joking	unbeholfen, linkisch	awkward
standhaft	firm, steadfast, steady	unbelehrbar	unteachable; *(stur)* obstinate, stubborn
starrsinnig	obstinate, stubborn	unbesonnen	thoughtless, inconsiderate
steif, förmlich	stiff, formal		
stolz (auf)	proud (of)	übereilt	rash
streitsüchtig	quarrelsome	unbestechlich	incorruptible
streng	severe	unbeugsam	inflexible, determined
genau	strict		
unnachgiebig	stern	undankbar	ungrateful (to)
unbeugbar	rigid	unehrlich	dishonest, insincere
stumpfsinnig	dull, stupid	uneigennützig	disinterested, unselfish
taktvoll	tactful, discreet		
tapfer	brave, *(hervorragend ~)* valiant	unentschlossen	irresolute, undecided
tätig	active; busy*	unerbittlich	inexorable*, rigorous
tatkräftig	energetic, vigorous		
tauglich (zu)	fit (for)	unermüdlich	indefatigable, untiring
Taugenichts	ne'er-do-well*, good-for-nothing	unerschrocken	intrepid, dauntless
teilnahmslos	apathetic, indifferent	ungebildet	uneducated
		unwissend	ignorant, illiterate
töricht, albern	foolish, silly	ungeschliffen	rough (a ~ fellow, ~ manners), ill-bred, low-bred
träge, faul	lazy		
lässig, bequem	indolent		
gleichgültig	unconcerned	ungeduldig	impatient
traurig	sad (to feel ~, a ~ look), mournful	ungehorsam	disobedient
		ungerecht	unjust, unfair
treu	faithful	unglücklich	unhappy; unlucky, unfortunate
treu ergeben	loyal		
treulos	unfaithful, faithless, perfidious	unhöflich	impolite; rude
		unparteiisch	impartial, fair
tüchtig	able, capable; efficient; qualified	unruhig, ängstlich	uneasy
		unstet, haltlos	unsteady, restless
tugendhaft, tugendsam	virtuous	unternehmungslustig	enterprising
		unübertrefflich	unrivalled, unequalled
überempfindlich	over-sensitive		
überrascht	surprised	unüberwindlich	invincible
bestürzt	(suddenly) dismayed, disconcerted	unvergleichlich	incomparable*
		unverschämt	impertinent, impudent, insolent
vollständig aus der Fassung gebracht	completely upset, all upset		
überspannt	eccentric; exaggerated, wild (ideas)	unversöhnlich	implacable, irreconcilable*

unwiderstehlich	irresistible	widerspenstig	refractory, rebellious
unzufrieden	discontented, dissatisfied	wild	wild, *(unzivilisiert)* savage, *(furchterregend)* fierce, *(brutal)* ferocious
verabscheuungswürdig	detestable		
verächtlich, verachtenswert	contemptible	wohltätig	charitable, beneficent
vergeßlich	forgetful	wohlwollend	benevolent, kind
verlegen	embarrassed	wortkarg	taciturn, (a man) of few words, tight-lipped
vernarrt (in)	infatuated (with)		
vernünftig, verständig	reasonable, sensible; judicious	würdevoll	dignified
verräterisch	treacherous*, perfidious	wütend	furious, enraged
		zaghaft	timid, faint-hearted
verrückt	mad, crazy	zäh	tough (worker, opponent), tenacious (will), stubborn
verschroben	eccentric, queer, odd		
verschwenderisch	wasteful; lavish, extravagant, spendthrift	zart	delicate (child, health), tender (conscience)
verschwiegen	discreet	gebrechlich	frail (health)
versöhnlich	conciliatory* (a ~ temper)	d. zarte Geschlecht	the gentle sex
		zartbesaitet	sensitive
verträumt, träumerisch	dreamy	zärtlich	loving, tender (heart, a mother's ~ care), fond
verwegen	daring, audacious		
verwirrt	perplexed, bewildered	zerstreut	absent-minded
		zornig	angry (at *or* about s-th; at *or* with s-o)
volkstümlich	popular		
vollkommen, vollendet	perfect	zufrieden	content
		befriedigt	satisfied
voreingenommen	prejudiced, biased	zügellos, ausschweifend	dissolute, licentious
vorsichtig	cautious, careful; *(klug)* prudent		
		zurückhaltend	reserved
wagemutig	daring, reckless	zuverlässig	reliable, dependable, trustworthy
wählerisch, schwer zu befriedigen	very particular (about), fastidious (about)		

5. Gesundheit und Krankheit

wendig	versatile; adaptable
wankelmütig	inconstant, fickle
weich, sanft	soft (a ~ heart; ~ and yielding)
weise	wise
weitblickend	far-sighted
weitherzig	broad-minded

Körperbeschaffenheit, Konstitution	constitution
schwächlich	frail
Gesundheit(szustand)	(state of) health
gut	good
schlecht	bad, ill
zart	delicate

schwach	weak	Krankheit	illness, *(bestimmte, mit Namen)* disease*; *(Kranksein; Übelkeit)* sickness; *(Leiden)* ailment; bad *(or* ill) health
unverwüstlich	robust		
gesund	healthy		
nicht krank	well, sound		
gesundheitsfördernd	healthful (climate), wholesome (food)		
		erblich	hereditary
Kraft, Stärke	strength	ansteckend	infectious, *(durch Berührung)* contagious
Lebenskraft	vigour, vitality		
kräftig, stark	strong		
widerstandsfähig	robust	Ansteckung	infection, *(durch Berührung)* contagion
lebenskräftig	vigorous		
kräftig gebaut, derb	sturdy	Bakterie	bacterium+
		Bazillus	bacillus+
Fehler, Gebrechen	defect (bodily ~, mental ~)	Virus	virus+
		Seuche, Epidemie	epidemic (disease)
angeboren	congenital	ausbrechen	to break out
Müdigkeit	weariness*, fatigue*	wüten	to rage
müde	tired, weary*	Opfer	victim
erschöpft	exhausted	Anfall	attack, fit (a fit of coughing, a fainting fit)
gähnen	to yawn		
(Bedürfnis) nach Ruhe	(need of) rest		
		Diagnose	diagnosis+
Schlaf	sleep	behandeln	to treat
gesund	sound	Behandlung	treatment; therapy
tief	deep	operieren	to operate on s-o (for appendicitis*)
leicht	light		
schlafen	to sleep	sich e-r Operation unterziehen	to undergo an operation
friedlich schlafen	to sleep peacefully		
sich ausschlafen	to have a good night's rest	Narkose	anaesthesia*, US anesthesia
Schläfer	sleeper	Narkotikum	anaesthetic*, US anesthetic
Schlummer	slumber		
schläfrig	sleepy, drowsy	ans Bett gefesselt sein	to be confined to one's bed, to be laid up (with a broken leg)
einschlafen	to fall asleep (I couldn't get to sleep last night)		
		Genesung	recovery, convalescence
schnarchen	to snore		
Traum, träumen	(to) dream	Rückfall	relapse
wecken	s. Kap. 3.1. (S. 24)	Zusammenbruch	breakdown, collapse
aufwachen	to wake (up), to awake	**Verletzung**	injury
		verletzen	to injure, to hurt
durch e-n langen Schlaf erquickt (erfrischt)	refreshed by a long sleep	Wunde	wound*
		wunde Stelle	sore
ganz wach sein	to be wide awake	quetschen	to bruise, to contuse
		bluten	to bleed
		verbinden	to dress
		Verband	dressing, bandage

Watte	BE cotton wool, US absorbent cotton	Schwitzkur	sweating-cure
Pflaster (Heft~)	plaster (sticking ~)	schwitzen	to sweat, to perspire
Narbe	scar	Erschöpfung	exhaustion
desinfizieren	to disinfect	Fieber	temperature (to have or run a t.); *(sehr hohes F.)* fever
sich erholen	to recover (from an illness)		
seine Gesundheit wiederherstellen	to restore one's health	Geisteskrankheit	mental illness; insanity
erkranken	to fall ill, to be taken ill (with a disease)	geisteskrank geistesgestört	mentally ill; insane (mentally) deranged
		Geschwulst	swelling
heilen	to cure (a disease, s-o of a disease); to heal (a wound*)	Geschwür	ulcer
		Gicht	gout
		Hautjucken	itching
impfen	to inoculate, *(bes. bei Pocken)* to vaccinate	kratzen	to scratch
		Heuschnupfen	hay fever
leiden (an)	to suffer (from)	Ischias	sciatica*
pflegen (Kranke)	to nurse	Katarrh	catarrh*
röntgen, durchleuchten	to X-ray, to take an X-ray of	Knochenbruch	fracture
		Kopfweh	headache*
Röntgenaufnahme, -bild	X-ray, radiograph	Krampf	cramp, spasm
		Zuckungen	convulsions
Allergie	allergy	befallen von	seized with (epilepsy)
allergisch	allergic		
Blinddarmentzündung	appendicitis*	Krebs	cancer
		Lähmung	paralysis
Blutvergiftung	blood-poisoning	spinale Kinder~	polio
Diphtherie	diphtheria*	Lungenentzündung	pneumonia*
Entzündung	inflammation	Malaria	malaria
entzünden	to inflame	Mandelentzündung	tonsillitis (US-l-)
Erkältung	a cold	Masern	measles (is a children's disease)
Schnupfen	a cold		
sich erkälten	to catch (a) cold		
erkältet sein	to have a cold	Nervenkrankheit	nervous disease
ich friere, mich friert	I'm cold, I feel cold	Nervosität	nervousness
		Ohnmacht	faint
niesen	to sneeze	Ohnmachtsanfall	fainting fit
Husten	cough*	in ~ fallen	to faint
husten	to cough*	das Bewußtsein verlieren	to go unconscious, to lose consciousness
sich räuspern	to clear one's throat		
Keuchhusten	whooping-cough*	das Bewußtsein wiedererlangen	to regain consciousness
Halsschmerzen haben	to have a sore throat		
Heiserkeit	hoarseness	bewußtlos	unconscious, senseless (he fell down s.)
Grippe	influenza, flu (a touch of the flu)		
		Pocken	smallpox
steif vor Kälte	stiff with cold	Rheumatismus	rheumatism

43

Scharlach	scarlet-fever, scarlatina*	Tropfen	drops
Schlaflosigkeit	sleeplessness, insomnia	Zahnpaste	toothpaste
		sich die Zähne putzen, bürsten	to brush one's teeth
Schlaganfall	(fit of) apoplexy*, (apoplectic) stroke	d. Mund ausspülen	to rinse (out) one's mouth
Schmerz	pain, (stark, dumpf) ache*, (stechend) cutting pain, smart	krank	ill (he is ~, he falls ~; to feel ~), sick (a ~ man); in bad (or ill) health, unwell; (Organ) diseased*
Schwindel(gefühl)	(feeling of) dizziness, giddiness*		
Sonnenstich	sunstroke	kränklich	sickly, in poor health
Tuberkulose	tuberculosis	unpäßlich, schwach	indisposed, unwell s. Kap. 4.2. (S. 39)
tuberkulös	tuberculous		
Unterernährung	malnutrition	gebrechlich, altersschwach	infirm, decrepit*
Unpäßlichkeit, Unwohlsein	indisposition		
		unterernährt	undernourished
Verdauungsstörung	indigestion	bleich	pale
Windpocken	chicken-pox	erschöpft	exhausted, worn out
Zahnweh	toothache*	schwindlig	dizzy, giddy*
e-e geschwollene Backe	a swollen cheek	blind	blind (in the left eye)
		kurzsichtig	short-sighted, near-sighted
plombieren (e-n hohlen Zahn)	BE to stop, to fill (a hollow tooth)	weitsichtig	long-sighted
Plombe, Füllung	filling	schielen	to (have a) squint
bohren	to drill	bucklig	hunchbacked
ziehen	to extract	kahlköpfig	bald(-headed)
Krone	crown	lahm	lame
Brücke	bridge	gelähmt	paralysed (US-lyzed)
künstliches Gebiß	dentures	Behinderter	handicapped person
Zuckerkrankheit	diabetes*	an Krücken gehen	to go (walk) on crutches
Diabetiker	diabetic*		
Arznei, Heilmittel	medicine, remedy, medicament	künstliche Glieder, Prothesen	artificial limbs
Dosis	dose	stumm	dumb, mute
Dosierung	dosage	taub	deaf*, (auf einem Ohr) of an ear, in one ear)
Gift	poison		
Rezept	prescription		
rezeptpflichtig	available only on prescription	schwerhörig	hard of hearing
		taubstumm	deafmute, deaf and dumb
verordnen	to prescribe (s-th for s-o)	mir ist übel	I feel sick
Pille	pill	Übelkeit	nausea*
schlucken	to swallow	belegte Zunge	furred tongue
Pulver	powder	ich habe mir den Magen verdorben	I've got an upset stomach*
Salbe	ointment		
Tablette	tablet		

starker Kaffee bekommt mir nicht	strong coffee does not agree with me	Gang	course (a one- ~ meal)
Diät einhalten	to keep to a (strict) diet, to be on a diet	Gericht Nachspeise, Nachtisch	dish BE sweet, dessert*
seine Kräfte schonen	to spare one's strength	Imbiß Festessen, Schmaus	light meal, snack feast
schone deine Augen	save your eyes!	Leibspeise	favourite dish
sich schonen	to take care of o. s.	frühstücken zu Mittag essen zu Abend essen	to (have) breakfast to (have) lunch to dine, to have dinner (supper)

6. Nahrung

Ernährung	nourishment, *(wissenschaftl.)* nutrition	**Kochkunst** Kochbuch	cookery, cuisine* BE cookery book, US cookbook
Nahrung	food (solid, liquid ~), nourishment	Kochrezept Zutaten	recipe* ingredients
Nahrungsmittel	food, foodstuffs	**essen**	to eat
Nahrungsmangel	lack of food	sich satt essen (an)	to eat one's fill (of)
Lebensmittelknappheit	food shortage	ich bin satt	I have had enough; I'm not hungry
reichlicher (dürftiger) Vorrat an	an ample (a scanty) supply of (food)	beißen	to bite
vegetarische, fleischlose Kost	vegetarian, meatless diet	(hinunter)schlucken	to swallow
leben von, s. nähren von	to live on (fruit)	verdauen	to digest*
Hunger	hunger	**trinken**	to drink
stillen	to appease	betrunken	drunk (he is ~), drunken (a ~ man); intoxicated
Hungersnot	famine	schlürfen	to sip
Appetit, Eßlust	appetite (for) (a healthy, keen, good, poor ~)	saugen	to suck
		Gasthaus	inn; restaurant
hungrig sein	to be (*or* feel) hungry	Gast	guest
verhungern	to die of hunger, to starve (to death)	Wirt, Wirtin	s. Kap. 10.2. (S. 60)
		Kellner	waiter
fasten	to fast	Café	café*
Durst	thirst	Speisekarte	menu*
löschen, stillen	to quench	Rechnung	bill, US check
durstig	thirsty	**Brot**	bread
Getränk	beverage, drink (warm, hot, cool, cold, refreshing)	e. Laib Brot Schwarzbrot	a loaf of bread brown (*or* black) bread
alkoholfreie Getränke	non-alcoholic drinks, soft drinks	Stück, Scheibe Rinde, Kruste	slice crust
Erfrischung(en)	refreshment(s)	belegtes Brot	(open) sandwich*
Mahlzeit	meal	**Butter**	butter
kräftig, reichlich	substantial	ein Butterbrot	a slice of bread and butter
dürftig, kärglich	scanty		

Ei	egg	Semmel	roll
frisch(gelegt)	newlaid	Zwieback	rusk, zwieback*
faul	rotten	**Geflügel**	poultry (s. Kap. 26.1.a, S. 111)
roh	raw		
hart-, weichgekocht	hard-boiled, soft-boiled	**Gelee**	jelly
Eidotter, Eigelb	yolk*	**Gemüse**	vegetables (s. Kap. 26.2, S. 116)
Spiegelei	fried egg		
Rührei	scrambled eggs	**Gewürz**	spice
Eierkuchen	omelet(te)*	Anis	aniseed
Eingemachtes	preserves	Bohnenkraut	savory
Fett	fat; *(ausgelassenes)* grease	Borretsch	borage
		Curry	curry
Bratenfett	dripping	Dill	dill
Schweineschmalz	lard	Ingwer	ginger
Fisch	s. Kap. 26.1.a (S. 113)	Kaper	caper
		Knoblauch	garlic
Fleisch	meat	Kümmel	caraway (seed)
fett	fat	Majoran	marjoram
mager	lean	Muskatnuß	nutmeg
zart	tender	Nelke	clove
zäh	tough	Petersilie	parsley
Kalbfleisch	veal	Pfeffer	pepper
Rindfleisch	beef	Schnittlauch	chive
Schweinefleisch	pork	Vanille	vanilla
Hammelfleisch	mutton	Zimt	cinnamon
Braten	roast (meat) (~ mutton, ~ goose, ~ hare)	**Grieß, Weizengrieß**	BE semolina*, US farina*
		Haferbrei	porridge
Kotelett (Schwein, Hammel)	chop	**Honig**	honey
Kalbsschnitzel	(veal) cutlet	**Kartoffel**	potato
Gebäck (feines ~)	pastry	Kartoffelbrei	mashed potatoes
Kuchen	cake	**Käse**	cheese
Mürbegebäck	shortcake	Rinde	rind
Torte	cake, gateau*+; *(Obst-)* tart	Quark	curds, curd cheese
		Kompott	stewed fruit, compote*, US *a.* sauce
Teig	paste, *(bes. Hefe-)* dough*, *(Rühr-)* batter		
		Konserven	canned (BE *a.* tinned) food (*or* goods); preserves
kneten	to knead		
Korinthe	currant		
Rosine	raisin	**Margarine**	margarine*
Rosinenkuchen	fruit-cake	**Marmelade**	jam (four-fruit ~)
Krapfen	doughnut	Orangen ~	(orange) marmalade
Pfannkuchen	pancake	**Mehl (feines ~ , Weizen ~)**	flour
Lebkuchen	gingerbread		
Keks	biscuit(s), US cookie; *(ungesüßt)* cracker(s)	grobes ~	meal
		Obst, Beeren	s. Kap. 26.2, (S. 116)

Salat	salad	Limonade, Zitronen ~	lemonade
Kopfsalat	lettuce (a head of ~)	Fruchtsaft	fruit juice*, BE squash (lemon ~, orange ~)
Salz	salt		
Schinken	ham		
Speck	bacon	Milch	milk
Speckscheibe	BE rasher (US slice) of bacon	Vollmilch	whole milk
		Magermilch	skimmed milk, bes. US skim milk
Schokolade	chocolate		
e-e Tafel ~	a bar of chocolate	abrahmen	to skim
Senf	mustard	Buttermilch	buttermilk
Süßigkeiten	sweets, US candy	Kondens-, Büchsen-Milch	evaporated milk, *(gesüßt)* condensed milk
Bonbon	sweetmeat, bonbon*		
Wildbret	game, venison*		
Wurst	sausage*	Rahm, Sahne	cream
Würze	seasoning, flavouring, *(bei Tisch)* condiment	Schlagsahne	whipped cream
		Öl	oil (salad-oil, olive oil)
Zucker	sugar*	Saft	juice* (fruit ~, tomato ~)
Stück	lump, cube		
Pilz, Tomate, Weintraube; Banane, Reis	s. Kap. 26.2. (S. 116/117)	Selterswasser, Sprudel	mineral water, soda-water
Flüssigkeit	liquid*	Soße, Tunke	sauce
alkoholische Getränke	alcoholic drinks	scharf	sharp, pungent, *(angenehm ~)* piquant*
Weinbrand	brandy		
Spirituosen	spirits	Fleischsaft, Bratensoße	gravy
sich betrinken	to get drunk		
Trunkenheit	drunkenness	Speiseeis	ice-cream
Apfelsaft	apple-juice, US (sweet) cider	Eis mit Früchten	sundae*
		Suppe	soup
Bier	beer	gebundene ~	cream
englisches Bier, hell	ale	Tee	tea
		Kräutertee	herb tea
~ ~, dunkel	porter	Wein	wine
Starkbier	strong beer; stout	Weißwein	white wine
Schaum	froth	deutscher Weißw.	hock
brauen	to brew	Rotwein	red wine
Essig	vinegar*	französ. Rotw.	claret
Fleischbrühe (Suppe)	broth	Champagner, Schaumwein, Sekt	champagne*
Kraftbrühe	beef tea		
Grog	grog, toddy	schäumend	sparkling
Kaffee	coffee	herb	dry
Kaffeebohne	(coffee) bean	auspressen (Saft)	to squeeze out, *(Zitrone, Orange)* to squeeze
Kakao	cocoa*, (hot) chocolate		
		backen	to bake
Likör	liqueur*	Backpulver	baking-powder

Hefe	yeast	duftend	fragrant
braten	to roast	**ausgezeichnet, vor-**	excellent, exquisite
in der Pfanne ~	to fry	**züglich**	
auf dem Rost ~	to grill	köstlich	delicious
durchgebraten	well done	lecker, fein	delicious (dish,
nicht ganz ~	underdone, US rare		wines), dainty
eingemacht, konser-	preserved	**knusprig**	crisp
viert		**nahrhaft**	nourishing, nutri-
in Dosen ~	canned (BE *a.*		tious
	tinned)	**roh, ungekocht**	raw, uncooked
mahlen	to grind	**saftig**	juicy*
mischen	s. Kap. 3.1 (S. 22)	**schmackhaft**	savoury, tasty
Mischung	mixture; blend	Geschmack,	(to) taste
reiben	to rub	schmecken	
rösten (Brot)	to toast	fade, geschmack-	tasteless, insipid
(Kaffee) ~	to roast	los	
schälen (Frucht)	to pare, to peel	**Wohlgeschmack,**	pleasant taste, (fine)
schmoren	to stew	**Würze**	flavour, savour
schneiden	to cut	würzig	spicy
tranchieren, zerle-	to carve		
gen		## 7. Kleidung	
hacken	to chop		
klein ~, zerhacken	to mince	**Kleidung**	clothing, wear
süßen	to sweeten		(children's w., ladies'
(um)rühren	to stir		w., men's w.)
würzen	to flavour, to season	Konfektion	ready-made clothes
kochen	to cook, to make	Schnitt	cut, pattern
	(tea, coffee, cocoa);	Machart	make
	(zum ~ bringen) to	Kleider	clothes*
	bring to a (the) boil;	abgetragen	worn
	(sieden) to boil	schäbig	threadbare, shabby
e-e Mahlzeit zube-	to prepare a meal	Kleidungsstück	garment
reiten		Garderobe	clothes*, wardrobe
fertig, bereit	ready (lunch is ~)	Verkleidung	disguise
auftragen, servie-	to serve	(sich) verkleiden	to disguise (o. s.)
ren		**Material, Stoff**	(dress) material, fab-
den Tisch decken	to lay (*or* set) the		ric
	table	Tuch	cloth*
abdecken	to clear the table	grob	coarse
spülen (d. Ge-	to wash (the dishes)	Stoffreste	remnants
schirr)		Webwaren	textiles
appetitanregend,	appetizing	weben	to weave
appetitlich		Gewebe	tissue*, fabric
Aroma	aroma, flavour	Leinen, Leinwand	linen*
e. feines ~	a delicate flavour	Futter	lining
Duft, Wohlgeruch	perfume, fragrance	füttern	to line
		Wolle	wool
		Baumwolle	cotton

(echte) Seide	(real) silk
Kunstseide	artificial silk
Kunstfasern	man-made fibres
Samt	velvet
Brokat	brocade
Gabardin	gabardine*
Popelin	poplin
Musselin	muslin
Leder	leather
Stoffmuster	pattern
Anzug, Kostüm	suit
Maßanzug	tailor-made, cus-tom(-made) suit
Konfektionsanzug	ready-made suit
Straßenanzug	lounge suit, US business suit
Sportanzug	sports (US sport) suit
anprobieren	to try on
umändern	to alter
passen, sitzen	to fit
gut stehen	to suit (does this hat ~ me?)
passen	to match (a shirt with a tie to ~)
Damenkleid	dress, frock, *(besonderes)* gown (tea ~, dinner ~)
Modellkleid	model (dress)
Morgenrock	dressing-gown
Schneiderkostüm	tailored suit
Gesellschafts-kleid(ung)	formal dress
Cut(away)	morning coat
Gehrock	frock-coat, US Prince Albert
Abendkleid	evening dress, ~ gown, US formal
Frack	tail coat, tails
Smoking	dinner suit, US tuxedo*
Mode	fashion
die neueste Mode	the latest fashion
modern	fashionable
altmodisch	old-fashioned
Ärmel	sleeve
Manschette	cuff
Manschettenknöpfe	cuff-links
Badehose	swimming trunks

Badeanzug	bathing-costume, swimsuit
Bademantel	bathrobe
Band (zur Verzierung)	ribbon (a silk ~)
Bluse	blouse* (shirt ~, lace ~)
Gürtel	belt (wide, narrow, leather ~)
Halstuch	(silk) scarf+
Umhang, Schultertuch	shawl
Handschuh	glove
Glacéhandschuh	kid-glove
welche Größe (Nummer)?	what size?
Handtasche	handbag, US *a.* purse
Aktentasche	briefcase
Hemd, Herren ~	shirt
Unterhemd	BE vest, US undershirt
Hose	(a pair of) trousers, US *coll.* pants
Sporthose	slacks
kurze Hose, Shorts	shorts
Reithose	breeches*
Unterhose	pants, US underpants, *(ganz kurz)* briefs, *(lang)* long pants, long johns
Hosenträger	BE braces, US suspenders
Arbeitsanzug	overalls
Strumpfhose	BE tights, pantyhose
Hut	hat
Filzhut	felt hat
Strohhut	straw hat
weicher Herrenhut	BE trilby, US fedora
steifer Hut, Melone	bowler (hat), US derby*
Zylinder	silk hat, top hat
Jacke	jacket
Sportjacke	sports jacket, blazer
Anorak	parka, anorak
Kopftuch	head-scarf+

49

Kragen	collar	Überschuhe	overshoes, galoshes, rubbers
Kragenknopf	collar-stud	Hausschuh, Pantoffel	slipper
Mantel	(over)coat		
Regenmantel	mackintosh, raincoat	Sohle	sole (leather, crepe* ~)
Wintermantel	winter coat	Absatz	heel (high, flat ~)
Pelzmantel	fur coat	Schnürsenkel	shoelace; bootlace; US shoestring
Kapuze	hood		
Mütze	cap	zuschnüren	to lace, to tie
Baskenmütze	beret+	**Schürze**	apron, *(Kinderschürze)* pinafore
Pullover	jersey, sweater		
Herren ~	pullover	**Strickjacke**	cardigan
Damen ~	jumper	**Strumpf**	stocking
Pullunder	tank top, slipover	Strumpfhaltergürtel, Hüfthalter	BE suspender belt, US garter belt
Reißverschluß	BE zip-fastener, zipper		
		Socke	sock
Rock, Frauen ~	skirt	**Tasche (im Anzug)**	pocket
Unterrock	slip, underskirt	**Taschentuch**	handkerchief
Schal (Woll-)	scarf+	**Wäsche**	linen*
Schirm	umbrella	Unterwäsche	underwear
Hülle	cover	**Weste**	BE waistcoat*, US vest
Schlafanzug	pyjamas, US pajamas		
		Brieftasche	wallet, US billfold
Schlips, Krawatte	tie, necktie	**Geldbeutel**	purse
Fliege	bow-tie*	**Notizbuch**	notebook
Schmuck, Putz	finery	**Brille**	(a pair of) glasses, spectacles, *(coll.)* specs
Juwelen	jewelry, BE *mst.* jewellery, jewels		
Perle (echt)	pearl (real)	Futteral	case
Zuchtperle	culture pearl	**Taschenuhr**	(pocket)watch
Perlen(hals)kette	string of pearls	Armbanduhr	wrist-watch
Glasperle	bead	**Spazierstock**	walking-stick, US cane
(Uhr- etc.) Kette	chain		
Halskette	necklace*	**anziehen (Kleidungsstück)**	to put on
Ohrklips	earclip		
Ohrring	earring	(j-n, sich) anziehen	to dress (up)
Armband	bracelet	sich fertig machen	to get ready
Ring	ring	barfuß	barefoot(ed)
Brillantring	diamond ring	nackt	naked*
Brosche	brooch*	**ausziehen (etwas)**	to take off
Schuh (Halb ~)	shoe, oxford	(j-n, sich) ausziehen	to undress
Pumps	BE court shoes, *bes* US pumps		
		sich umziehen	to change (one's clothes)
hoher Schuh, Stiefel	boot, US (high) shoe		
Schaftstiefel	high boot, US boot	**tragen**	s. Kap. 3.1 (S. 23)
mein Schuh drückt mich	my shoe pinches		

ausbessern	to mend, to repair
Flicken, flicken	(to) patch
bleichen (Wäsche)	to bleach
bügeln	to iron*, to press
elektr. Bügeleisen	electric iron
bürsten	to brush, to give s-th a brush
färben	to dye (a white dress brown)
nähen	to sew*
Nähnadel	needle
Steck- oder Haarnadel	pin
Zwirn, Faden	thread
e-e Rolle Nähgarn	a reel of (sewing-) cotton *or* thread
Naht	seam
Knopf	button
Nähmaschine	sewing*-machine*
reinigen	to clean
chemische Reinigung	dry-cleaning
ein Schmutzfleck	a stain (on the tablecloth, ink stains)
Schuhe putzen, wichsen	to clean, to polish one's shoes
stopfen	to darn (darning-cotton, -needle, -ball)
stricken	to knit
Stricknadel	knitting-needle
trocknen	to dry (one's clothes)
waschen	to wash
sauber	clean (shirt, shoes)
schmutzig	dirty; filthy, soiled

8. Haus und Wohnung

8.1. Haus

Gebäude	building; *(stattlich)* edifice; *(Bauwerk, allgem.)* structure
stattlich, imposant	imposing
Bauplatz, Lage	site
Haus	house
Wohnhaus	(dwelling-)house
Fertighaus	prefabricated house, *(coll.* prefab)
Etagen-, Mietwohnung	BE flat, US apartment
Mietshaus	tenement (house)
Wohnblock	BE block of flats, US apartment house
Hochhaus	multi-story building, highrise building
Palast	palace
Schloß, Burg	castle
Landsitz	country seat
Landhaus	cottage
schmuck, nett	neat, handsome
bescheiden	humble
Doppelhaus(hälfte)	semidetached house
Einfamilienhaus	detached (family) house
Eigentumswohnung	BE owner-occupied flat, US condominium
Hütte	hut
elend, erbärmlich	miserable
ungesund	insanitary
Elendsviertel	slums
Wohnwagen	BE caravan*, US trailer
Obdach	shelter
obdachlos	homeless
die Wohnungsfrage	the housing problem
bauen	to build, to construct
Baugerüst	scaffolding
aufstellen	to put up, to erect
Stange	pole
Brett	board, *(dickes)* plank
Balken	beam
Bauholz	timber, US lumber
Pfosten	post
Stein	stone
Back-, Ziegelstein	brick
Dachziegel; Fliese	tile
Zement	cement
Mörtel	mortar
Beton	concrete
Stahlbeton	reinforced concrete
ausbessern	to repair
reparaturbedürftig	in need of repair
in gutem (schlechtem) baulichem Zustand	in good (bad) repair

baufällig	dilapidated, out of repair	Erker	bay
ab-, niederreißen	to pull down, to demolish	Erkerfenster	bay window
		Fahrstuhl, Aufzug	BE lift, US elevator
(an)streichen (Tür usw.)	to paint	Fenster	window
		Fensterbrett, Fenstersims	window-sill
frisch gestrichen!	wet paint!	Fensterscheibe	pane
tünchen	to whitewash	Flügelfenster	casement-window
moderne Einrichtung	modern furnishings (furniture)	Schiebefenster	sash-window
		Jalousie	venetian blind
ständiger Wohnsitz	domicile, residence	Rollo, Rouleau	(roller-)blind
zeitweiliger Aufenthaltsort	whereabouts (his ~ is unknown)	Feuerleiter (Nottreppe)	fire-escape
Hausbesitzer(in)	house-owner	Flur	(entrance-)hall
Vermieter	landlord, landlady	Fundament	foundation
Hausbewohner	occupant, resident	Fußboden	floor
Hausgenosse, Mitbewohner	fellow lodger or tenant	scheuern, schrubben	to scrub
		Bürste	brush
Hausmeister	caretaker, janitor	Staubsauger	vacuum cleaner, BE hoover (to vacuum, BE a. to hoover; mst. clean the carpet with the hoover)
Mieter	tenant		
Untermieter	subtenant, lodger, US roomer		
Miete	rent		
Badezimmer	bathroom	Gang	corridor, hallway
Badewanne	bath-tub	Garage	garage*
Brause, Dusche	shower	Gewölbe	vault
Boiler	water-heater	Säule	column
Balkon	balcony	Pfeiler	pillar
Loggia	loggia*	Giebel	gable
Beleuchtung	lighting	Hof	(court)yard
elektrisches Licht	electric light	Keller	cellar
Brunnen	well	Kellergeschoß	basement
Pumpe	pump	Klosett	lavatory, toilet
pumpen	to pump	Küche	kitchen
Dach	roof	Kleinküche, Kochnische	kitchenette*
flach	flat		
Strohdach	thatched roof	Spülbecken	sink
Dachboden	loft, attic	Mansarde	attic, (dürftig) garret
Dachrinne	gutter	Mauer, Wand	wall
Schornstein, Kamin	chimney	Zimmerdecke	ceiling
fegen	to sweep	Schuppen	shed
Eingang	entrance	Treppe	(flight of) stairs, stair-case
eintreten	to enter		
Schwelle	threshold	die Treppe hinaufgehen	to go upstairs
Fußmatte	doormat		
Achtung Stufe!	mind the step!		

Treppengeländer	banister
Treppenabsatz	landing
Treppenhaus	BE staircase, stairwell
Stufe	step
Stock(werk)	story, floor
Erdgeschoß	ground floor, US first floor
erster Stock	BE first floor, US second floor
ein dreistöckiges Haus	a three-storied house
Tor	gate
Tür	door
Haustür	front door
Türschild	door-plate
klopfen	to knock
Klingel	bell
klingeln	to ring (the bell)
auf den Knopf drücken	to press the button
Schloß	lock
Vorhängeschloß	padlock
Schlüssel	key
schließen	s. Kap. 3.1 (S. 23)
ab-, verschließen	to lock
Veranda	verandah, porch
Glas-, Verandatür	French window
Wasserleitung	water-pipes, plumbing; water-supply
Wasserleitungsrohr	water-pipe
Wasserhahn	tap, US faucet
Stöpsel	plug
Zaun	fence
Zentralheizung	central heating
Heizkörper	radiator
Zimmer, Raum	room
geräumig	spacious
Wohnzimmer	living-room
Schlafzimmer	bedroom
Gästezimmer	guest-room
möbliertes Zimmer	furnished room
Arbeitszimmer	study
Kinderzimmer	nursery
Bewohner	occupant
sauber	clean
aufgeräumt, ordentlich	tidy
Staub, abstauben	(to) dust
Staubtuch	duster, US dustcloth
Behaglichkeit und Bequemlichkeit	comfort and convenience
bequem, angenehm	comfortable
gemütlich, behaglich	snug (corner), cosy (room)
kündigen	to give s-o (a month's) notice
mieten	to rent (a room, a car), to hire
umziehen nach	to move to
vermieten	to let, (Sachen) to hire (out)
wohnen	to live, to stay
sich niederlassen, s-n Wohnsitz nehmen	to settle (in Munich, in the country)

8.2. Hausrat

Hausrat	household goods
Möbel	furniture
ein Möbelstück	a piece of furniture
möblieren	to furnish
möblierte Wohnung	furnished lodgings
Bett	bed
Bettwäsche	bed-linen*
Bettlaken, Bettuch	sheet
Bettdecke	blanket, bedspread, counterpane
Steppdecke	quilt, US comforter
Daunendecke	continental quilt
Kopfkissen	pillow
Matratze	mattress
Wärmflasche	hot-water bottle
Heizkissen	electric heat pad
Bild	picture
Rahmen	frame
Couch	couch
Bettcouch	studio*+ couch, bed settee
Kühl-, Eisschrank	refrigerator, fridge
auftauen	to defrost
Flurgarderobe	hallstand

Fön	(electric) hair-dryer	Becher	cup, mug
Kehrichteimer, Müll-	BE rubbish bin, *bes*	Schale	bowl*
eimer	US ashcan	Weinglas	wineglass
Mülltonne	BE dustbin, US garbage can	Trinkglas (ohne Henkel und Fuß)	tumbler
Kehricht, Abfall,	rubbish, refuse,	Flasche	bottle
Müll	garbage	Thermosflasche	thermos flask
Müllabfuhrwagen	BE dustcart, US garbage truck	Kanne, Krug großer Bierkrug	jug, pitcher tankard, beer mug
Besen	broom	irdenes, gläsernes	jar
Schaufel	shovel	Gefäß mit breiter	
kehren	to sweep	Öffnung, mit oder	
Kinderwagen	BE pram, US baby carriage	ohne Henkel, Krug, Topf	
Klavier	piano	Einmachglas	preserving-jar
Flügel	grand (piano)	Eimer	pail, bucket
Kommode	BE chest of drawers,	Kaffeemühle	coffee-grinder
	US bureau*+	Konservendose	can, BE *a.* tin
Schublade	drawer	Zitronenpresse	lemon-squeezer
Korb	basket	Fleischwolf	(meat) mincer, US meat grinder
Papierkorb	BE wastepaper basket, waste basket	Mixer	mixer, blender
Küchengeräte	kitchen utensils	Korkenzieher	corkscrew
Kessel	kettle	Nußknacker	nutcrackers, US -er
Kochtopf	pot, saucepan*	Sieb	sieve*, strainer
Pfanne	pan	Trichter	funnel
Stiel-, Bratpfanne	frying-pan	Waage	(a pair of) scales, a balance
Teekanne	teapot	wiegen	to weigh
Besteck	knife, fork and spoon	Lampe	lamp
Messer	knife+	Stehlampe	floor lamp
scharf	sharp	Taschenlampe	(electric) torch, US flashlight
stumpf	blunt	Glühbirne	(electric) bulb
Schneide	edge	Kerze	candle
Gabel	fork	Taschenfeuerzeug	lighter
Löffel	spoon (soup- ~, tea ~, egg-spoon)	(e-e Zigarre, Lampe) anzünden	to light (a cigar, lamp)
irdenes Geschirr	crockery	Streichholz	match
Steingut	earthenware	anzünden	to strike, to light
Porzellangeschirr	china	(Streichholz-)	(match)box
Tasse	cup	Schachtel	
Untertasse	saucer	Leiter	ladder
Teller	plate (flat, deep ~)	Sprosse	rung
Schüssel	dish, bowl*	Netz (elektr.)	electric wiring, BE mains
Suppenschüssel	tureen		
Service	set, service	Netzstrom	BE mains current, US (city) current
Gefäß	vessel		
füllen	to fill		
leeren	to empty	Steckdose, Stecker	s. Kap. 18.7 (S. 94)

Schukostecker	three-pin plug
Verlängerungsschnur	extension lead
Ofen	stove
Backofen	oven*
Gasofen	gas fire, *(Küche)* gas stove
Elektroofen	electric fire, el. stove
Kamin (im Zimmer)	fireplace
Kochherd	cooker, stove
Gasherd	gas-cooker
Feuer	fire
anzünden	to light
auslöschen	to put out, to extinguish
brennen, ver~	to burn
Flamme	flame
Funke	spark
Rauch	smoke
rauchen	to smoke (the chimney is smoking)
Asche	ashes
heizen	to heat (a room; the stove ~s well)
Brennstoff	fuel
Brennholz	firewood
hacken	to chop
Kohle	coal
Koks	coke
Radioapparat, Fernsehapparat	s. Kap. 18.7 (S. 94/95)
Schrank (f. Geschirr und Eßwaren)	cupboard*
Geschirrschrank	china cupboard*
Wäscheschrank	linen cupboard*
Kleiderschrank	wardrobe
Kleiderbügel	coat-hanger
Bücherschrank	bookcase
Büfett, Anrichte	sideboard
Tablett	tray
Aschenbecher	ash-tray
Sofa	sofa, *(kleines)* settee
Kissen	cushion*
Spiegel	(looking-)glass, mirror
Stuhl	chair
wacklig	rickety
Polsterstuhl	upholstered chair
Sessel	armchair, easy chair
Schaukelstuhl	rocking-chair
Hocker	stool
Tapete	wallpaper
tapezieren	to paper
Teppich	carpet, *(klein, länglich)* rug
Teppichboden	carpeting
Tisch	table (square, round, oval; dinner-~)
Tischtuch	tablecloth*
Schreibtisch	desk
Nachttisch	bedside table
Uhr	clock
Standuhr	grandfather clock
Zifferblatt	dial, clock-face
Wecker(uhr)	alarm-clock
Vase	vase*
Vorhang	curtain
Wandbrett, Schrankbrett	shelf+
Regal	shelf+, shelves
Waschtisch	washstand
Waschbecken	wash basin, washbowl
Waschlappen	BE face-cloth, BE flannel, US washrag
Schwamm	sponge*
Seife	soap (toilet-~; a tablet of ~)
Handtuch	towel
(sich) waschen	to wash
(sich) (ab)trocknen	to dry
(sich) kämmen	to comb
Frisur	haircut, hairdo, hair style
(sich) frisieren	to do one's hair
Kamm	comb*
Krem, Creme	(beauty) cream
Nagellack	nail varnish, nail polish
Lippenstift	lipstick
Kosmetika	cosmetics
Nagelreiniger	nail-cleaner
Nagelschere	nail-scissors
Toilettentisch, Frisiertoilette	BE dressing-table, US dresser

Rasierapparat	safety razor, *(elektr.)* electric razor	Ehescheidung	divorce
Rasierpinsel	shaving-brush	scheiden (von)	to divorce (from)
(sich) rasieren	to shave	er ließ sich von ihr scheiden	he divorced her
Zahnbürste	tooth-brush		
Zahnpaste	tooth-paste	**Eltern**	parents
sich die Zähne putzen	to brush one's teeth	Vater	father
		Mutter	mother
(sich) den Mund (aus)spülen	to rinse one's mouth	Großeltern	grandparents
		Urgroßeltern	great-grandparents
Mundwasser	mouthwash	**Erbe (der)**	heir*
		Erbin	heiress
		Erbschaft	inheritance

9. Name, Familie, Verwandtschaft

Name	name	erben von	to inherit (from)
nennen	s. Kap. 3.5 (S. 29)	hinterlassen	to leave
Familienname	family name, surname	vermachen	to bequeath
		Testament	testament, (last) will
Vorname	BE Christian name, first name, US given name	**Erwachsener**	grown-up, adult
		Gatte, Ehemann	husband, spouse
		Gattin, Ehefrau	wife+, spouse
Spitzname	nickname	**Geburtstag**	birthday (~ present)
Namenstag	name-day	**Generation**	generation (his descendants in the third ~ ; future ~s)
Familie	family (member of the ~ ; ~ life)		
Haushalt	household	**Geschwister**	brothers and sisters
Haushaltführung	house-keeping	**Hochzeit**	wedding (silver, golden, diamond ~)
Verwandtschaft	relationship		
ein Verwandter	a relative, a relation	feiern	to celebrate
wir sind nahe (weitläufig) verwandt	we are close (distant) relatives	Feier	ceremony
		heiraten (j-n)	to marry
verwandt mit	related to (how are you ~ to her?)	sich verheiraten	to marry, to get married
verschwägert	related by marriage	die Neuvermählten	the newly-weds
Angehörige	dependants (US -dents), *coll.* (my) folks*	Mädchenname	maiden name
		Frau Brown, geb. White	Mrs. Brown, née* White
Bräutigam	fiancé*, *(am Hochzeitstag)* bridegroom	Flitterwochen	honeymoon (to honeymoon in Spain)
Braut	fiancée*, *(am Hochzeitstag)* bride	**Jubiläum**	jubilee
		Jahrestag	anniversary
Ehe, Heirat	marriage	Glückwunsch	s. Kap. 3.5 (S. 28)
Trauung, Hochzeit	wedding (~-day, ~-dress, ~-ring; ~-eve)	**Jugendlicher**	adolescent, youth, young person
Ehestand	matrimony	**Junggeselle**	bachelor (~ flat)
Ehepaar	married couple	**Kind**	child
Eheleben	married life	ehelich	legitimate
		unehelich	illegitimate

Kleinstkind, Säugling	baby		Vorfahr	ancestor
Kleinkind (unter 7 Jahren)	infant		~en, Ahnen	ancestors, forefathers
Knabe, Junge	boy; youngster		Ahnenforschung	research into ancestry
Mädchen	girl		Stammbaum	family tree
Sohn	son		Stammtafel, Ahnentafel	genealogical table, pedigree
Tochter	daughter		abstammen von	to be descended from
Zwillinge	twins			
Drillinge	triplets		Vormund	guardian
Enkelin	grand-child (grandson, granddaughter)		Mündel	ward
ledig	unmarried, single		**Waise(nkind)**	orphan (~boy, girl)
Mitgift	dowry		Waisenhaus	orphanage
Aussteuer	trousseau*		**Witwe(r)**	widow(er)
Nachkomme	descendant			
Nachkommenschaft	issue, offspring			

10. Berufsleben

10.1. Allgemeines

Neffe	nephew*
Nichte	niece*
Onkel	uncle
Tante	aunt
Pate	godfather, sponsor
Patin, Patentante	godmother
Patenkind	godchild
Schwager	brother-in-law
Schwägerin	sister-in-law
Schwiegersohn	son-in-law
Schwiegertochter	daughter-in-law
Schwiegereltern	parents-in-law
Stiefmutter	stepmother
Stiefvater	stepfather
Vererbung	heredity
erben (von)	to inherit (from)
vererben	to transmit by heredity (to)
erblich	hereditary
Verlobung	engagement
sich verloben (mit)	to get (*or* become) engaged (to)
er machte ihr e-n Heiratsantrag	he proposed to her
Heiratsantrag	proposal
Verlobter	fiancé*
Verlobte	fiancée*
Vetter	cousin (boy ~)
Kusine	cousin (girl ~)

Beschäftigung	occupation, job
Beruf	occupation, *(akademisch)* profession, *(handwerkl.)* trade
er hat s-n ~ verfehlt	he has missed his vocation
ausüben	to practise (US -ice)
Handwerk, Gewerbe	trade
was sind Sie von Beruf?	what's your occupation (trade, profession)?
von Beruf Arzt (Bäcker, Hausfrau)	a doctor by profession (a baker by trade, a housewife by occupation)
Berufsberater	careers adviser
e-e Laufbahn einschlagen	to enter upon a career
Bewerbung (um e-n Posten, e-e Stelle)	application (for a post, a situation, *coll.* a job)
e-e freie Stelle	a vacancy
Bewerber	applicant
sich bewerben um	to apply for
sich wenden an	to apply to
Zeugnisabschriften	copies of certificates
Schulzeugnisse	s. Kap. 18.1 (S. 86)
Empfehlungsschreiben	letter of recommendation*

empfehlen	to recommend*
feste Stellung	permanent position
Einkommen	income
Durchschnitts~	average ~
Gehalt	salary
Honorar (Arzt), Gebühren (Anwalt)	fee
Lohn	wages
Lohnempfänger	wage-earner
Lohnforderungen	wage claims
Lohnerhöhung	wage increase, ~ rise
Lohnkürzung	wage cut
verdienen	to earn (money, one's living, £600 a year); to deserve (good work ~s good pay)
Trinkgeld	tip
Lebensunterhalt, Existenz	livelihood, living
Lebenshaltung	standard of living
sein Brot verdienen (mit), sich ernähren (von)	to earn one's bread (by), to make a living (out of s-th)
Gewerbe	trade
ausüben, betreiben	to carry on
Gewerbetreibender	tradesman+
Handwerk	trade
Kunsthandwerk	handicraft, craft
Handwerker	craftsman+
Kunsthandwerker	artisan
Meister, Geselle, Lehrling	s. Kap. 11.1 (S. 60)
Arbeitgeber	employer, *coll.* boss
beschäftigen	to employ s-o
Arbeitnehmer	employee
Angestellter	(salaried) employee
Belegschaft	workers (and employees) of a factory, workforce
Personal	staff, personnel
Mitbestimmungsrecht	right of co-determination
Betriebsrat	works committee
Gewerkschaft	trade union, US labor union
Arbeiter	worker (a manual ~, a brain ~), workman+ (a skilled ~); labourer (agricultural ~); hand (factory ~s; farm ~s)
Kurzarbeiter	short-time worker
Teilzeit-	part-time (job, employee)
Vorarbeiter	foreman+
Überstunden machen	to work overtime
kündigen	to give notice; to give s-b his notice
entlassen	to dismiss, *coll.* to fire, to sack
Mangel an Arbeitskräften	manpower shortage
arbeitslos	unemployed
er ist arbeitslos	he is out of work
Arbeitslosenunterstützung beziehen, stempeln gehen	to draw unemployment benefit, to be on the dole

10.2. Berufe und Gewerbe

Arzt	doctor, *bes* US physician (s. Kap. 18.2, S. 88)
Ärztin	woman doctor
praktischer Arzt	general practitioner, GP
Facharzt	specialist
Chirurg	surgeon
Zahnarzt	dentist, dental surgeon
als Kassenarzt zugelassen	BE on the panel
Praxis	practice
Sprechstunde	consultation hour, BE surgery
Sprechzimmer	BE surgery, *(Facharzt)* BE consulting room; US (physician's) office
Wartezimmer	waiting-room
Tierarzt	veterinary* surgeon, US veterinarian, *coll.* vet

Apotheker	pharmacist; *bes* BE (pharmaceutical) chemist*, *bes* US druggist	Einzelhändler	retailer, shopkeeper, US storekeeper
		Blumenhändler	florist
		Buchhändler	bookseller
Jurist	lawyer; jurist	Eisenwarenhändler	BE ironmonger, US hardware dealer
Rechtsanwalt	lawyer, *(plädierend)* BE barrister, *(meist nur beratend)* BE solicitor; US counselor, US attorney* (at law)	Fischhändler	BE fishmonger, US fish dealer
		Gemüsehändler	BE greengrocer
		Juwelier	jeweller, US -ler
		Lebensmittelhändler	grocer
Notar	notary public	Schreibwarenhändler	stationer
Beamter	official, officer, Civil Servant		
		Tabakhändler	*bes* BE tobacconist, dealer in tobacco
Bibliothekar	librarian		
Geistlicher	s. Kap. 23 (S. 106)	Stoffhändler, Tuchhändler	draper, US textile dealer (t. store)
Theologe	theologian		
Lehrer(in)	teacher	Weinhändler	wine merchant
Dolmetscher	interpreter	Hausierer	BE pedlar, US peddler
Journalist	s. Kap. 14.1 (S. 74)		
Schriftsteller	author, writer	mit etwas hausieren	to peddle s-th
Übersetzer	translator		
Baumeister	architect; building contractor	Kassier(er)	cashier
		Bankkassierer	teller
Bildhauer	sculptor	Kaufmann	s. Geschäftsmann; Händler; Verkäufer
Ingenieur	engineer		
Maler (Kunst ~)	painter, artist	Korrespondent	correspondent (foreign language ~)
Musiker	musician		
Schauspieler	s. Kap. 18.6 (S. 93)	Sekretär(in)	secretary; clerk*
Techniker	technician, engineer	Stenotypist(in)	shorthand typist
Bankier	banker	Verkäufer	BE shop assistant, salesman+, US (sales) clerk*
Betriebsleiter, Geschäftsführer, Direktor (e-r Firma)	manager, managing director		
		Verkäuferin	BE shopgirl, saleswoman+, US salesgirl
Buchhalter	book-keeper; accountant		
		Bäcker	baker
Büroangestellter	office worker, clerk*	Bäckerei	s. Kap. 15 (S. 78)
Fabrikant	manufacturer	Bergmann	miner
Geschäftsmann	businessman*+	Brauer	brewer
Geschäftsreisender, Handelsvertreter	commercial traveller, US traveling salesman+	Brauerei	brewery
		Bote	messenger
		Buchbinder	bookbinder
Händler	trader, dealer	Drucker, Buch ~	printer
Großhändler	wholesaler	Elektriker	electrician

Elektrotechniker	electrical engineer
Fischer	fisherman+
Förster	forester
Friseur	hairdresser
Herrenfriseur	barber
Gärtner	gardener
Handels~	market-~, US truck farmer
Hausangestellte	domestic servant
Dienstmädchen	housemaid
Haushälterin	housekeeper
Hausmeister	caretaker, janitor
Hebamme	midwife+
Installateur	plumber*; fitter
Elektro~	electrical fitter
Kellner	waiter
Kellnerin	waitress
Oberkellner	head-waiter
Kindermädchen	nurse
Klempner	s. Spengler
Koch, Köchin	cook
Krankenschwester	(sick-)nurse
Maler, Anstreicher	painter
Mannequin	model
Maurer	bricklayer
Mechaniker	mechanic
Metzger, Schlachter	butcher*
Monteur	fitter
Müller	miller
Optiker	(dispensing) optician
Photograph	photographer
Putzfrau	cleaner, cleaning lady
Putzmacherin, Modistin	milliner
Schlosser	locksmith
Schmied	blacksmith
Schmiede	forge, smithy
Schneider	tailor
Damenschneiderin	dressmaker
Schornsteinfeger	chimney-sweep
Schreiner, Tischler	joiner
Möbeltischler, Kunstschreiner	cabinet-maker
Schriftsetzer	compositor, typesetter
Schuster	shoemaker
Seemann	s. Kap. 13.3 (S. 72)
Soldat	s. Kap. 22 (S. 102)
Spediteur	forwarding agent, carrier
Möbel~	remover
Spengler, Klempner	plumber*
Uhrmacher	clockmaker, watchmaker
Wirt (Gast~)	innkeeper, landlord
Wirtin	landlady
Zimmermann	carpenter

11. Wirtschaftsleben

Wirtschaft	economy
Wirtschaftsaufschwung	economic upswing
Hochkonjunktur	boom
Wirtschaftsblüte, Wohlstand	prosperity
Wirtschaftskrise	economic crisis
Geschäftsrückgang	(business) depression, recession

11.1. Handwerk und Industrie

Handwerk, Gewerbe	s. Kap. 10.1 (S. 58)
Meister	master (~ tailor, ~ carpenter)
Geselle	journeyman+ (~ tailor)
Lehrling, Auszubildender	apprentice
Werkstatt	workshop, *(Autos)* garage*
Reparatur	repair
Werkzeug	tool
Gerät	implement (garden ~s); instrument, device
Axt	axe, US ax
Bohrer	drill
Feile	file
Hammer	hammer

Hebel	lever*	Maschine (An-	engine, *(elektrisch)*
Hobel	plane	triebs~)	motor
Kette	chain	angetriebene ~	machine*
Meißel	chisel	Werkzeug~	machine tool
Nagel	nail	Ausrüstung	equipment
Säge	saw	Apparat, Vorrich-	apparatus+,
Schere	(a pair of) scissors	tung, Gerät	appliance (house-
schleifen	to grind		hold, electrical ~s),
Schraube	screw		device (for s-th)
Schraubenzieher	screw-driver	bedienen	to operate
Schraubenschlüs-	wrench, *bes* BE	Drehbank	lathe
sel	spanner	Kran	crane
Schraubstock	vice, US vise	**Rohstoff**	raw material
Schweißbrenner	welding torch	Ersatzstoff	substitute
Zange, Greif~	(a pair of) tongs	minderwertig	of inferior quality
Beißzange	pincers	Metall, Erz, Ton	s. Kap. 27 (S. 118)
Flachzange	pliers	usw.	
Industrie	industry	**Schicht**	shift (to work in
Grundstoffindu-	primary industry		three ~s; night ~)
strie		**Stillegung, Betriebs-**	shutdown
Schwerindustrie	heavy industry	**einstellung**	
Industrieerzeugnis	industrial product	Aussperrung	lockout
Industriezweig	(branch of) industry	**Streik**	strike
Industriestadt	industrial town	Generalstreik	general strike
Bergwerk	mine	in den Streik treten	to go on strike
Kohlenbergwerk	coal-mine, BE col-	streiken	to (be on) strike
	liery	**Textilindustrie**	textile industry
Schacht	pit, shaft	Strickwaren	knitwear
Durchschnittsför-	average output	Webwaren	woven goods
derung			
Fabrik	factory, mill (cotton	**11.2. Handel**	
	~, paper-~), works		
	(an iron-~, a glass-	**Handel**	trade
	~, a gas-~)	blühend	flourishing
Fabrikanlage	industrial plant	Einzelhandel	retail trade
Spinnerei	spinning-mill	Großhandel	wholesale trade
Weberei	weaving-mill	Außenhandel	foreign trade
Walzwerk	rolling-mill	Tauschhandel	barter
Fabrikation, fabri-	(to) manufacture	Handelsverkehr	trade
zieren		**Handelsgesellschaft**	commercial com-
Fabrikmarke	trade-mark		pany
fabrikneu	brandnew	Konzern	combine
Fertigwaren	finished products	Kartell	cartel, syndicate
Fließband, Monta-	assembly line	Aktie(ngesell-	s. Kap. 11.3 (S. 65)
ge~		schaft)	
Hochofen	blast-furnace	GmbH	limited company
Laboratorium	laboratory*	**Handelskammer**	Chamber of Com-
Konfektion, Beklei-	clothing industry		merce
dungsindustrie			

Handelskorrespondenz	commercial correspondence	Bedingungen	terms
Geschäft	business*	Außenstände	outstanding debts
ein rentables ~	a paying concern	Forderungen (Schuld ~)	claims
Laden, Geschäft	BE shop, US store	Einfuhr und Ausfuhr	importation and exportation, import and export (of goods)
Ladeninhaber	owner (of a shop), proprietor		
Auslage	display (of goods)		
Selbstbedienungsladen	self-service shop	die ein- u. ausgeführten Waren	imports and exports
Supermarkt	supermarket	Erzeugung, Ertrag	output, production
Filialbetrieb	branch	erzeugen	to produce
Ladentisch	counter	Erzeuger	producer
Schaufenster	shop window	Faktura, Warenrechnung	invoice
(Waren) ausstellen	to display		
Geschäfts-, Ladenschluß	closing-time	ausstellen	to make out
Einkäufe machen	to go shopping, to do one's shopping	Fracht	freight
		Frachtkosten	freight charges
Warenhaus, Kaufhaus	department store	Gewähr, Garantie	guarantee*
		~ leisten für etw.	to guarantee s-th
Branche, Geschäftszweig	line (of business)	Gewicht	weight
		Brutto ~	gross weight
Firma	firm	Netto ~	net weight
Inhaber	owner	Tara	tare
Filiale, Zweiggeschäft	branch (establishment)	wiegen	to weigh (a parcel; it ~ed 10 lb.)
Absatz	s. Verkauf, Markt (s. S. 64)	Gewinn	profit(s)
		Reingewinn	net profit
e-e ~möglichkeit finden für	to find an outlet for	Nettoertrag	net proceeds
		Inventar, Bestand(sverzeichnis)	inventory*
Anfrage	inquiry		
Auskunft	information	Inventur, Bestandsaufnahme	stock-taking
streng vertraulich	strictly confidential		
Erkundigungen einziehen über	to make inquiries about	Irrtum	error
		berichtigen	to rectify
Angebot	offer	e-n Fehler verbessern	to correct a mistake
annehmen	to accept		
Angebot und Nachfrage	supply and demand	Irrtum vorbehalten	errors and omissions excepted (E. O. E.)
Ansichtssendung	consignment (sent) on approval	Katalog	catalogue, US mst. catalog
Auftrag, Bestellung	order	Kauf	purchase, buy (a good ~)
erteilen	to give		
ausführen	to execute	Konkurrent	competitor
zurückziehen, streichen	to cancel	Konkurrenz, Wettbewerb	competition
Probeauftrag	trial order	Kontor, Büro	office

Papier	paper	**Preis**	price
Schreibblock	writing-pad	neueste ~ liste	latest price-list
Bleistift	pencil	Durchschnittspreis	average price
Feder	pen	Preisnachlaß, Rabatt, Skonto	discount (to allow a five per cent discount for cash)
Federhalter	penholder		
Füllfederhalter	fountain pen		
Kugelschreiber	ballpoint pen, BE biro	feste Preise	fixed prices
		mäßiger Preis	moderate, reasonable price
Filzstift	felt-tip (pen)		
Mine	refill	Preisherabsetzung	reduction in price
Tinte	ink	Selbstkostenpreis	cost-price
Stempel	stamp	Herstellungskosten	production cost
vervielfältigen	to duplicate, to mimeograph*	**Provision**	commission
		Qualität	quality (of excellent, inferior, poor ~)
Abschrift, Kopie	copy		
Kopiergerät	photocopier	erstklassig	first-rate, first-class
kopieren	to photocopy		
Schreibmaschine	typewriter	**Quittung**	receipt* (he ~ ed the bill)
Maschinenschreiben	typewriting		
		Rate	instalment, US -ll
Blindschreiben	touch typing	Ratenkauf	BE hire-purchase, US (purchase on the) installment plan
(Akten)Ordner	(document) file		
Kartei	card-index		
Karteikarte	file card	auf Raten kaufen	to buy in instalments, BE on hire purchase
Kunde	customer		
ständiger Abnehmer	regular customer		
		Räumungsausverkauf	clearance sale
Lager, Vorrat	stock, store (we have plenty of food in store)	räumen	to clear
		Rundschreiben	circular
		Schadenersatz	compensation, indemnity
Lagerhaus, Magazin	warehouse, storehouse		
		auf Schadenersatz verklagen	to sue for damages
aufspeichern	to store (up)		
Lieferschein	delivery note	~ leisten	to pay damages
Bezahlung bei Lieferung, Nachnahme	cash (US collect) on delivery, C.O.D.	Beschwerde	complaint
		Schlußverkauf	end-of-season sale
		Sommer ~	summer sales
Mahnbrief	reminder	Winter ~	winter sales
Markt	market (~ -day, ~ place; new ~ s for s-th; there is no ~ for these goods)	**Sendung, Lieferung**	consignment, shipment
		Auslieferung	delivery
		Speditionsfirma	forwarding agency
Menge	quantity	**Spesen, Auslagen**	charges, expenses
Messe	fair (industrial ~, book ~)	**Teilhaber**	partner
		stiller ~	sleeping (US silent) partner
Muster, Probe	sample		
Probestück	specimen	**Termin**	(appointed or fixed) time (date, day)
Schnittmuster, Stoffmuster	pattern		

Umsatz	turnover	Kurzwaren	BE haberdashery, US notions
Jahresumsatz	annual turnover		
Umsatzsteuer	turnover tax	**Warenzeichen**	trade-mark
Mehrwertsteuer	value added tax, VAT	gesetzl. geschützt, eingetragen	registered
Verbrauch	consumption	Etikett	label
verbrauchen	to consume	**Werbung, Reklame,**	publicity, advertis-
Verbraucher	consumer	**Propaganda**	ing
Verkauf, Absatz	sale, return(s)	**Wert**	s. Kap. 2 (S. 12)
dieses Buch findet guten Absatz	this book is selling well	anbieten	to offer
Verlust	loss	ausgeben (Geld)	to spend
Verpackungsmaterial	packing material	begleichen (Rechnung)	to settle (an account)
Behälter	container	bestellen	to order
enthalten	to contain	den Empfang bestäti-	to acknowledge re-
Beutel	bag	gen	ceipt (of s-th)
Tüte	(paper) bag	entschädigen (für	to compensate (s-b
Blechbüchse, -dose	can, BE *a.* tin	**Verluste)**	for s-th)
Faß	barrel	ermäßigen (Preis)	to reduce
Holzkiste	wooden case	**handeln (mit etwas)**	to deal (in), to trade (in)
Sack	sack, *(Papier-, Plastik-)* bag	kaufen	to buy, to purchase
Pappschachtel, Karton	cardboard box	konkurrieren (mit)	to compete (with)
Hülle	envelope	kosten	to cost (it ~ me £50)
Bindfaden	string	liefern	to send; to supply, to furnish; *(aus~)* to deliver
Draht	wire		
Holzwolle	wood-wool, US excelsior		
verpacken	to pack	mieten	to hire (a car), to rent
Packpapier	wrapping paper, brown paper	senden	to send
einwickeln	to wrap	absenden (Waren)	to dispatch, to forward
Versand	dispatch, shipment		
Transport, Beförderung	transport(ation), conveyance	zurücksenden	to return
		umtauschen (gegen)	to exchange (for)
Schiffsladung	cargo+	verkaufen	to sell
Versorgung, Zufuhr	supply	verschiffen, versenden	to ship
Waren	goods, *(die einzelne ~)* article, *(Gebrauchsartikel)* commodity; *(Handels~)* merchandise, ware (iron ~, hard ~, earthen ~; to advertise one's ~s)		
		versorgen (mit)	to supply (with)
		versteigern	to put s-th up for auction, to sell by auction
		der Meistbietende	the highest bidder
		beiliegend	enclosed
		Beilage	enclosure
		billig	cheap, inexpensive
Neuheit	novelty	spottbillig	dirt-cheap
Textilien, Textilwaren	textile fabrics, textiles		

fabrikneu	brandnew		Ausgaben	expenses
gewinnbringend, einträglich	profitable		kürzen	to cut down
			Bank	bank
gratis, unentgeltlich	free of charge, gratuitous (information, help), gratis		(Bank)Konto	(bank) account
			eröffnen	to open
			Kontoauszug	statement of account
teuer	expensive, dear		Banküberweisung	bank transfer
umgehend	by return (of post), by return mail		Sparkasse	savings-bank
			Geld sparen	to save money
			Filiale	branch-office
im voraus	in advance		Einlage	deposit
vorrätig	in store, in stock		Kassenschalter	counter
Zustand	condition		Geldschrank	safe
in gutem ~	in good condition		feuersicher	fireproof
cif(-Klausel) (Warenpreis einschl. Verladungskosten, Versicherung u. Seefracht, alles vom Absender getragen)	c.i.f., cost, insurance, freight		**Bankrott, Konkurs**	bankruptcy
			in Konkurs geraten (gehen)	to go bankrupt
			Betrag	amount
			fällig am 1. Juli	due July 1st
			Bilanz	balance-sheet
			Saldo	balance
fob(-Klausel) (im Warenpreis sind die Einschiffungskosten eingeschlossen)	f.o.b., free on board		e-e B. aufstellen	to draw up a balance-sheet
			Börse, Effekten ~	(stock-)exchange
			Börsenmakler	stock-broker
			Börsenspekulant	speculator
Geschäft, ~sgang	business*		Kursnotierung	(market) quotation
~ ist flau, schleppend	business is dull, slack		**Buchführung**	book-keeping
			doppelte ~	double-entry ~
~ geht flott, ist lebhaft	business is brisk		Soll und Haben	debit and credit
			Darlehen	loan
der Markt ist übersättigt	the market is overstocked (or glutted)		**Devisen**	foreign currency, foreign exchange
die Preise erholen sich	prices are recovering			
			Dividende, Gewinnanteil	dividend
steigende Nachfrage (nach)	increasing demand (for)		ausschütten	to distribute, to pay
			Einnahmen	receipts*
11.3. Geldwesen			**Geld**	money
			e-e beträchtliche Geldsumme	a considerable sum of money
Aktie, Anteilschein	share, US stock			
Aktionär	shareholder, US stockholder		Geldsendung	remittance
			geldknapp sein	to be short of money
Aktiengesellschaft	BE joint-stock company, US (stock) corporation		Bargeld	ready cash
			Kleingeld	(small) change
			Wechselgeld	change
Jahresbericht	annual report		Können Sie mir e-e £5-Note wechseln?	Can you give me change for a five-pound note?
Aktiva	assets			
Anleihe	loan			

65

Banknote	bank-note, US bill
Gläubiger	creditor
Hypothek	mortgage*
Kapital	capital
verfügbar	available
Geldmittel	funds
reichliche Geldmittel	ample means
Kaufkraft	purchasing power
Konto	account
Passiva	liabilities
Posten (e-r Rechnung u. dgl.)	item
Rechnung	bill
ausstellen, schreiben	to make out
s. belaufen auf	to amount to
Begleit~, Warenrechnung	invoice
Rückstände	arrears (of rent, of wages)
Scheck	cheque*, US check
Schuld	debt*
Schuldner	debtor
Sicherheit(sleistung), Kaution	security (to give or stand ~)
Stundung, Zahlungsaufschub	extension of credit
Überschuß	surplus
Vermögen	fortune (to make a ~)
Besitz	property, assets
Versicherung	insurance
Haftpflicht	liability insurance, third-party insurance
Prämie	premium
Vorschuß	advance
gewähren	to grant
Währung	currency
~seinheit	monetary unit: 1 pound sterling (£) = 100 pence (p.); früher = 20 shillings; 1 s. = 12 pence (d.); U.S.A.: 1 dollar ($) = 100 cents (c)
Wechsel	bill (of exchange)
gezogener ~, Tratte	draft
Wechselkurs	rate of exchange
Zahlung	payment
Barzahlung	cash (payment)
Zahlungsempfänger	payee
Zins(en)	interest (to pay 10 per cent. ~ on a loan)
Zinsfuß, ~satz	rate of interest
abheben (Geld)	to withdraw (money from the bank)
anlegen (Geld)	to invest (in)
ausgeben (Geld)	to spend (on)
bezahlen	to pay (for)
e. Rechnung ~	to settle an account
buchen, verbuchen, eintragen	to book; *(Buchhaltung)* to enter
einnehmen	to receive
einzahlen	to deposit, to pay in
gutschreiben	to credit (I have credited you for the amount of ...)
kündigen (Kapital)	to call in, to recall
rechnen	s. Kap. 3.1 (S. 22)
schulden	to owe (he ~s him £10)
tilgen (Schuld)	to pay
überweisen (Geld)	to transfer, to remit
zählen	to count

12. Naturwissenschaft und Technik, Elektrizität

(Natur)Wissenschaft und Technik	science and technology (s. Kap. 18.2, S. 87)
wissenschaftlicher Fortschritt	scientific progress (*or* advance)
Experiment, Versuch	experiment
Laboratorium	laboratory*
Mikroskop	microscope*
Linse	lens+

Gegenstände vergrößern	to magnify objects	elektrischer Strom	electric current
Maschine	s. Kap. 11.1 (S. 61)	Gleichstrom	direct current, D.C.
Dampfkraft	steam power	Wechselstrom	alternating current, A.C.
Motor	engine, *(bes. elektr.)* motor	Drehstrom	three-phase current
Pferdestärke (PS)	horse-power (h. p.)	Stromkreis	circuit*
Ingenieurwesen (Hoch-, Tief-, Maschinenbau)	engineering	Glühbirne ~nfassung	(electric) bulb socket
Elektrotechnik	electrical engineering	Hochspannung	high tension
		Isolator	insulator
Ingenieur	engineer	isolieren	to insulate
Techniker	(technical) engineer, technician	Kabel	cable
erfinden	to invent	Kurzschluß	short circuit*
ausdenken, ersinnen	to devise, to contrive	Leiter	conductor
Erfinder	inventor	Blitzableiter	lightning-conductor
Erfindung	invention	Leitungsdraht	conducting wire
Vorrichtung	device	Schalter	switch
arbeitsparende ~	a labour-saving device, contrivance	einschalten (Licht)	to switch on
		ausschalten	to switch off
sinnreich	ingenious*	Schalttafel	switchboard
die erste praktische Anwendung e-r	the first practical application of a	Schlag, elektrischer	an electric shock
Entdeckung	discovery	Sicherung	fuse
anwenden	to apply	die Sicherung ist durchgebrannt	the fuse has blown, BE the light has fused
Apparat	apparatus+, appliance (s. S. 61)		
aufsehenerregend	sensational	Widerstand	resistance
zeitgemäßes (modernes) Verfahren	an up-to-date method	**Computer**	Computer
veraltet, altmodisch	out-of-date, old-fashioned	computergesteuert	computer-controlled
		Bildschirm	screen
Kernenergie, Atomenergie	nuclear energy, atomic energy (s. Kap. 27, S. 117)	Daten	data
		Datenverarbeitung	data processing
		Datenschutz	data protection
Kernkraftwerk	nuclear power station	EDV	EDP, electronic data processing
das Atomzeitalter	the atomic age	Hardware	hardware
Elektrizität	electricity	Programm	program
Elektrizitätswerk	power station	Programmierer	programmer
Dampfkraftwerk	steam power station	Software	software
Wasserkraftwerk	hydroelectric power station	Speicher	memory, store
		speichern	to store
Akkumulator	accumulator, storage battery	Terminal	terminal
laden	to charge		

13. Verkehr

Verkehr	traffic (s. Kap. 15, S. 77)
stark	heavy
Verkehrsmittel	means of transport
Verkehrsstau	traffic jam
Verkehrsunfall	road accident
Fahrzeug	vehicle*
Personen- und Güterbeförderung	carriage of passengers, transport (-ation) of goods
befördern	to transport, to carry
Reise	journey, trip
See~, Luft~	voyage
Vergnügungs~	pleasure trip
Gesellschafts~	group tour
Reiseandenken	souvenir
Reiseführer	guide(-book)
Reiseziel	destination
Reisender	traveller, passenger
Reisebüro	travel agency, tourist office
Reisepaß	passport
Visum	visa* (entrance ~, exit ~)
reisen	to travel, to go to...
Ausflug	s. Kap. 17, S. 83
Camping	s. Kap. 17, S. 84
Kurort	s. Kap. 15, S. 76
Gasthaus	s. Kap. 6, S. 45

13.1. Eisenbahn

Eisenbahn	railway, US railroad
Drahtseilbahn (Standbahn)	funicular (railway), cable railway
Abfahrt, Abreise	departure
Ankunft	arrival
Anschluß	connection (from, to) (The trains to Dover run in connection with the Channel steamers. Our train connects with the 10.15 train at N.)
Bahnhof	(railway, US railroad) station
Haupt~	main station
Bahnhofswirtschaft	station restaurant
Wartesaal	waiting-room
Bahnsteig	platform
Fahrgeld, Fahrpreis	fare
ermäßigt	reduced
Ermäßigung	reduction
Fahrkarte	ticket
einfache ~	single (US one-way) ~
Rückfahrkarte	BE return ticket, US round-trip ticket
Zeitkarte	BE season(-t.), US commutation ticket
~ninhaber	BE season ticket holder, US commuter
Fahrkartenschalter	ticket office
e-e Fahrkarte lösen	to buy a ticket, to book (for)
Kontrolleur	ticket-collector
Schaffner	BE guard, US conductor
lochen, knipsen	to clip, to punch
Fahrplan	time-table, US schedule*
Kursbuch	(railway) time-table
Gepäck	BE luggage, baggage
Gepäckaufbewahrung(sstelle)	BE left-luggage office, US checkroom
Gepäckschein	BE luggage ticket, US baggage check
Handkoffer	suitcase
Handtasche	handbag
Reisetasche	travelling bag
Mappe, Aktentasche	briefcase
Pappschachtel	cardboard box
sein Gepäck aufgeben	to register one's luggage, US to check one's baggage
Grenzstation	frontier-station
Zollamt	custom-house
Schranke	barrier
Zollabfertigung	customs examination
Zoll, Zölle, Abgaben	duty, duties

erheben	to levy
zollpflichtig	liable to duty, dutiable
haben Sie etwas zu verzollen?	have you anything to declare?
Zug	train
Personenzug	passenger train
Schnellzug	express train
Sonderzug	special train
Vorortzug	suburban train
Güterzug	BE goods train, US freight train
Lokomotive	engine
Lokführer	engine-driver, US engineer
Wagen	coach, car, BE carriage
Personenwagen	passenger coach, BE a. carriage, US passenger car
Schlafwagen	sleeping-car, sleeper
e. Bett im ~ belegen	to book a berth
Liegewagen (platz)	couchette
Speisewagen	BE restaurant car, dining-car, US diner
Gepäck-, Packwagen	luggage van, US baggage car
Güterwagen	BE goods truck, US freight car
Notbremse	emergency brake
Klimaanlage	air-conditioning (system)
mit ~	air-conditioned
Abteil	compartment
Nichtraucher	non-smoker
Triebwagen	rail-car
Schiene	rail
Gleis	track
Weiche	BE points, US switch (to throw a ~)
rangieren	to shunt, US to switch
Rangierbahnhof	BE marshalling yard, US switchyard
Knotenpunkt	junction
Pendelverkehr	shuttle-service
Signal	signal
Stellwerk	BE signal-box, US switch tower
Tunnel	tunnel (railway ~, road ~)
Verspätung haben	to be late
~ aufholen	to make up time
Zusammenstoß	collision
Frontal ~	head-on ~
abfahren, abreisen (nach), aufbrechen	to depart, to start, to leave (for), to set out for; *(Zug)* to start, to leave
abholen (am Bahnhof)	(to go *or* come) to meet s-o at the station
begrüßen, willkommen heißen	to welcome
ankommen	to arrive
aussteigen	to get out, to get off the train
befördern	to convey
besetzt	*(Wagen)* full up, *(Platz)* occupied
belegt	reserved
überfüllt	crowded
leer	empty
einsteigen	to get in(to)
Abschied nehmen	to take one's leave (of s-o)
umsteigen (nach)	to change (for)
verpassen (Anschluß)	to miss (one's connection)
gerade noch erreichen	to catch (just in time)
Aufenthalt	stop
wie lange haben wir hier Aufenthalt?	how long do we stop here?

13.2. Kraftfahrzeug

Autobahn	BE motorway, US freeway, US expressway
Auto, Kraftwagen, PKW	BE (motor-)car, US automobile car
Limousine	BE saloon, US sedan
Kabriolett	convertible
Lastwagen, LKW	BE lorry, truck

Kombiwagen	station wagon	den 2. Gang einlegen	to change into (shift to) second
Taxe (Taxi)	taxi, cab	e-e Steigung im 3. Gang nehmen	to take a hill on third (US on high)
Fahrgeld	fare	Rückwärtsgang	reverse (gear)
Traktor, Zugmaschine	tractor	**Hupe**	horn (to sound the ~, to honk)
Motorrad	motor-cycle	**Karosserie**	body
~fahrer	motor-cyclist	**Kofferraum**	BE boot, US trunk
Roller	(motor) scooter	**Lenkrad**	(steering-)wheel
Beiwagen	side-car	**Lichtmaschine**	(light) generator
Anhänger	trailer	Anlasser	starter
Wohnwagen	BE caravan*, US trailer	Zündkerze	sparking-plug, US sparkplug
Armaturenbrett	dashboard, instrument panel	**Motor**	engine, US *a.* motor
Autobus	s. Kap. 15 (S. 77)	anlassen	to start
Autofahrer	motorist, driver	abstellen	to stop
Autofahrt, -reise	motoring trip	auseinandernehmen	to dismantle, to take apart
Bremse	brake	Motorhaube	BE bonnet, US hood
versagen	to fail	Kupplung	clutch
Bremsweg	stopping distance	~spedal	clutch pedal
Brennstoff	fuel	**Nummernschild, Kennzeichen**	BE number-plate, US license plate
Benzintank	fuel tank	**Panne**	breakdown
Brennstoffverbrauch	fuel consumption	Reifenpanne	puncture, blowout
Benzin	BE petrol, US gasoline (*coll.* gas)	**Parkplatz**	s. Kap. 15 (S. 76)
unser B. ist knapp	we are short of petrol	**Rad**	wheel
das B. ist uns ausgegangen	we have run (we are) out of petrol	**Reifen**	tire (BE *a.* tyre)
Gaspedal	accelerator	aufpumpen	to pump up, to inflate
Ersatzteil	spare part	Luftschlauch	tube
Fahrer	driver, motorist	Mantel	cover
Führerschein	BE driving-licence, US driver's license	schlauchlos	tubeless
Fahrprüfung	BE driving test, US driver's test	**Reparaturwerkstatt**	(repair) workshop, BE garage*
Fahrgestell	chassis*+	**Schalthebel**	gear lever
Fahrrad, Rad	bicycle, *coll.* bike	**Scheinwerfer**	headlight, headlamp
Radfahrer	cyclist	**Schlußlicht**	rear light
Garage	garage*	**Schutzblech**	mudguard, US fender
Geschwindigkeit	speed	**Soziussitz (auf dem Motorrad)**	pillion (seat)
Höchst~	top speed		
erlaubte Höchst~	speed limit	**Steuer(rad)**	(steering-) wheel (he was at the wheel)
Durchschnitts~	average speed		
erster, zweiter, dritter Gang	first (bottom, US low) gear, second g., third (top, US high) gear	betrunken am ~ sitzen	to be drunk in charge of a car

Straße	s. Kap. 15 (S. 77)
Landstraße	country road, highway
Fahrbahn	roadway, BE carriageway, *(Spur)* lane
Umleitung	detour*, BE diversion
Umweg	roundabout way, detour*
Fernverkehrsstraße	BE trunk road, BE arterial road, US (arterial) highway
Wegweiser	signpost
Tachometer	speedometer*
Tankstelle	filling station, BE garage*, US gas (*or* service) station
tanken	to tank up
Verkehrsschild, -zeichen	road sign
Windschutzscheibe	windscreen, US windshield
Zündung	ignition
Zündschlüssel	ignition key
abblenden	to dip the headlights, US to dim ~ ~
abschalten	to switch off
aufblenden	to turn the headlights on full
abschleppen (Auto)	to tow (off)
beschädigen	to damage
bremsen	to brake (a car), to put on (*or* apply) the brakes
einholen (j-n)	to catch up with s-o
überholen	BE to overtake, to pass
fahren	to drive (a car, in a car; can you ~ ?); to ride (in a bus, tram, train; to ~ a bicycle); to go (by train, bus, car; this train goes to Oxford); to run (trains ~ in every direction); *(abfahren)* to start, to leave; *(reisen)* to travel
halten, an ~	to stop
steuern (Auto)	to drive (a car)
überfahren	to run over
überholen, ausbessern	to overhaul
rücksichtsloses Fahren	reckless driving
rücksichtsloser Fahrer	road-hog

13.3. Schiffahrt

Schiffahrt	navigation
Schiff	ship, *(bes als Transportmittel)* vessel, *(klein)* boat, *(groß und klein)* craft+
Deck	deck
Mast	mast
Schornstein	funnel
Reling	railing
Bug	bow*
Heck	stern
Backbord	port
Steuerbord	starboard
Laderaum	hold
Dampfkessel	boiler
Tau, Seil	rope
Bullauge	porthole
Kajüte	cabin
Koje	berth, bunk
Anker	anchor*
vor Anker gehen	to cast (*or* drop) a.
die Anker lichten	to weigh anchor
Boje	buoy*
Boot	boat
Segel ~	BE sailing-boat, US sailboat
Ruder ~	BE rowing-boat, US rowboat
Ruder, Riemen	oar
Brandung	surf, breakers
Welle	wave
Schaum	foam
Dampfer	steamer
Dock	dock (dry ~ ; floating ~)

Fähre	ferry(-boat)	Überfahrt	passage
Floß	raft	**Segel**	sail
flößen	to raft	Segelschiff	sailing-ship
Hafen	harbour, *(natürl. od. künstl. mit ~ anlagen; ~ stadt)* port	Takelwerk	rigging
		Steuermann (Rudergänger)	helmsman+, man at the wheel
Mole	mole, pier, jetty	**Steuer**	helm
Kai (Ufermauer)	quay*, wharf+	**Werft**	dockyard, shipyard
Hafenanlagen	port installations	**Wind, Brise, Bö**	s. Kap. 25 (S. 111)
Handelsschiff	trading ship	**Wrack**	wreck
Handelsflotte	merchant fleet	**an Land gehen**	to go ashore
Jacht	yacht*	**anlaufen**	to call at (a port)
Segelsport	yachting*, sailing	**auslaufen, in See stechen**	to put to sea, to sail
Kapitän	captain, *(Handelsschiff)* master	**beladen**	to load
Laderaum	hold	**bergen (Schiff, Ladung)**	to salvage
Leck	leak		
dichten	to stop	**beschädigen**	to damage
Leuchtturm	lighthouse	s. **einschiffen (nach)**	to embark (for)
Lotse	pilot	**ertrinken**	to (be) drown(ed)
Mannschaft	crew	**kentern**	to capsize*
Matrose	sailor	**löschen, ausladen**	to unload (*or* discharge) (a ship)
Schiffskellner	steward		
Passagier, Fahrgast	passenger	**rudern**	to row, to pull
blinder ~	stowaway	**schleppen (Schiff)**	to tow, to tug
Pirat, Seeräuber	pirate	**seekrank werden**	to get seasick
Rettungsboot	life-boat	**segeln**	to sail (up the coast, into a harbour)
aussetzen	to launch		
Rettungsgürtel	life-belt, US life-preserver	**sinken, versenken**	to sink
Schiffbruch	shipwreck	**vom Stapel lassen**	to launch
Schiffskompaß	ship's compass*	**steuern**	to steer (by the stars)
der Kurs eines Schiffes	the course of a ship	**stranden**	to run aground; to be wrecked
Schiffsladung, Fracht	cargo+, freight	**verstauen**	to stow (cargo in a ship's holds)
Schlepper	tug(boat)	**schwerer Seegang**	heavy sea
Lastkahn	barge	bewegte See	rough sea
Seemann, Matrose	sailor, seaman+	glatt	smooth
Seekarte	chart	ruhig	calm
Seemeile	nautical mile s. Kap. 29 (S. 122)	**seichtes Wasser**	shallow water
Knoten	knot (i. e., a nautical mile per hour)		
Seereise	voyage		

13.4. Flugwesen

Flugwesen	aviation
Aktionsradius, Flugreichweite	range (of flight)
Ballon	balloon
Fessel~	captive balloon
Gondel	gondola
Besatzung	crew
Flugzeugführer	pilot
Fallschirm	parachute*
Flug	flight
Fluggast	(air-)passenger
Flugplatz	airfield
Flughafen	airport
Startbahn	runway
Schuppen, Flughalle	hangar*
Flugzeug	BE aeroplane, US airplane, plane, aircraft+
viermotorig	four-engined
Verkehrsflugzeug	airliner
Düsenflugzeug	jet (plane)
Überschallgeschwindigkeit	supersonic speed
Tragfläche	wing
Brennstofftank	fuel tank
Propeller	propeller, air-screw
Höhenmesser	altimeter*
Kompaß	compass*
Steuerknüppel	control column
Hubschrauber	helicopter
Landung	landing
glatte ~	smooth landing
Zwischen~	stopover
Notlandung	forced (or emergency) landing
Bruchlandung	crash landing
Absturz	crash
Segelflugzeug	glider, (leicht) sailplane
Segelflieger	glider pilot
Segelfliegen	gliding
Start	take-off (to take off)
abstürzen	to crash
brennend	in flames
fliegen	to fly
(in der Luft) schweben	to hover*
landen	to land
steuern	to pilot
tanken	to refuel
zurücklegen (Entfernung)	to cover

14. Nachrichtenwesen

Nachrichtenwesen	communications

14.1. Zeitung

Zeitung	(news)paper
Tageszeitung	daily (paper)
Wochenzeitung	weekly (paper)
Amtsblatt	gazette, official journal
Boulevardpresse	popular press
Sensationspresse	yellow press
Zeichnung	drawing
Karikatur(enzeichner)	cartoon(ist)
Zeitschrift	periodical, (unterhaltend) magazine, (bes. fachl.) journal
Zeitungsartikel	(newspaper) article
Nachricht, Zeitungsnotiz	news item, item of news
Leitartikel	BE leader, editorial
Stellungnahme, Stellung nehmen (zu etwas)	(to) comment* (on)
Zeitungshändler	newsagent, US newsdealer
Zeitungskiosk	newsstand, newspaper kiosk
Zeitungsstil	journalese
Zeitungswesen	journalism, the press
zuverlässige und umfassende Berichterstattung	reliable and complete information (or coverage)
abonnieren	to subscribe (to a paper)
Abonnent	subscriber
Abonnement	subscription

73

halten, beziehen	to take (a paper)	Überschrift	heading
Anzeige, Inserat	advertisement* (*coll.* ad)	**Schriftleiter, Redakteur**	editor
Kleinanzeigen	classified advertisements, *coll.* small ads	Redaktion	editorial staff; editorial office
Chiffre	box number	**Spalte (Zeitung)**	column
inserieren	to advertise*	Seite	page
Reklame	advertising	Zeile	line
Auflage	edition		
Auflagenhöhe, Verbreitung e-r Zeitung	circulation	**14.2. Post- und Fernmeldewesen**	
		Post, ~beförderung, ~sachen	post (send it by ~; please reply by return (of ~); the ~ has come; take it to the post); mail (I had a lot of ~ last week; ~-bag, ~-train, ~-boat, ~plane, air ~)
Ausgabe	edition (morning, Sunday, late, special ~), issue*		
Beilage	supplement		
drucken	to print		
illustrieren	to illustrate		
setzen	to compose, to set up (type)		
veröffentlichen	to publish	**Absender**	sender('s name and address*), return address
herausgeben (Zeitung)	to edit		
erscheinen	to appear	**aufgeben (Brief)**	to post, US to mail
Druckerei	printing office, printery	**befördern**	to handle (letters), to send
Druckerpresse	(printing-)press	**Brief**	letter
Zeitungspapier	newsprint	Briefwaage	letter scales
Extrablatt, Sonderausgabe	special edition	Briefwechsel	correspondence
		e. Bogen Briefpapier	a sheet of notepaper (writing-paper)
Journalist	journalist, newspaperman+	zusammenfalten	to fold
		Umschlag	envelope
Berichterstatter	reporter, correspondent	Anschrift	address*
		bei Smith	c/o Smith
Bildberichter	photo reporter, press photographer	Einschreiben	Registered
		durch Eilboten	Express (Paid)
Leserbrief	letter to the editor	Luftpost	(By) Air Mail
Lettern	letters, types	Drucksache	Printed Matter
Großbuchstaben	capital letters (to capitalize)	bitte nachsenden	please forward, US please redirect
Fettdruck	bold(-faced) type	Beilage	enclosure
Kursiv-, Schrägdruck	italics (to italicize)	beilegen	to enclose
Presse	press	**Briefkasten**	BE post-box, BE pillar-box, US mailbox
Pressefreiheit	freedom of the press		
Pressekonferenz	press conference	~ an der Haustür	BE letter-box, US mailbox
Schlagzeile	headline	den Briefkasten leeren	to collect the letters (US the mail)

Leerung	collection	postwendend antworten	to reply by return of post (*or* return mail)
Briefmarke, Postwertzeichen	(postage) stamp	Warenprobe	(trade) sample
gummiert	adhesive	zustellen (Post)	to deliver
Gebühr	fee, rate (letter rate, parcel ~)	Zustellung	delivery (your letter came by the first ~)
Eilbrief	express letter, US special delivery letter	Fernsprechwesen	telephony
		Fernmeldewesen	telecommunications
		Fernsprecher, Telefon	telephone (*coll.* phone)
Einschreibebrief	registered letter		
Einschreibegebühr	registration fee	einrichten	to install
Empfänger	addressee*, recipient	~ anschluß haben	to be on the phone
entwerten	to cancel	telefonieren	to (tele)phone
Formular	form, US blank (to fill in a form, *bes* US fill out)	Fernsprechamt, Vermittlung	(telephone) exchange
		Fernsprechleitung	telephone line
		Fernsprechnetz	telephone network
gegen Nachnahme	cash (US collect) on delivery, COD	Fernsprechstelle (öffentliche)	BE public call-office
Nachnahmepaket	COD parcel	Fernsprechzelle	BE callbox, (tele)phone box, *bes* US telephone booth
Paket	parcel, *bes* US package		
Päckchen	small parcel	Hörer	(telephone) receiver
Paketkarte	parcel-form	abnehmen	to lift
Porto	postage	auflegen	to put back (*or* down), to replace
portofrei	BE postfree, postage paid	Selbstanschlußtelefon	automatic telephone, dial telephone
Postamt	post office		
Haupt~	main post office	Wählscheibe	dial
Schalter	counter	wählen	to dial
(Schalter)Beamter	(post-office) clerk	Selbstwählfernverkehr	BE subscriber trunk dialling, STD, US direct distance dialing
Postanweisung	money order		
Überweisung	remittance		
Postbote, Briefträger	postman+, US mailman+	Störung (technische ~, Betriebs ~)	fault, breakdown
Postkarte	postcard, US postal card	d. Leitung ist gestört	the line is out of order
Ansichtskarte	picture postcard	Teilnehmer	caller, telephone user
postlagernd	to be (left till) called for, Poste Restante*	Telefonbuch	telephone directory
Postleitzahl	BE post(al) code, US zip code	e-e Nummer nachschlagen	to look up a number
		mein Telefon ist 23056, Apparat 447	my telephone number is 23056, extension 447
Postgiroamt	BE Giro office (G. account, G. cheque)		
Post(schließ)fach	post-office box, PO box	Telefongespräch	(telephone-)call (urgent, emergency, priority ~)
Poststempel	postmark		

75

Ortsgespräch	local call
Ferngespräch	BE trunk call, long-distance call
anrufen	BE to ring (up), to call (up), to phone
d. Leitung (Nummer) ist belegt	the line (number) is engaged (US is busy)
unterbrechen	to interrupt
verbinden Sie mich mit...	put me through to...
falsch verbunden	wrong connection (number)
hier Braun!	this is Mr. B.; Mr. B. speaking
bleiben Sie am Apparat!	hold the line, please
sprechen Sie noch? (Sind Sie fertig?)	Have you finished? US *a.* Are you through?
Wen möchten Sie sprechen?	Who do you want to speak to?
(selbst) am Apparat	speaking
einhängen	to hang up
Telefonist(in)	telephone operator
Fernschreiber	BE teleprinter, US teletype(writer)
Fernschreiben	telex
Telegraf(ie)	telegraph(y)
Telegramm	telegram, *bes* US wire
Telegrammformular	telegraph form
Telegrammstil	telegraph style, telegraphese
Funkspruch	radio message
telegrafieren	to telegraph, *bes* US to wire

15. Die Stadt

Stadt	town, *(bedeutsam)* city
Weltstadt	metropolis
benachbart	neighbouring
Stadtviertel	quarter
Vorstadt, Vorort	suburb
am Rande der Stadt	on the outskirts of the town
Umgebung	neighbourhood, surroundings
umgeben	to surround
Einwohner	inhabitant
Adreßbuch	directory
Städter	town-dweller, city-dweller
Kurort	health-resort
Badeort	spa, *bes* BE watering-place
Seebad	seaside resort
Fremdenverkehr	tourist traffic
Reisebüro	s. Kap. 13 (S. 68)
Fremdenheim (-pension)	guest-house, pension
Verpflegung und Unterkunft	board and lodging, room and board
Brücke	bridge
Unterführung	BE subway, underpass
Kanalisation (e-r Stadt)	sewerage* system
Abzugskanal	sewer*
Park(anlagen)	park
gepflegt	well-kept
Bank	bench
Rasenfläche	lawn
Springbrunnen	fountain
Parkplatz	BE car-park, *bes* US parking lot
Parkuhr	parking meter
parken	to park (where can we ~ *?or* ~ our car?)
Parken verboten	No parking
Politesse	traffic warden
Platz	square, *(rund)* BE circus, US circle
Marktplatz	market-place
Verkaufsstand	stand, *bes* US stall
Reklametafel	hoarding, US billboard
Plakat	poster, bill
Plakatsäule	advertisement* pillar
Ankleben verboten!	Stick (US post) no bills!
Sehenswürdigkeiten	sights
Denkmal	monument, memorial

errichten	to erect, to raise	Hauptverkehrs-	rush-hours
zur Erinnerung an	in memory of	stunden	
Standbild	statue (to set up a ~)	Lärm	noise
Museum	museum	Menschenmenge	crowd
Tiergarten, Zoo	zoological garden	Fußgänger	pedestrian
Wolkenkratzer	skyscraper	Fußgängerzone	pedestrian precinct
Wahrzeichen	landmark	Vorsicht!	BE Take care! Caution!
Straße	road, *(im Ort)* street, *(viel benutzte Land-)* highway, *(gut ausgebaut)* BE highroad, *(Durchgangs-)* thoroughfare*	**Straßenbahn**	BE tram, US streetcar
		Anhänger	second car
		Straßenbahnhaltestelle	stop
		Strecke	BE tramline, US streetcar line
Einbahn~	one-way street	Fahrgeld	fare
Stadtautobahn	BE urban motorway, US urban freeway	**Autobus, Omnibus**	bus, *(im Fernverkehr)* BE coach
Gasse	alley, lane		
Sackgasse	blind alley	mit dem Bus fahren	to go by bus, to take a ~
Allee	avenue		
Straßenkreuzung	BE crossroads, US intersection	Obus	trolley-bus
		Untergrundbahn, U-Bahn	underground (railway), *(in London)* the tube, US subway
überschreiten	to cross		
Ecke	turning, corner		
Kurve	bend		
Pflaster	pavement	Rolltreppe	escalator
pflastern	to pave	**Verkehrsinsel**	BE (traffic) island, US safety zone, safety island
Bürger-, Gehsteig	BE pavement, US sidewalk		
Bordstein	BE kerb, US curb		
Gosse	gutter	**Zebrastreifen**	zebra crossing
Gully	gully-hole	**Apotheke**	chemist's* shop, pharmacy, US drugstore
Fahrbahn	roadway		
e-n kleinen Umweg machen	to make a slight detour*		
		Bibliothek, Bücherei	library
		Leihbücherei	lending library
Verkehr	traffic (s. Kap. 13, S. 68)	**Drogerie**	BE druggist's shop, US drugstore
Straßen~	road ~		
Verkehrsregelung	traffic control	**Kirche**	church
Verkehrspolizist	traffic policeman+	Kapelle	chapel
Verkehrszeichen	road sign	Turm	tower (church- ~)
Verkehrsampel	traffic lights (red, amber, green)	**Krankenhaus**	hospital
		Krankenauto	ambulance
grüne Welle	phased traffic lights	Sanatorium, Heilanstalt	sanatorium+, *bes* US sanitarium+
Fahrzeug	vehicle		
Auto, Motorrad, Fahrrad, Parkplatz, Tankstelle, Taxe (Taxi)	s. Kap. 13.2. (S. 69/70/71)	**Postamt**	s. Kap. 14.2. (S. 75)
		Rathaus, Polizeirevier, Feuerwehr	s. Kap. 20 (S. 99)
Kutsche	coach	**Schule**	s. Kap. 18.1 (S. 84)

Kindergarten	kindergarten, nursery school	**Bauer, Landwirt**	farmer, peasant
Theater, Kino	s. Kap. 18.6 (S. 93/94)	Pächter	tenant
Konzertsaal	s. Kap. 18.5 (S. 92)	Landarbeiter	agricultural labourer, farm hand
Waisenhaus	orphanage	Landleute	country people, country folk*
Schwimmbad, Sportplatz, Stadion, Turnhalle	s. Kap. 17 (S. 82/83)	**Bauernhof**	farm
		Geflügelfarm	poultry farm
		Viehfarm	US ranch
Elektrizitätswerk	power station	Pflanzung, Plantage	plantation (cotton, sugar, tobacco ~)
Gaswerk	gas-works		
Schlachthaus	slaughterhouse	**Bauernhaus**	farmhouse
Wasserwerk	water-works	Scheune	barn
~ versorgung	water-supply	Schuppen	shed
Fabrik	s. Kap. 11.1 (S. 61)	Stall	stable
Gasthaus	s. Kap. 6 (S. 45)	Kuhstall	cow-house, cowshed, US cow barn
Geschäft (= Laden)	s. Kap. 11.2 u. 10.2, s. Händler (S. 62/59)	Schweinestall	pigsty, pigpen
		Hundehütte	kennel, doghouse
Bäckerei	bakery	**Geräte**	implements
Bäckerladen	BE baker's shop, US bakery	Axt	axe, US ax
		Beil	hatchet
Lebensmittelgeschäft	BE grocer's shop	Hacke	hoe
		Heu-, Mistgabel	pitchfork
Molkerei	dairy	Pflug	plough, US plow
Milchgeschäft	dairy	Rechen, Harke	rake
Modesalon	fashion house	Schaufel	shovel
Schuhgeschäft	shoe shop	Sense	scythe*
Süßwarengeschäft	BE sweet shop, US candy store	Sichel	sickle
		Spaten	spade
Wäscherei	laundry	Gießkanne	BE watering-can, US sprinkling can
Warenhaus, Kaufhaus	s. Kap. 11.2 (S. 62)		
		Schlauch	hose
		Maschine	s. Kap. 11 (S. 61)

16. Dorf und Landwirtschaft

		Mähmaschine	mower
Landleben	country life	Mähdrescher	combine (BE a. combine-harvester)
ländlicher Bezirk	rural district		
Landstraße	s. Straße, Kap. 15 (S. 77)	Traktor, Zugmaschine, Schlepper	tractor
Wegweiser	signpost	**Wagen (Pferde-)**	carriage, waggon, bes US wagon
Fußweg	(foot-)path		
Dorf	village	zweirädriger Wagen, Karren	cart
Mühle	mill (windmill)		
Sägewerk	sawmill	Peitsche	whip
Landwirtschaft, Akkerbau	agriculture, farming	Schubkarren	wheelbarrow
		Boden	ground
landwirtschaftliche Erzeugnisse	agricultural produce	Acker ~	soil
		Feld	field

Wald	(klein, durchforstet) wood(s), (groß, wild) forest	s. ansiedeln	to settle
		bebauen, bestellen	to cultivate, to till
		bewässern	to water, to irrigate
Wiese	meadow	gießen	to water
Weideland	pasture	düngen	to manure
Weinberg	vineyard*	ernten	to harvest; to reap
Weinrebe	vine	erzeugen	to produce
Weintraube	grape	(Ertrag) liefern	to yield (~ a heavy crop)
Dünger, Dung	dung, manure		
Kunstdünger	fertilizer	fällen (Baum)	to fell
Jauche	liquid manure	sägen	to saw
Ernte(zeit)	harvest	füttern	to feed
Ernteertrag	harvest, crop (rich, abundant, average, bad, poor ~)	graben	to dig
		Graben	ditch
		mähen	to mow, to reap, to cut
Garten	garden		
Blumengarten	flower garden	mahlen	to grind
Gemüsegarten	kitchen garden, vegetable garden	mästen	to fatten
		melken	to milk
Obstgarten	orchard	pachten	to rent (s-th from s-o)
Bäume, Beeren, Blumen, Gemüse, Obst, Sträucher	s. Kap. 26.2 (S. 115/116)	verpachten	to rent (s-th to s-o), to lease
Blumenbeet	flower-bed	pflücken	to pick, to pluck, to gather
Hecke	hedge		
Rasen	lawn	pflügen	to plough, US plow
Zaun	fence	Furche	furrow
Gartenbau	gardening	säen	to sow
Treibhaus	hot-house	Samen	seed
Getreide(arten)	s. Kap. 26.2 (S. 115)	Saatkorn	seed-corn
Stroh	straw	d. Saat steht schön	the crops look well
Haustiere	s. Kap. 26.1 (S. 111)	wachsen	to grow
Bienenzucht	bee-keeping	weiden, grasen	to graze
Imker	bee-keeper		
Honig	honey		
Geflügelzucht	poultry-farm(ing)	**17. Erholung, Spiel, Sport**	
Viehbestand	livestock (horses, cows, pigs, sheep, etc.)	Erholung	recreation
		Entspannung	relaxation
		Ruhe	rest
Viehfutter	fodder, feed	Ablenkung, Zerstreuung	diversion
Rindvieh	cattle		
5 Stück ~	five head of cattle	s. langweilen	to feel bored
Viehherde	herd of cattle	eintöniges Leben	monotonous* life
Viehzucht	cattle-breeding, US stock raising	Lieblingsbeschäftigung	favourite occupation
anbauen, pflanzen	to plant, to grow, to raise	Steckenpferd, Liebhaberei	hobby

Freizeit, Muße-stunden	leisure* (time), spare time, (in my) off time	Gesellschaftstanz	ballroom dance (e.g., foxtrot, tango+, cha-cha*, boogie-woogie, rumba)
e. freier Tag	a holiday, a day off		
Urlaub (persönl.) Ferien	leave holiday (to go on ~ ; to take a month's ~), US vacation	Walzer	waltz (Viennese ~ ; slow or English ~)
		Vergnügung	entertainment, amusement, pleasure
Urlauber, Ferien-reisender	holiday-maker, US vacationist	Vergnügungsindu-strie	entertainment industry
Scherz, Spaß	joke, fun, jest	Vergnügungsreise	pleasure trip, *(Schiff)* cruise
scherzen, spaßen	to jest, to joke		
spaßig, drollig	funny	s. vergnügen	to enjoy o.s., to have a wonderful time
ein Witz	a joke		
abgedroschen	stale	**Karneval**	carnival (~ proces-sion, ~ prince)
Unterhaltung, Zeit-vertreib	entertainment, pas-time, amusement	Jahrmarkt	(BE fun) fair
j-n (kurzweilig) unterhalten	to entertain, to amuse	Bude, Stand	stall
		Zirkus	circus+
Gespräch	talk, conversation	Vorführung	performance
rauchen	to smoke (a cigar, a cigarette, a pipe)	akrobatisches Kraft-, Kunststück	acrobatic feat
Festlichkeit	festival, festivity	Seiltänzer	rope-walker
Gesangverein	choral society	Clown, Hanswurst	clown
geselliges Beisam-mensein	social gathering	Taschenspieler, Zauberkünstler	conjurer* (s. Kap. 23 S. 107)
		Kniff, Kunstgriff	trick
Klub	club	Karussell	*bes* BE roundabout, merry-go-round
Mitglied	member		
Abendgesellschaft	evening party	Riesenrad	Ferris wheel, big wheel
Einladung	invitation		
einladen	to invite	Berg- u. Talbahn, Achterbahn	BE big dipper, BE switchback, US roll-er coaster
Gastgeber(in)	host(ess)		
Gast	guest		
willkommen	welcome	Geisterbahn	BE ghost train, US spook ride
ungebeten	uninvited		
empfangen	to receive	Autoskooter	dodgem, bumper car
begrüßen	to welcome	Kasperltheater	Punch and Judy show
e. herzlicher Emp-fang (Willkomm)	a hearty welcome		
einführen, vorstel-len	to introduce	**Spiel**	play, *(nach Regeln)* game (of tennis, football, chess; in-door, outdoor ~s)
Einführung	introduction		
s. verbeugen	to bow* (to s-o)		
e-e leichte (e-e tie-fe) Verbeugung	a slight (a low) bow*	Wettspiel	*bes* BE match (foot-ball, tennis, golf ~)
auf Wiedersehen!	good-bye!	Regel	rule
Tanz, tanzen	(to) dance	Spieler	player
Ball	ball	Mitspieler (Kar-tenspiel, Tennis)	partner

Einsatz	stake
Glücksspiel(er)	gamble(r)
Billard	billiards
~stock	billiard cue
Kugel	ball
Damespiel	BE draughts* (a game of ~), US checkers
Damebrett	BE draught-board, US checkerboard
Feld	square
Stein	piece, man+
Dame	king
Federball	badminton
Ball	shuttlecock
Schläger	racket
Schach (spielen)	(to play) chess
~partie, ~spiel	a game of chess
Schachbrett	chessboard
Feld	square
Schachfigur	chessman+, piece
König	king
Dame	queen
Läufer	bishop
Springer	knight
Turm	castle (*or* rook)
Bauer	pawn
ziehen, e-n Zug machen	to (make a) move
Schachmatt, matt setzen	(to) checkmate (*or* (to) mate)
Kartenspiel	game of cards
Herz	hearts
Karo	diamonds
Pik	spades
Kreuz	clubs (the ace of hearts, the ten of clubs, etc.)
Farbe	suit
Trumpf	trump (hearts are ~s)
mischen	to shuffle
geben, austeilen	to deal
Kegelspiel	BE skittles, ninepins, US bowls
Kegel	BE skittle, ninepin
Kugel	ball
Kegelbahn	BE skittle-alley, *bes* US bowling alley
Tischtennis	table-tennis, ping-pong
würfeln	to throw (dice)
ein Würfel	one of the dice, a dice
Rätsel	riddle
Kreuzwort~	crossword puzzle
Lösung	solution
lösen	to solve
(er)raten	to guess
Wette	bet
Fußballtoto	football pools (he won on the pools, a fortune from the pools; did you do the pools last week?)
Lotto	national lottery (to do the n.l.)
Spielzeug	toy, playthings
Ball	ball
e-n Drachen steigen lassen	to fly a kite
Puppe	doll
Roller	scooter
Rollschuh	roller-skate
Schaukel(n)	(to) swing
Schaukelbrett, Wippe	seesaw
Wurfpfeil	dart
Sport	sports, athletics
~ treiben	to do *or* to go in for sport(s)
Angeln	angling, fishing
Baseball	baseball
Basketball	basket-ball
Bergsteigen	mountain-climbing, mountaineering
Boxen	boxing (~-gloves, ~-match, ~-ring)
Kricket	cricket (~-match)
Diskuswerfen	discus-throwing
Fechten	fencing
Fußball	football
deutscher ~	association f., *coll.* soccer
amerikanischer ~	American football; Rugby
Gewichtheben	weight-lifting
Golf	golf

~platz	golf-course	sportsmännisch, sportlich (Verhalten usw.)	sporting, sportsmanlike, *(Figur)* athletic (man, build)
~schläger	golf-club		
~spieler	golfer		
Loch	hole	Sportlerin	sportswoman+
Handball	handball	Berufsspieler	professional
Hockey	hockey (ice-~)	Schulung, Ausbildung, Übung	training
Jagd	hunting (fox-~)		
~ auf Niederwild	shooting	(Sport-)Abzeichen	(sports) badge
Kugelstoßen	shotputting, putting the shot	**Gymnastik**	keep-fit exercises, callisthenics, US cali-*
Kugelstoßer	shotputter		
Laufen	running, racing		
Dauerlauf	jog(ging) (to ~)	**Höchstleistung, Rekord**	record
Motorsport	motor sport		
Autorennen	motor race	e-n Rekord aufstellen	to set up a record
Rennwagen	racing car		
Pferderennen	horse race	innehaben	to hold
Radsport	cycle racing, cycling	brechen	to break
Ringen	wrestling	hervorragende Leistung	outstanding performance
Rodeln	sledging, sledding, coasting downhill on a sled(ge)		
		Weltrekord	world record
Schlitten	sledge, sled, toboggan	**Leibesübungen**	physical training, P.T.
		Leichtathletik	track and field athletics
Rodelbahn	toboggan run		
Schlittschuhlaufen	skating	**Turnen**	gymnastics, *coll.* gym (to do gym)
Schlittschuh	skate		
Eiskunstlauf	figure skating	Turner	gymnast
Rollschuhlaufen	roller skating	Turnhalle	gymnasium*+, gym
Schwimmen	swimming (breast stroke, back stroke, crawling)	Turnhose	gym shorts
		Turnschuhe	gym shoes, US sneakers
Tauchen, Turmspringen	diving	**Mannschaft**	team
		Fußball~, Elf	football team
Segelfliegen	s. Kap. 13.4 S. 73	Trainer	coach
Segeln, Segelsport	sailing, yachting*	Torwart	goalkeeper (to keep goal)
Skisport, Skilaufen	skiing*		
~läufer	skier*	Verteidigung	defence, US -nse
Sprungschanze	ski-jump	Läuferreihe	half-backs
Skilift	ski-lift	Sturm	forwards
Sessellift	chair-lift	Stürmer	forward
Piste	ski run	schießen, kicken	to kick (a goal; penalty kick, free kick, corner kick)
Speerwerfen	throwing the javelin*		
Springen	jumping (high jump; long, *bes* US broad jump)	Abseits	offside
		Meister	champion
Tauziehen	tug of war	Meisterschaft	championship
Wasserball	water polo	Weltmeister	world champion
Sportler	sportsman+, athlete	Titel	title

Niederlage	defeat
besiegen, schlagen	to defeat, to beat
er war nicht auf der Höhe	he was not up to the mark
Punktzahl, Ergebnis	score
Wie steht das Spiel?	What's the score?
er gewann fünf Läufe für unsere Mannschaft	he scored five runs for our team
Unentschieden	draw, tie (the game ended in a d., in a t.)
Schiedsrichter	umpire; *(Fußball)* referee (Who refereed the football match?)
Entscheidung	decision
Schwerathletik	heavy athletics (wrestling, weightlifting, judo)
Sieg	win (our team has had five wins; a win by four goals to one), victory
siegreich	victorious
Goldmedaille	gold medal
Pokal	cup
siegen	to win, to be victorious
den ersten Preis gewinnen	to win the first prize
Sieger	winner
nach Punkten	on points
das Spiel endete mit e-m 3:0 Sieg für...	the match *(bes* US the game) resulted in a 3-0 win for...
das Ergebnis war 3:0	the result was 3-0 (three nil, three nothing)
Spielplatz	playground
Sportfest	sports meeting
Sportplatz	sports ground *or* field
Aschenbahn	cinder track
Fußballplatz	football field, US gridiron
Tennisplatz	(tennis) court
Tennisschläger	(tennis) racket
Rennbahn (Pferde-)	race-course
Rennstrecke (Auto-)	race-track
Wettrennen	race
Stoppuhr	stop-watch
Ziel	finish
Tribüne	grandstand
Sportverein	sports club
Liga, Verband	league
Stadion	stadium+
Wettkampf	contest (athletic ~s)
einen ~ austragen	to contest an event
Zuschauer	spectator
Beifall	applause
tosend	roaring
Beifall klatschen	to applaud
Beifallsrufe	cheers
Ausflug	trip, outing, *(mit Reisebüro)* excursion
Ausflügler	tripper
Tourist	tourist
Wanderung	walking-tour, hike
wandern	to walk, *(sportl.)* to hike
(ohne Ziel) umherwandern, umherstreifen	to wander about, to ramble (to r. from place to place; to r. in the forest)
Rucksack	rucksack
Rast	rest
Picknick	picnic (to have *or* go for a ~)
Jugendherberge	youth hostel
baden (im Freien)	to bathe, to have a bathe (BE) *or* a swim
schwimmen	to swim
Schwimmer	swimmer
tauchen	to dive
Sprungbrett	diving-board
Kunstspringen	fancy diving
Kopfsprung	header
Salto	somersault
Schwimmbad, Badeanstalt	*(Gebäude)* swimming-baths, *(im Freien)* swimming-pool
Becken	basin
rudern	to row

Wassersport	water sports
Wellenreiten, Surfen	surfing
Surfbrett	surfboard, *(mit Segel)* sailboard
(Wind)Surfing	windsurfing
Gartenarbeit	gardening
jagen	to hunt, *(Niederwild)* to shoot
Jäger	hunter, huntsman+, sportsman+
klettern	to climb
Kletterer	climber
Bergführer	mountain guide
Seil	rope
reiten	to ride (on horseback)
ausreiten	to go for a ride
Sattel	saddle
Zügel	rein(s)
Hufeisen	horseshoe
schießen	to shoot (at a target; to ~ hares)
Gewehr	gun, rifle
zielen (auf)	to take aim, to aim (at)
Schuß	shot
das Ziel treffen	to hit the mark
das Ziel verfehlen	to miss the mark (*or* one's aim)
spazierengehen	to go for a walk, to take a walk
im Freien	in the open air, out of doors
frische Luft und Sonnenschein genießen	to enjoy fresh air and sunshine
Sonnenbad	sun-bath (to take a ~, to sun-bathe)
spielen	to play (do you ~ cricket? will you ~ me at chess? to ~ a trump, one's ace of diamonds)
springen	to jump, *(mit e-m Satz)* to spring, *(in großen Sätzen)* to bound
laufen, rennen	to run
hüpfen (auf einem Bein)	to hop
trainieren	to train
in Form bleiben	to keep fit (*or* in form)
Zelt	tent
aufschlagen	to pitch
Camping	camping (we want to go ~ next summer)
Campingplatz	campsite
Luftmatratze	air mattress
Picknickkoffer	picnic case

18. Bildung, Wissenschaft und Kunst

18.1 Schule

Erziehung, Bildung	education
Allgemeinbildung	general background
Unterricht	instruction, *bes* BE tuition
Einzel ~	individual tuition
Fern ~	BE postal tuition, correspondence course
berufliche Ausbildung	vocational education (*or* training)
Schule	school
staatl., öffentl. ~	State s., BE county s., US public school
Höhere Privatschule mit Internat	BE public school
Privatschule	private school
Volks-, Grundschule	elementary school, primary school, US grade school
höhere Schule, Oberschule, Gymnasium	secondary school, US high school
Berufsschule	vocational school
Technikum	college of technology
Handelsschule	commercial school
Heimschule, Internat	boarding school
Kost u. Wohnung	board and lodging
Analphabet	illiterate

Anschlagtafel, schwarzes Brett	notice-board, US bulletin board
Aufgaben	homework, assignment
Lektion	lesson
e-e Aufgabe stellen	to set a task, to give homework
Aufsatz	composition, essay
Thema	subject
Entwurf	draft
Reinschrift	fair copy
Satzzeichen	punctuation marks
Anführungszeichen	quotation marks, quotes, BE inverted commas
Apostroph	apostrophe*
Ausrufezeichen	exclamation mark, bes US exclamation point
Bindestrich	hyphen (these words are, this compound is, hyphened)
Doppelpunkt	colon
Fragezeichen	question mark, US interrogation point
Gedankenstrich	dash
Klammern	parentheses*+, round brackets
eckige Klammern	(square) brackets
Komma	comma
Punkt	BE full stop, period
Semikolon	semicolon
Direktor	headmaster, US principal
Direktorin	headmistress
Einschreibung	enrolment, US enrollment
einschreiben	to enrol, US enroll
Ferien	holidays, vacation
Klasse	BE form, class, US grade
Klassenarbeit	written test
Lehrplan	curriculum+
~stoff	subject matter
Unterrichtsplan	syllabus+
Leibesübungen	s. Kap. 17. (S. 82)
Spielnachmittag	games afternoon
Note, Zensur	mark, US grade
zensieren	to mark, US to grade
Prüfung	examination, coll. exam (written, oral)
e-e ~ machen	to sit for an exam (or test)
Aufnahmeprüfung	entrance examination
Abschlußprüfung	final exam, finals
Prüfling	examinee
Prüfungsordnung	examination syllabus (and regulations)
Abitur	school-leaving examination, BE GCE. (advanced level) (GCE. = General Certificate of Education), US high school diploma
Abiturient	secondary-school leaver
Schlußfeier	BE speech-day, US graduation (ceremony), US commencement
Aula	assembly-hall, US auditorium
Schüler	pupil, schoolboy, US a. student
Mitschüler	BE schoolfellow, schoolmate, classmate
Schulbuch	school-book
Lehrbuch	textbook
Handbuch	handbook, manual
Wörterbuch	dictionary
Heft	(exercise-)book
e-e saubere Handschrift	a neat handwriting
Klecks	blot
Löschpapier	blotting-paper
Schulgebäude	school building
Schulgeld	tuition, school fee(s)
Schulzimmer	schoolroom, classroom
Wandtafel	blackboard
Schwamm	sponge*
Kreide	chalk
Lineal	ruler

85

Zirkel	pair of compasses*, US *a.* compass	Wahlfach	optional subject, US elective subject
Pult	desk	alte Sprachen	classical languages (Latin, Greek)
Landkarte	map		
Atlas	atlas	neue Sprachen	modern languages (English, French, Russian)
Schultasche, -mappe	school-bag		
Filzschreiber	felt-tip (pen)	Geschichte	history (ancient, medieval*, modern)
Füll(federhalt)er	fountain pen		
Kugelschreiber	ballpoint(pen), BE biro	Geographie	geography
		Mathematik	mathematics, coll. maths (arithmetic*, algebra, geometry)
Bleistift	pencil		
Schuldisziplin	school discipline		
Betragen, Führung	conduct (he got 'good' for ~)	Naturwissenschaften	(natural) science (physics, chemistry*, biology*)
grobe Disziplinlosigkeit	gross misdemeanour		
		Staatsbürgerkunde	civics
Unfug treiben	to get up to mischief*	Kunsterziehung	art (~ education; drawing, singing)
Strafe, Tadel	s. Kap. 2. u. 3.5. (S. 16/26)	Religion	religious instruction
		Zeugnis	report, certificate
Strafarbeit	lines (I have to do lines)	Abgangs~	leaving certificate
		Fleiß	effort, diligence (good, satisfactory, not satisfactory)
Stundenplan	time-table, US schedule*		
Unterrichtsstunde	*(bes. als Stoffeinheit)* lesson, *(bes. als Zeiteinheit)* period	Leistungen	results, proficiency (very good, good, fair, satisfactory, poor, unsatisfactory)
Pause	break, US recess		
Übung	exercise	**in der Schule gut mitkommen**	to do well at school
Aussprache	pronunciation*		
aussprechen	to pronounce	auffallende (schnelle, erstaunliche, geringe) Fortschritte machen	to make remarkable (rapid, astonishing, little) progress
Rechtschreibung	spelling		
buchstabieren	to spell		
Diktat	dictation		
Grammatik	grammar		
Regel	rule	Kenntnisse, Wissen	knowledge*
Beispiel	example		
Übersetzung	translation	gründlich	thorough*
frei	free	oberflächlich	superficial
wörtlich, wortgetreu	literal	**aufpassen**	to pay attention (to)
		behandeln (Thema)	
Fehler	mistake	geschickt	skilfully, US skillfully
schuldhafter, ernster ~	error (in addition, a grammatical ~)	**benoten**	to mark, US to grade
dummer ~	blunder	**bestehen (Prüfung)**	to pass (an examination)
Flüchtigkeits~	slip		
Unterrichtsfach	subject	durchfallen	to fail (in an examination)
Pflichtfach	compulsory subject		

besuchen (e-e Schule)	to go to (or to attend) a school	vorsagen	to prompt
(be)treiben	to study, (bes. Hobby) to go in for (golf, stamp-collecting)	**18.2. Wissenschaft**	
		Wissenschaft	science
		Wissenschaftler	scientist, scholar
ermahnen	to admonish (s-o not to be careless)	wissenschaftliche Forschung	scientific research
erziehen	to educate	untersuchen	to investigate (or to inquire into) (the causes of natural phenomena)
Eselsbrücke (Übersetzungshilfe u. dgl.)	coll. crib (to use a ~), US coll. pony (or trot)		
abschreiben von	to crib from	gründliche Untersuchungen anstellen	to make thorough* inquiries (or investigations)
faulenzen	to be lazy; to take it easy		
seine Pflicht vernachlässigen	to neglect one's duty	Methode	method
		Lehre	doctrine
die Schule schwänzen	to play truant, US to play hooky	Theorie	theory
		Abhandlung	treatise
lehren, unterrichten	to teach (s-o a subject)	erforschen	to explore
		entdecken	to discover
lernen	to learn (French; one's lessons), to study	Entdeckung	discovery
		alle Zweige menschl. Wissens	all branches of human knowledge*
auswendig ~	to learn by heart	Naturwissenschaft(en)	natural science(s)
wiederholen	to repeat		
sich abmühen	to work hard, to toil	Sozialwissenschaft(en)	social science(s)
büffeln	BE to swot, bes US to bone, to grind (for an exam)		
		Geisteswissenschaft(en)	humanities
loben	s. Kap. 3.2. (S. 26)	Akademiker	university graduate, professional man
Lob	s. Kap. 2. (S. 16)		
nachsitzen lassen	to keep in	akademisch	academic (subjects; the ~ year: October to June)
nachsitzen müssen	to be kept in, to have detention		
prüfen	to examine, (Kenntnisse) to test	Bibliothek, Bücherei	library
		Hand ~ (zum Nachschlagen)	reference ~
tadeln	s. Kap. 3.5. (S. 26)	leihen	to lend (s-o s-th)
üben	BE to practise, US to practice, to drill	sich etwas leihen	to borrow s-th from s-o
verbessern (Fehler)	to correct	Aus- u. Rückgabe v. Büchern	issue and return of books
Verbesserung	correction		
ausstreichen	to strike (or cross) out	Experiment, Versuch	experiment
		Beobachtung	observation
ausradieren	to rub out, to erase	Fachmann	expert
Radiergummi	BE rubber, eraser	Fachausdruck	technical term
vorrücken, versetzt werden	to be put up, US to be promoted	Laie	layman+

Gelehrter	learned man+, scholar
Gelehrsamkeit	learning, scholarship
Laboratorium	laboratory*, lab
Mikroskop	microscope*
Reagenzglas	test-tube
Universität	university
Gelände, Gebäude e-r ~	campus
Rektor	Vice-Chancellor, US President
Rektor ehrenhalber	Chancellor
Fakultät	faculty
Dekan	Dean
Ordinarius, ord. Univ. Prof.	professor in ordinary
Lektor, Dozent	lecturer, assistant professor
Lehrstuhl	chair
Studium	study
studieren	to study
Hauptfach	chief (*or* principal) subject, US major
Nebenfach	subsidiary subject, US minor
Immatrikulation	matriculation
Student	student
~ im 1. Jahr	freshman+
~ bis zum ersten Examen	undergraduate
Studentin	(girl *or* woman) student, US *coll.* co-ed
Studentenverbindung	students' club, US fraternity
Studentinnenvereinigung	women-students' club, US sorority
Debattierklub	debating society (*or* club)
Semester	term
Vorlesung halten	to deliver (give) a lecture (on s-th)
hören	to attend
Hörsaal	lecture room (*or* hall)
Vorlesungsverzeichnis	lecture timetable
Stipendium	scholarship
Dissertation	thesis+
akad. Grad	academic degree
Inhaber e-s akad. Grades	graduate
e-n akad. Grad erwerben	to take a degree
absolvieren, das Abschlußexamen machen (in)	to graduate (he graduated at Oxford; US he was graduated from...)
promovieren (in Philosophie)	to do a doctorate (in philosophy)
Promotion	(receiving a) doctorate
Diplom	diploma
verleihen	to confer (a degree upon), to grant (a diploma to)
Technische Universität (Hochschule)	*bes* BE Institute (*or* College) of Technology, *bes* US Technological Institute
Astronomie	astronomy
Astronom	astronomer
Biologie	biology*
Biologe	biologist
Botanik	botany
Botaniker	botanist
Chemie	chemistry*
Chemiker	(analytical) chemist*; chemical engineer
Pharmazeut	(pharmaceutical) chemist*
Erdkunde	geography
Geograph	geographer
Forschungsreisender	explorer
Forstwirtschaft	forestry science
Geologie	geology
Geologe	geologist
Geschichte	history (universal ~, prehistory)
Historiker	historian
Archiv	archives*
öffentl. Urkunde	public record
Chronik	chronicle
Mathematik	mathematics
reine ~	pure mathematics
angewandte ~	applied m.

Mathematiker	mathematician	Sprachforscher,	linguist
Medizin	medicine, medical	Sprachenkenner	
	science	Philologie	philology; language
Mediziner	medical man+		and literature
Augenheilkunde	ophthalmology*	Philologe	philologist
Augenarzt	ophthalmologist,	Sprache	language
	oculist	Fremdsprache	foreign language (s.
Chirurgie	surgery		Kap. 3.6., S. 29)
Chirurg	surgeon	**Technik**	technical science(s)
Facharzt (für)	specialist (in)	angewandte ~	engineering
Geburtshilfe	obstetrics*	techn. Wissen-	technology
Geburtshelfer	obstetrician*	schaft	
innere Medizin	internal medicine	**Theologie**	theology
Kinderheilkunde	paediatrics*, US	Theologe	theologian
	pedi-	**Tierarzneikunde**	veterinary* science
Kinderarzt	paediatrician*, US	Tierarzt	s. Kap. 10.2. (S. 58)
	pedi-	**Völkerkunde**	ethnology
Nervenheilkunde	neurology*	**Volkskunde**	folklore*
Nervenarzt	neurologist	**Volkswirtschafts-**	economics
Orthopädie	orthopaedics*, US	**lehre**	
	-pedics	Volkswirtschaftler	(political) economist
Orthopäde	orthopaedist, US	**Zoologie**	zoology*
	-pedist	Zoologe	zoologist
Zahnheilkunde	dentistry		
Zahnarzt	dentist	**18.3. Buch**	
Naturwissenschaft	(natural) science		
Naturwissen-	scientist	**Buch**	book
schaftler		Format	size
Pädagogik, Erzie-	educational science	Einband	cover
hungswissenschaft		binden	to bind
Pädagoge	*bes* BE educationist,	**Buchhandel**	book trade
	educator	Buchhandlung	bookshop, US
Erziehungswissen-	educationalist		bookstore
schaftler		Antiquariatsbuch-	second-hand
Philosophie	philosophy	handlung	bookshop
Philosoph	philosopher	**Anhang**	appendix+
Physik	physics	**Anmerkung**	annotation
Kern ~	nuclear physics	Fußnote	footnote
Physiker	physicist	Kommentar	commentary
Psychologie	psychology*	erläuternde Be-	explanatory remark
Psychologe	psychologist	merkung	(*or* note)
Rechtswissenschaft	legal science, juris-	Abkürzung	abbreviation
	prudence	**Auflage**	edition
Jurist	jurist, lawyer	verbesserte und	revised and enlarged
Soziologie (Gesell-	sociology	erweiterte Auflage	edition
schaftslehre)		Exemplar	copy
Sprachwissenschaft	linguistics	Ab-, Neudruck	reprint
Sprachwissen-	linguistician, linguist	unverändert	unaltered
schaftler			

Druck	s. Kap. 14. (S. 74)	Epos	epic (poem)
Ausgabe	edition (pocket ~)	**Gedicht**	poem
Volksausgabe	popular edition	vortragen	to recite
Herausgeber	editor	Dichter	poet
herausgeben	to edit	Dichtkunst	poetry
Band	volume (a two-~ edition)	Lyrik, lyrische Dichtung	lyric poetry
Druckfehler	misprint	Vers	stanza, strophe*, verse, *(Zeile)* line
Korrekturfahne	proof	melodisch, wohlklingend	melodious
Einleitung, Einführung	introduction (to a book)	Reim	rhyme
Ergänzung	supplement	Kinderreim, -lied	nursery rhyme
Inhaltsverzeichnis	table of contents	Kehrreim	refrain, chorus
Sachregister	subject index+	Strophe	stanza, strophe*
Kapitel	chapter	Versmaß	metre, US meter
Seite	page	**Geschichte, Erzählung**	story, *(märchenh.)* tale
Abschnitt, Absatz	paragraph	Märchen	fairy-tale
Leser	reader	aufregend	exciting, thrilling
Nachschlagewerk	reference book	fesselnd, spannend	fascinating
nachschlagen (in)	to consult (a book), to look up (a word)	rührend	touching
Konversationslexikon	encyclopaedia*, US -pedia	handeln von	to deal with
		Inhalt und Form, Gehalt und Gestalt	substance and form
Titel, Buch~	title	**Kritik**	criticism
Verfasser	author	Besprechung	review (of a new novel)
verfassen	to write (a book)		
veröffentlichen	to publish; to issue*	kritisieren	to criticize
Veröffentlichung	publication	rezensieren	to review
vergriffen	out of print	Kritiker, Rezensent	critic, reviewer
Verlag(sfirma)	publishing house		
Verleger	publisher	Stellungnahme zu	comment* on
Verlagsrecht	copyright	**Lebensbeschreibung**	biography
Vorwort	preface*, foreword	**Prosa**	prose
Zitat	quotation	prosaisch	prosy; *(fig.)* prosaic (a ~ life)
e-e Stelle zitieren	to quote a passage		
		Prosadichtung	prose writing, fiction
18.4. Literatur		**Rede**	speech (to make a ~ on, about s-th)
Literatur, Schrifttum	literature	aufrütteln, packend	stirring
schöne Literatur	belles-lettres*, literature		
Schriftsteller(in)	author(ess), writer	Hauptpunkt, Kern	gist*, essence
literarisch	literary	Ansprache	address*
Abhandlung	*(literar.)* essay, *(wissenschaftl.)* treatise	Vortrag	lecture
		Plauderei	talk
Drama	drama (s. Kap. 18.6. S. 93)	Redner	speaker, orator*
		langatmig, weitschweifig (Redner, Rede)	lengthy

die (Zu)Hörer	the audience
Roman	novel
Romanschriftsteller	novelist
Romanliteratur	fiction
Fortsetzungsroman	serialized novel
Tendenzroman	novel with a purpose
Kriminal~, Detektivgeschichte	detective novel, (crime) thriller
Schauerroman	shocker, thriller
Fortsetzung folgt	to be continued
Sprichwort	proverb
Stil, Ausdrucksweise	style, mode of expression
kurz und bündig, knapp	concise
flüssig	fluent, flowing
klar	lucid
anschaulich	graphic
ausdrucksvoll	expressive
sorgfältig ausgearbeitet, kunstvoll	elaborate
vollendet	polished
langweilig	tedious
dunkel, schwer verständlich	obscure
schwerfällig	heavy, ponderous
gekünstelt	affected
geschraubt, gespreizt	stilted
nachlässig, schlampig	slipshod
erhabene Sprache	sublime language
die Wahl der Worte	the choice of words
Tagebuch	diary (to keep a ~)
Überblick über	survey of
Zusammenfassung	summary
Exzerpt, Auszug	excerpt, extract (from a book)
gekürzte Ausgabe	abridged (*or* condensed) edition
Werk	work (his best ~ ; the complete edition of his ~s)

18.5. Bildende Künste, Musik

Kunst	art
bildende Kunst	fine arts
ausüben	to practise, US -ice
blühen	to flourish
verfallen	to decay
Kunstakademie	art college
Kunstausstellung	art exhibition
Kunsthändler	art dealer
Kunststil	style of art
künstlerisch	artistic
Künstler(in)	artist
Atelier	studio*+
Dilettant	dilettante*
Kunstwerk	work of art
Schmuck, Zierde, Verzierung	ornament, decoration
Technik (e-r Kunst, e-s Künstlers)	technique*
Ausstellung	exhibition
Galerie	gallery
Museum	museum
Sammlung	collection
Baukunst	architecture
romanisch	Romanesque
gotisch	Gothic
Renaissance	Renaissance*
Barock	baroque*
Rokoko	rococo*
architektonisch	architectural
Bildhauerei	sculpture*
Bildhauer	sculptor
Statue	statue
Relief	relief
Holzschnitt	woodcut
Holzschnitzerei	wood-carving
Malerei	(art of) painting
Gemälde	painting
Bild	picture (the ~ represents...)
Motiv	motif*
Bildnis	portrait
in Lebensgröße	life-size
Kunstmaler	artist, painter
Plastik	plastic arts, sculpture*
e-e ~	sculpture*, statue

Radierung	etching
Stich	engraving
Kupferstich	copperplate (engraving)
Zeichnung, Zeichnen	drawing
zeichnen	to draw
Entwurf	draft, outline
Skizze	sketch
Musik, Tonkunst	music
(musikal.) Ton	BE note, US tone (e.g., a whole ~)
das Reich der Töne	the realm* of music
Tonleiter	scale
Klang	tone, sound
Note	note
Melodie	melody
Harmonie	harmony
Akkord	chord
Rhythmus	rhythm
vertonen	to set to music
komponieren	to compose
Komponist	composer
Komposition	composition
Musiker	musician
Musikinstrumente	musical instruments
Blasinstrumente	wind instruments
Blechbläser	brass-wind instruments
Saiteninstrumente	stringed instruments
Schlaginstrumente	percussion instruments
stimmen	to tune
verstimmt	out of tune
Akkordeon	accordion
Blockflöte	recorder
Cello	cello*+, violoncello*+
Cembalo	harpsichord
Dudelsack	bagpipes
Fagott	bassoon
Flöte	flute
Flügel	grand (piano)
Geige	violin
Bogen; Saite	bow*; string
Gitarre	guitar*
Harfe	harp
Kastagnetten	castanets
Klarinette	clarinet*
Klavier	piano* (pianist*)
Taste (Tastatur)	key (keyboard)
Kontrabaß	double-bass*
Mundharmonika	mouth-organ, harmonica
Oboe	oboe
Orgel	organ
Posaune	trombone
Saxophon	saxophone
Trommel	drum (to beat a ~)
Trompete	trumpet (to blow a ~)
Xylophon	xylophone*
Zither	zither
Musikfest	music festival
Musikstück	musical composition, piece of music
Ouvertüre	overture
Marsch	march
Sinfonie	symphony
Sonate	sonata
Satz	movement
Lied	song
singen	to sing
Sänger	singer
Volkslied	folk*-song
Weihnachtslied	Christmas carol
Opern-, Konzertchor	chorus*
Kirchenchor	choir*
Solist	soloist
Sopran	soprano*+
Alt	alto*+
Tenor	tenor*
Baß	bass*
Schlager	pop song, hit song
Konzert	concert
Konzertsaal	concert-hall
Aufführung	performance
Kammermusik	chamber* music
Spieler	player
Notenschrift	musical notation
Dur	major
Moll	minor
Tonart	key
Takt	time (waltz time, two-four time, 4/4 time)
Orchester	orchestra*
Kapelle	band

Blasorchester	brass band	Operette	operetta
Tanzkapelle	dance band	Libretto	libretto+
Schlagzeug	percussion	Ballett	ballet*
Kapellmeister	bandmaster	**Pause**	interval, intermission
Dirigent	conductor		
dirigieren	to conduct	**Platz (Sitz)**	seat (the second ~ in the third row)

18.6. Theater, Film, Photographie

		Loge	box
Theater	theatre	bestellen	to book
Freilichtbühne	open-air theatre	belegen	to reserve
Varieté	variety theatre, BE music-hall, US vaudeville* theater	**Programm, Spielfolge, -plan**	programme, US -am
		Publikum	audience
Vorführung	show	Theaterbesucher	playgoer
Aufführung, Vorstellung	performance	Zuschauer	spectator, looker-on
		Regisseur, Spielleiter	producer, (stage-)director
Theater ~	theatrical ~		
Premiere	first night	inszenieren, herausbringen	to (put on the) stage, to produce
Matinee	morning performance		
		Regie	direction
Nachmittagsvorstellung	matinée*	~ führen	to direct
		Schauspieler	actor
Probe	rehearsal	Schauspielerin	actress
General ~	dress rehearsal	Rolle	role, part
aufführen, geben, spielen	to perform, to act	das Ensemble	the (entire) cast
		e-e gute Besetzung	a good cast
Beifall	applause	**Schauspielkunst**	drama(tic art)
Beifall klatschen, (j-n, etw.) beklatschen	to applaud, to clap	**Souffleur**	prompter (~ 's box)
		Theaterkarte	ticket
auspfeifen, -zischen	to boo off the stage	~ kasse	(theatre) box-office
		Theaterstück	play
Bühne	stage	Schauspiel	play, drama
Bühnenbild	(stage-)set	Trauerspiel	tragedy
die Kulissen	the scenery, the wings	Lustspiel	comedy
		Schwank, Posse	farce
Kostüm(e)	costume(s)	Schauplatz, Szene	scene
Schminke	make-up	Handlung (Fabel)	plot
Vorhang	curtain (the c. rises, drops)	Zwiegespräch	dialogue*
		Held	hero*+
Bühnendichter, Dramatiker	dramatist, playwright	Heldin	heroine*
		für d. Bühne bearbeiten	to adapt (for the stage)
Garderobe	BE cloakroom, US checkroom	**Film**	BE cinema; film, (motion) picture, US coll. movie
Intendant, Direktor	superintendent, theatre-manager		
		Stummfilm	silent film
Oper	opera	Tonfilm	sound film
große ~	grand opera	Farbfilm	colour film

93

(gezeichneter) Trickfilm	(animated) cartoon	Film empfindlich	film (roll-film) sensitive
Hauptfilm	feature film	Empfindlichkeit	sensitivity, speed
Kurzfilm	short feature	entwickeln	to develop
Kulturfilm	documentary (film)	Negativ	negative
ein Film mit N.N. in der Hauptrolle	a film starring (featuring) N.N.	Abzug, Bild, Kopie	print
Filmleinwand	screen	Fotokopie, Ablichtung	photocopy (to ~)
(etw.) filmen	to film		
Drehbuch	(film) script, scenario*+	Dia(positiv)	slide
		e-n Film einlegen	to load a camera
Atelier	studio*+	Objektiv	objective
Frei-, Außengelände	location	Sucher	view-finder
		belichten	to expose
Kino, Lichtspieltheater	BE cinema, US motion picture theater, US movie house	Belichtung	exposure
		Blitzlicht(aufnahme)	flash(light) (to take a ~)
ins K. gehen	to go to the pictures (*or* movies)	Blitzlichtgerät	flashgun
Kinobesucher	film-goer, BE cinema-goer, US movie goer	**18.7. Rundfunk, Fernsehen**	
		Rundfunk	broadcasting, radio
Filmregisseur	film (*or* US movie) director	**Antenne**	aerial*
		atmosphärische Störungen	atmospheric* disturbances, atmospherics
e-n Film drehen	to produce, to shoot a film		
		entstören	to suppress
Notausgang	emergency exit	**Radioapparat, -gerät**	radio (set)
Platzanweiser(in)	usher(ette)	Empfänger	receiving set, receiver
Publikum	audience		
synchronisieren	to dub, to synchronize	Lautsprecher	loudspeaker
		Verstärker	amplifier
Untertitel	subtitle	Plattenspieler	record-player
Vorschau	trailer	Tonabnehmer	pick-up
Vorstellung	show, performance	Tonbandgerät	tape-recorder
Wochenschau	newsreel	Kassettenrecorder	cassette recorder
Photographie	photography	Wiedergabe, Abspielen	playback
Foto, Aufnahme	photo(graph) (colour~, trick~), snap(shot)	Steckdose	BE (wall) socket, US outlet
e-e A. machen	to take a photo (a picture, a snap, a snapshot)	Stecker	plug
		hineinstecken	to plug in, to insert
		herausziehen	to pull out
Fotoapparat	camera	**Rundfunkprogramm, Sendefolge**	broadcasting programme (US -am)
Spiegelreflexkamera	reflex camera		
(Film-)Kamera	BE cine-camera, US motion-picture camera	Nachrichtensendung	news broadcast, newscast
		Kommentar	commentary
		Sportbericht	sport(s) report

Hörspiel	radio play
Darsteller	performer
Schallplatte	record, disc
Bandaufnahme	tape-recording
CD(-Platte)	compact disc, CD
CD-Spieler	CD player
Ansager	announcer
Sprecher	speaker
Radio hören	to listen to the radio
Hörer	listener
Hörerschaft	audience
Rundfunkreklame	radio advertising
Rundfunksender	broadcasting station
Sendernetz	network
Sendung	broadcast
senden	to broadcast
übertragen	to transmit
Senderaum	studio*+
Mikrophon	microphone*
Wellenlänge	wave-length (long wave, medium w., short w., ultra-short w.)
UKW	VHF (very high frequency), US frequency modulation, FM
einschalten	to switch on
ausschalten	to switch off
einstellen (auf e-n Sender)	to tune in (on *or* to Munich)
Klangregler	tone control
Empfang	reception (to receive)
Lautstärke	volume (to adjust the radio to room ~)
Trennschärfe	selectivity
stören (e-n Sender)	to jam (jamming station)
Fernsehen	television, TV
Fernsehsendung	television broadcast, telecast
Fernsehsender	TV station
Fernsehkamera	TV camera
Fernsehstudio	TV studio*+
Empfänger, Fernseher	television set, TV set, BE *coll.* telly
Bild	image
Bildschirm	television screen
Fernsehteilnehmer	(tele)viewer
fernsehen	to watch television
im Fernsehen übertragen	to televise, to telecast
Zuschauer	(TV) viewer

19. Der Staat

(Verwaltung, Regierung, Politik)

Staat	state
souverän	sovereign
Souveränität	sovereignty
Unabhängigkeit	independence
Autonomie	autonomy
Staatsmann	statesman+
politische Gemeinschaft	political community
Bundesstaat	federal state
Bundesrepublik	federal republic
Staatenbund	confederacy
die Großmächte	the Great Powers
Reich	empire, kingdom, realm*
Land	country
Grenze	boundary
~gebiet, Rand	border
politische Grenze	frontier*
Gebiet, Fläche	area
Provinz	province
Bezirk, Kreis	district
Hauptstadt	capital
Heimat	native country, n. place
in der Heimat	at home
im (ins) Ausland	abroad (to live ~, to go ~)
Monarchie	monarchy
Fürst, Prinz	prince
der Herrscher	the sovereign
Kaiser	emperor
König	king
Königin	queen
Prinzgemahl	Prince Consort
Krönung	coronation
Hof	court
ein treuer Untertan	a loyal subject
Republik	republic
Gemeinwesen	commonwealth (the British C~ of Nations)

95

d. Bundesrepublik Deutschland	the Federal Republic of Germany
Deutsche Demokratische Republik	German Democratic Republic
Präsident	president
Amtszeit	term of office
Bevölkerung	population
einheimisch	native
städtisch	urban
ländlich	rural
Einwohner	inhabitant
Eingeborener	native
Einwanderer	immigrant
Volkszählung	census
Auswanderer	emigré*
Emigrant	emigrant
Flüchtling	refugee
Ausländer(in)	foreigner, *(nicht eingebürgert)* alien*
Asyl	(political) asylum*
j-m Asyl gewähren	to grant s-o asylum*
Asylant	person seeking political asylum*
Bürger	citizen
Mitbürger	fellow ~
Oberschicht	upper classes
Mittelstand	the middle classes
Arbeiterklasse	working class
die breite Masse	the populace, the masses
Adel	nobility, *(hoher)* aristocracy
Demokratie	democracy
die Rechte des Volkes	the people's rights
Diktatur	dictatorship; totalitarian system
Diktator	dictator
Einzelwesen und Gemeinschaft	s. Kap. 2. (S. 12)
Gesellschaft	society
sozial	social
asozial	antisocial
Gesetzgebung	legislation
Gesetz	law, statute; Act of Parliament*, Act of Congress
Gesetzbuch	statute book; *(Bürgerliches ~)* Civil Code
Gesetzesvorlage	bill
annehmen, verabschieden	to pass
ablehnen	to reject
zum G. erheben	to enact into law
Antrag	motion
beantragen	to move
internationale Beziehungen	international relations
Völkerrecht	international law
Diplomatie	diplomacy
Diplomat	diplomat*
Botschafter	ambassador
Botschaft	embassy
Gesandter	minister, envoy
Gesandtschaft	legation
Attaché	attaché*
Vertrag	treaty
geheim	secret
schließen	to conclude
verletzen	to violate
Bruch	breach
Bündnisvertrag	treaty of alliance
Handelsvertrag	commercial treaty
Abkommen	agreement
Handels ~	trade agreement
Nichtangriffspakt	non-aggression treaty (*or* pact)
verhandeln	to negotiate
die Vereinten Nationen	the United Nations (Organization), UN
die Generalversammlung	the General Assembly
der Sicherheitsrat	the Security Council
d. Generalsekretär	the Secretary General
der (Genfer) Völkerbund	(1919-1946) the League of Nations
Nationalfeiertag	national holiday
gesetzlicher Feiertag	BE bank holiday, US legal holiday
Nationalflagge	national flag
Sternenbanner	the Star-Spangled Banner, Stars and Stripes
Nationalhymne	national anthem
öffentliches Leben	public life
öffentliche Meinung	public opinion

Presse, Zeitungswesen	s. Kap. 14.1. (S. 73)	(unter)stützen	to support
Tagung	conference (to hold a ~)	stürzen	to overthrow
		zurücktreten	to resign
Versammlung	assembly	regieren	to govern, to rule; to reign
Zusammenkunft	meeting		
Sitzungsperiode	session	Herrschaft	rule; reign
an e-r Sitzung teilnehmen	to attend a meeting	Macht	power (to come into ~, to rise to ~; the party in ~)
Delegierter	delegate	gesetzgebende, richterliche, vollziehende Gewalt	legislative, judicial, executive power
Tagesordnung	agenda* (an item of the ~)		
aufstellen	to draw up	Kabinett	cabinet
e-e Sitzung eröffnen	to open a meeting	Regierungschef	head of the government
Verfahren	procedure*	Ministerpräsident	Prime Minister, Premier*
Protokoll, Niederschrift	minutes*		
		Kanzler	chancellor
Bericht	report	Minister	minister *(in England z. T.)* Secretary of State, *(in USA)* Secretary
Beschluß	decision		
~ fassen	to take a decision		
Entschließung	resolution		
~ annehmen	to pass, to adopt a r.	Ministerium	ministry, *(in England z. T.)* Office, Board, Department, *(in USA)* Department
Partei	party		
unter der Führung von	under the leadership of		
Bewegung	(political) movement	Außenministerium	Foreign Ministry, BE Foreign Office, US State Department
Koalition	coalition		
Block	bloc		
Mitglied	member		
Anhänger	supporter, sympathizer	Außenminister	Foreign Minister, BE Secretary of State for Foreign Affairs, Foreign Secretary, US Secretary of State
Gegner	opponent		
politische Ansichten	political views		
(Partei-)Programm	(party) programme, US -am, platform		
		Finanzministerium	Ministry of Finance, BE the Exchequer, US Treasury Department
Politik	*(als Tätigkeit)* policy, *(als Gebiet, Kunst, Ansicht)* politics		
		Finanzminister	Minister of Finance, BE Chancellor of the Exchequer, US Secretary of the Treasury
Sozialpolitik	social policy		
soziale Sicherheit	social security		
Wirtschaftspolitik	economic policy		
Marktwirtschaft	free-enterprise economy, market e.		
Planwirtschaft	planned economy	Handelsministerium	Ministry of Commerce, BE Board of Trade, US Department of Commerce
verstaatlichen	to nationalize		
Regierung	government, *bes* US administration		

Handelsminister	Minister of Commerce, BE Trade Secretary, US Secretary of Commerce	Staatsdienst	Civil Service
		Vorgesetzter	superior, senior
		Untergebener	subordinate
		ernennen	to appoint
Innenministerium	Ministry of the Interior, BE Home Office, US Department of the Interior	Gehalt	salary
		in den Ruhestand treten	to retire
		Volk	people, nation
		das einfache ~	populace
Innenminister	Minister of the Interior, BE Home Secretary, US Secretary of the Interior	nationale Einheit	national unity
		Volksvertreter, Abgeordneter	representative (of the people)
Justizministerium	Ministry of Justice, US Department of Justice	~ in England	Member of Parliament*, M. P.
		~ in USA	Representative
Justizminister	Minister of Justice, BE Lord High Chancellor, US Attorney General	Bundestag	Bundestag
		Landtag	diet, *(heute)* Landtag
		gesetzgebende Körperschaft	legislative body
Revolution, Umsturz	revolution	e. Sitz im Parlament	a seat in parliament*
Unruhen	unrest, riots		
Aufstand	insurrection, revolt, rebellion	Ausschuß	committee
		e-e Rede halten	to make a speech
niederschlagen, unterdrücken	to put down, to suppress, to crush	Debatte	debate
		Wahl	election
die Ordnung wiederherstellen	to re-establish order	Wahlrecht, Stimmrecht	(right to) vote, suffrage
Staatshaushalt(splan), Etat	budget	Wahlbezirk, Wählerschaft	constituency*
Steuer	tax	Gesamtwählerschaft	electorate
erheben	to levy, to collect		
Steuersatz	(tax) rate	Wahlkampf	election campaign
Titel	title	Wahlversammlung abhalten	election meeting to hold
Auszeichnung	decoration		
Orden	order	Kundgebung	demonstration
verleihen	to confer (an order) on s-o, to award s-o (a medal)	Abstimmung	vote, poll*
		abstimmen (über)	to vote on a question, for, against s-th
Verein, Verband, Gesellschaft	association, union, society, club	wählen	to elect (s-o to an office; he was elected president)
Gewerkschaft	trade union, US labor union	in geheimer Wahl abstimmen	to vote by (secret) ballot
Verfassung	constitution	Stimmzettel	voting-paper, ballot(-paper)
Grundrechte	basic rights		
Freiheit	s. Kap. 2. (S. 19)	Wähler	voter
Verwaltung	administration	Wahlzelle	polling-booth
Amt, Büro	office, agency	Wahlurne	ballot-box
amtlich	official	Stimme	vote
Beamter	official, Civil Servant		

~ abgeben	to cast a vote
stimmen	to vote (for, against)
Stimmenmehrheit	majority of votes
überwältigend	overwhelming
Minderheit	minority
Volksabstimmung, Volksentscheid	plebiscite*
Volksbefragung	referendum

20. Gemeinde

Gemeinde	municipality, *(die Menschen)* community
Land ~	rural community
Stadt ~	municipality, urban community
Stadt	s. Kap. 15. (S. 76)
Amt, Büro	office
öffentliches Amt	public office (s. Kap. 19., S. 98)
Gemeindebeamter	municipal officer
amtlich	official
zuständig (für)	competent (for)
Urkunde	document
Siegel	seal
Stempel, stempeln	(to) stamp
Unterschrift	signature*
unterschreiben	to sign
Behörde	authority; agency, office
örtlich	local
städtisch	municipal
Fundbüro	BE Lost Property Office, US Lost and Found Office
Gesundheitsamt	Public Health Office
Grundbuchamt	Register of Landed Property
Standesamt	registry office
Bürger	citizen; town-dweller
Polizei	police
Polizeipräsidium	police headquarters
Einwohnermeldeamt	registration office
Polizeirevier	police station
~ beamter	policeman+, BE *coll.* bobby, US *coll.* cop
Feuerwehr	fire-brigade, US fire department
Feuerspritze	fire-engine
Schlauch	hose
Rathaus	town hall, *(Großstadt)* city hall
Stadtrat (Körperschaft)	town (*or* city) council
~ (Person)	town (*or* city) councillor, US -ilor
Ausschuß	committee
Vorsitzender	chairman+
Bürgermeister	mayor*, *(Deutschland)* a. burgomaster
gemeindliche Steuern, Abgaben	BE local rates, US municipal taxes
Verwaltung	administration
Bekanntmachung, öffentl. Anschlag	public notice
Zeugnis	certificate
Geburtsschein	birth certificate
Trauschein	marriage certificate
es wird hiermit bestätigt, daß...	this is to certify that...
Formblatt, Formular, Vordruck	form, blank
ausfüllen	to fill in, *bes* US to fill out
Fragebogen	questionnaire*
Liste, Verzeichnis	list
aufstellen	to make out
Paßwesen	passport matters
Personalausweis, Kennkarte	identity card
ausstellen	to issue*
gültig	valid
Fingerabdruck	fingerprint
sich ausweisen	to prove one's identity
Passierschein, Ausweis	pass
Reisepaß	s. Kap. 13. (S. 68)

21. Rechtswesen

Rechtsprechung	jurisdiction, administration of justice
Recht sprechen	to administer justice
Gesetz, Recht	law
bürgerliches Recht	civil law
geschriebenes Recht	statute law
ungeschriebenes engl. Recht (Gemeines Recht)	common law
gesetzmäßig	lawful, legal
gesetzwidrig	unlawful, illegal
gesetzestreuer Bürger	law-abiding citizen
Anklage	charge
~ erheben gegen	to bring charges against
der (die) Angeklagte	the accused
Beklagter	the defendant
Kläger	plaintiff, complainant
Beleidigung	offence, US -nse (to the eye), *(grob)* insult
Beweis	proof
überzeugend	convincing
schlagend, zwingend	cogent
Beweismaterial	evidence
Eid	oath+ (to take *or* swear an ~)
Meineid	perjury
Gericht(shof)	court (of justice), law-court; tribunal
Richter	judge
Staatsanwalt	public prosecutor
Gerichtsverfahren	legal proceedings
Gerichtsverhandlung	hearing, *(Straf-)* trial
Zivil- und Strafsachen	civil and criminal cases
Geständnis	confession (to make a full ~)
Haftbefehl	warrant of arrest
Prozeß, bürgerl.	lawsuit; action, case (to gain one's ~)
Rechtsstreit	
in e-n Rechtsstreit verwickelt	involved in a lawsuit
gegen j-n e-n Prozeß anstrengen	to bring an action against s-o
Rechtsanwalt, Verteidiger	s. Kap. 10.2. (S. 59)
Sachverständiger	expert
zu Rate ziehen	to consult
Gutachten	(expert) opinion
Strafe	punishment
Todes~	capital punishment
Gefängnis	prison, BE gaol*, jail
(Gefängnis-)Strafe	imprisonment
Zelle	cell
Gefangener	prisoner
Verhaftung	arrest
Gefängnishaft	confinement, detention; *(Strafe)* imprisonment
Bewährungsfrist	probation
er erhielt Bewährungsfrist	he was placed on probation
Geldstrafe	fine (he was fined ten pounds)
Unschuld	innocence
unschuldig	innocent, not guilty
Untersuchung, Nachforschung	investigation, inquiry (into s-th), probe (into s-th)
Urteilsspruch	sentence, judgment
fällen	to pass
Todesurteil	death sentence
aussprechen	to pronounce
hinrichten	to execute
Hinrichtung	execution
Verurteilung	condemnation, conviction
Vorstrafe	previous conviction
Freispruch	verdict of not guilty, acquittal
Berufung einlegen bei	to (make an) appeal to
Verbrechen	crime
abscheulich	abominable
begehen	to commit
Mord	murder
ermorden	to murder
Mörder	murderer

töten	to kill	betrügen	to defraud; to cheat
Totschlag	manslaughter	Betrug	fraud
Brandstiftung	arson, BE fire-raising	Betrüger	defrauder; swindler, *(Spiel)* cheat
Brandstifter	incendiary, arsonist	beweisen	to prove
Raub	robbery	bezeugen	to testify, to bear witness (that s-th is true)
Verbrecher	criminal		
Täter, Missetäter	offender, culprit	entführen	to kidnap
Mittäter, Mitschuldiger	accomplice	freilassen	to release
		gegen Bürgschaft	on bail
Schurke	villain, rascal, rogue	freisprechen	to acquit (s-o of a crime)
Verdacht	suspicion		
unbegründet	unfounded	gestehen	to confess (I ~ that I did it, I ~ to doing it)
verdächtig	suspicious (behaviour; under ~ circumstances)		
		sich (nicht) schuldig bekennen	to plead (not) guilty
j-n in Verdacht haben	to suspect s-o (of being a thief)		
Vergehen	offence (US -nse)	**leugnen, bestreiten**	to deny
Übertretung	violation *or* infringement (of the law)	**plädieren**	to plead (for *or* against)
Verhör	examination, *(polizeil.)* interrogation	**rauben, berauben**	to rob
		Räuber	robber
Vernehmung (v. Zeugen)	hearing	**rechtfertigen**	to justify
		schwören	to swear
Zeuge	witness (eye- ~)	**stehlen**	to steal
Zeugenstand	BE witness-box, US witness stand	Dieb	thief
		Diebstahl	theft
anklagen (wegen), beschuldigen	to accuse (of), to charge (with)	Taschendieb	pickpocket
		Einbrecher	burglar
aussagen	to testify, to give evidence against *or* for s-o	Einbruch(sdiebstahl)	housebreaking, burglary
gegen oder für j-n		**überführen**	to convict s-o of, to find guilty of
begnadigen	to pardon		
Begnadigungsgesuch	petition for mercy	**übertreten (Gesetz)**	to violate, to infringe
Amnestie, amnestieren	(to) amnesty	**unterschlagen (Geld)**	to embezzle
		verhaften	to arrest, to take into custody
beleidigen	to offend, *(grob)* to insult		
		verhören	to try; to (cross-)examine; to interrogate
beschlagnahmen	to seize, to confiscate		
bestätigen (Urteil)	to confirm	**verklagen**	to sue
bestechen	to bribe, to corrupt	auf Schadenersatz	for damages
Bestechung	bribery, corruption	**verteidigen (vor Gericht)**	to defend
Bestechungsgeld	bribe		
bestrafen	to punish (s-o for s-th with a fine)	**verurteilen**	to condemn, (~ *zu*) to sentence to

auf frischer Tat ertappen	to catch in the very act (*or* red-handed)
in Notwehr handeln	to act in self-defence (US -nse)

22. Heer, Flotte, Luftwaffe; Krieg

Streitkräfte, Wehrmacht	armed forces
Heer	army
im ~ dienen	to serve in the a.
Ausrüstung	equipment
Befehl	order, command
Befehlshaber	commander, commanding officer
Oberbefehlshaber	commander-in-chief
ernennen	to appoint
Dienst	service
im aktiven ~	on active ~
im ~ sein, ~ haben	to be on duty
nicht im ~	off duty
Urlaub	leave
Disziplin	discipline
Fahne	flag, colours
Garnison (Truppe, Standort)	garrison, US (military *or* army) post
Kaserne	barracks
Mannschaften u. Unteroffiziere	soldiers and non-commissioned officers (NCOs*), BE other ranks, US enlisted men
Manöver	manoeuvre*, US maneuver
Offiziere	(commissioned) officers
Leutnant	Second Lieutenant*
Oberleutnant	(US First) Lieutenant*
Hauptmann	Captain
Major	Major*
Oberstleutnant	Lieutenant-Colonel*
Oberst	Colonel*
Brigadegeneral	Brigadier*, US ~ General
Generalmajor	Major-General
Generalleutnant	Lieutenant-General
Generaloberst	General
Feldmarschall	Field-Marshal, US General of the Army
Parade, Truppenschau	parade, (military) review
Rang, Dienstgrad	rank
Soldat	soldier
Rekrut	recruit
Freiwilliger	volunteer
Löhnung, Sold	(soldier's) pay
Stab	staff (regimental ~), headquarters (battalion ~)
Generalstab	General Staff
Truppen	troops
Infanterie	infantry
Artillerie	artillery
Kavallerie	cavalry
Pioniere	engineers
Fernmelde-, Nachrichtentruppen	signal troops
Truppenteil	unit, outfit
Einheit	unit
Zug	platoon
Kompanie	company
Batterie	battery
Bataillon	battalion
Regiment	regiment*
Brigade	brigade
Division	division
Abteilung	detachment, detail
Truppenübungsplatz, Lager	training area
Exerzierplatz	drill-ground
ausbilden	*(Soldaten)* to train, to drill
Uniform	uniform
Stahlhelm	steel helmet
Feldstecher	field-glasses
Wache	guard
Wachtposten	sentry
bewachen	to watch, to guard
Parole, Losung	watchword, password
Waffe	weapon*, arms
Schußwaffe	fire-arm
Bajonett	bayonet*

(gezogenes) Gewehr	rifle	tauchen	to dive, to submerge
Reichweite	range	auftauchen	to surface
laden	to load	Sehrohr	periscope
Handgranate	hand grenade	U-Bootkrieg	submarine warfare
Geschütz	gun	**Aufrüstung**	rearmament
Maschinengewehr	machine* gun	Wettrüsten	armament race
Pistole	pistol	militär. Hilfsquellen, Kriegspotential	military resources, war potential
Maschinenpistole	submachine gun		
Panzer(kampfwagen)	tank	Abrüstung	disarmament
		Krieg	war
Munition	ammunition	Krieg führen gegen	to make war upon, to wage war against
Patrone	cartridge		
Kugel	bullet	Kriegsziele	war aims
Granate	shell	Angriffskrieg	war of aggression
Pulver	powder	Verteidigungskrieg	defensive war
Wehrpflicht (allgemeine)	compulsory military service, (universal) conscription	Krieg erklären	to declare war (on)
		Kriegserklärung	declaration of war
		Neutralität	neutrality
Luftwaffe	Air Force, (England) Royal Air Force, RAF	Feldzug	campaign, expedition
		Angreifer	aggressor
Flugzeug	s. Kap. 13.4. (S. 73)	Feind	enemy
Bomber	bomber*	Verbündeter	ally
Jäger	fighter	Bündnis	alliance
Kriegsmarine	navy	Kriegsschauplatz	theatre of war
Kriegsschiff	warship, naval vessel	Taktik und Strategie	tactics and strategy
Matrose	sailor, seaman+	Eroberung	conquest*
Flotte	fleet	Eroberer	conqueror*
Geschwader	squadron	**Angriff**	attack
Geleitzug	convoy	Eröffnung der Feindseligkeiten	opening of hostilities
Flugzeugträger	aircraft carrier		
Kreuzer	cruiser (light ~, heavy ~)	Gegenangriff	counter-attack
		Aufruhr, Aufstand	s. Kap. 19. (S. 98)
Minenleger	mine-layer	**Befestigung**	fortification
Minensuchboot, Räumboot	mine-sweeper	Festung	fortress
		Schützengraben	trench
		Minenfeld	minefield
Schlachtschiff	battleship	**Belagerung**	siege
Schnellboot	motor torpedoboat, MTB, mosquito* boat	Ausfall	sally, sortie
		Besatzungstruppen	occupation troops
		Beschlagnahme	confiscation
Schulschiff	training ship	Requirierung	requisition
Torpedoboot	torpedo-boat (to fire a torpedo+)	**Blockade**	blockade
		Bombe	bomb*
Zerstörer	destroyer	Sprengbombe	explosive bomb
Unterseeboot	submarine, *(dt. ~)* U-boat	Atombombe	atom(ic) bomb, A-bomb

Wasserstoffbombe	hydrogen* bomb, H-bomb	Luftschutz(maßnahmen)	air-raid precautions
Fallschirmtruppen	parachute troops, paratroops	Luftschutzraum	air-raid shelter
Fernlenkwaffe	guided missile*	Nachschub	supply
Feuer (Beschuß)	fire	Niederlage	defeat (to suffer ~)
schwer	heavy	Radar	radar (= radio detecting and ranging)
Schuß	shot		
Volltreffer	direct hit	Radarschirm	radar screen
Flakartillerie	anti-aircraft artillery	Rakete	rocket
Scheinwerfer	searchlight	abschießen	to launch
Fliegeralarm	air-raid warning, alert	Leuchtkugel	signal rocket
		Atomrakete	nuclear missile*
Verdunklung	blackout	Interkontinentalrakete	intercontinental missile*
Entwarnung(ssignal)	all-clear (signal)		
		Rückzug	retreat
Fliegerangriff	air raid	den Rückzug antreten	to (make a) retreat
Gaskrieg	chemical warfare		
Gasmaske	gas mask	Flucht	flight
verseuchen	to contaminate	Verfolgung	pursuit
entseuchen	to decontaminate	verfolgen	to pursue
Kampf, Gefecht	fight, combat*	Sanitätsoffizier	medical officer
Schlacht	battle	Sanitäter	medical orderly
entscheidend	decisive	Rotkreuzschwester	Red Cross nurse
ein verzweifelter (blutiger, grimmiger) Kampf	a desperate (bloody, fierce) fight	Sieg	victory
		den Sieg erringen, siegen	to gain a victory, to be victorious
Kampftruppen	combat* troops	Sieger	victor
Kapitulation, Übergabe	surrender	Spion	spy
		Spionage	espionage*
bedingungslos	unconditional	Nachrichtendienst	intelligence service
e-e Katastrophe überleben	to survive a catastrophe* (disaster)	(Spionage-)Abwehr(dienst)	counter-espionage (or intelligence service)
Kernwaffe	nuclear weapon	Stellung	position
Kernwaffenverbot	ban on n. weapons	halten	to hold
Kriegsdienstverweigerer	conscientious objector	Verhandlungen	negotiations
		aufnehmen	to enter into n.
Kriegsgefangener	prisoner of war, P.O.W.*	abbrechen	to break off
		wiederaufnehmen	to resume
Gefangenschaft	captivity	Bedingungen	conditions, terms
Kriegsgericht	court martial+	Verluste, Ausfälle	casualties
vor e. Kriegsgericht stellen	to court-martial s-o	gefallen	killed in action
		schwer (leicht) verwundet	severely (slightly) wounded*
Lazarett	(military) hospital	vermißt	missing (in action)
Luftlandetruppen	airborne troops	Verteidigung	defence, US defense
Luft- und Flottenstützpunkte	air and naval bases	Waffenstillstand	armistice, (zeitl. begrenzt) truce

Einstellung der Feindseligkeiten	cessation of hostilities
Widerstand	resistance
starken, entschlossenen Widerstand leisten	to offer stout resistance
auf Widerstand stoßen	to meet with resistance
Zerstörung	destruction
Schaden	damage
Ziel (für Beschuß)	objective; target
Zielraum	target area
Zivilist	civilian
Evakuierter	evacuee
Flüchtling	refugee
Internierter	internee
Friedensvertrag	peace treaty
unterzeichnen	to sign
Wiederaufbau	reconstruction
versehrt, (schwer) kriegsbeschädigt	war invalid, (seriously) disabled
abschießen (Flugzeug)	to shoot down, to down
abwehren, abschlagen (Angriff)	to repel, to beat off
abwerfen (Bomben, Flugblätter)	to drop
angreifen	to attack, to charge
ausrüsten	to equip, to arm
befestigen	to fortify
belagern	to besiege
beschädigen	to damage; to injure
beschießen (d. Feind)	to fire (at the enemy); to shell; to machine-gun
mit Bomben belegen	to bomb
besetzen	to occupy
besiegen, schlagen	to defeat, to beat, to conquer*
in die Flucht schlagen	to put to flight
in Deckung gehen	to take cover
einfallen (in ein Land)	to invade (a country)
entlassen (aus dem Militärdienst)	to discharge, *(disziplinär)* to dismiss (from the army)
freilassen (Gefangene)	to release
entwaffnen	to disarm
sich ergeben	to surrender
erobern	*(Land)* to conquer*, *(Festung, Stadt)* to take
fliehen	to flee
gefangennehmen	to take prisoner, to capture
kämpfen	to fight
marschieren, Marsch	(to) march
melden, Meldung, Bericht	(to) report
plündern	to plunder, to loot
räumen, evakuieren	to evacuate
schießen	to shoot (at), to fire (at)
abfeuern (Waffe)	to discharge, to fire off
zielen	to aim (at)
sprengen (in d. Luft)	to blow up
unterwerfen (Volk, Land)	to subdue, to conquer*
versenken (Schiff)	to sink
verteidigen	to defend
verwüsten	to ravage, to devastate, to lay waste
vorrücken	to advance
zerstören	to destroy; to demolish
zertrümmern	to smash
Zuflucht suchen	to seek refuge
zurückziehen (Truppen)	to withdraw, to retire
sich zurückziehen	to retire, to retreat

23. Weltanschauung, Religion, Kirche

Welt- oder Lebensanschauung	philosophy of life, world view; ideology
Philosoph	philosopher
Denker	thinker
Ethik, Sittenlehre	ethics

Moral	morals, (moral. Prinzipien) morality
Sittengesetz	moral law, m. code
Lebensführung	conduct of life
Religion	religion
Christentum	Christianity
Christenheit	Christendom
Christ, christlich	Christian*
Religionsgemeinschaft, Konfession, Bekenntnis	religious community, denomination
Kirche	church
Staatskirche	state church, Established Church
die anglikanische Kirche	the Anglican Church, (in England) the Church of England, (in USA) the Protestant Episcopal Church
Freikirche	free church
Dissident	nonconformist
die Gläubigen	the faithful
Konzil	council
Glaube	belief, (bes. religiös) faith
glauben an	to believe in
Glaubensbekenntnis	confession of faith, creed
Schöpfung	creation
Geschöpf	creature
Christus	Christ*
Heiland, Erlöser	(Our) Saviour
erlösen	to redeem
Erlösung	redemption
die göttliche Vorsehung	(Divine) Providence
Himmel	heaven
Paradies	paradise
Hölle	hell
verdammen	to damn
Engel (Erz~)	angel (arch~*)
Teufel	devil*
Geist	spirit (aber the Holy Ghost)
Lehre	doctrine
heilige Schriften	holy scriptures
Bibel	Bible
Prophet	prophet
Prophezeiung	prophecy*
prophezeien	to prophesy*
Apostel	apostle*
Jünger	disciple*
Evangelium	gospel
Geistlicher	clergyman+
Klerus	clergy
Priester	priest
Pfarrer	parish priest
evgl. freikirchlicher Prediger	minister, pastor
(anglikan.) Pfarrer	parson, rector; vicar
Pfarrei	parish
Dekan	dean
Bischof	bishop
Erzbischof	archbishop
Bistum, Diözese	diocese*
Papst	Pope
Kloster	monastery
Nonnenkloster	nunnery, convent
Mönch	monk
Nonne	nun
Abtei	abbey
Abt	abbot
Äbtissin	abbess
Oberin	Mother Superior
Laie	layman+
weltlich	secular (~ interests, ~ music), temporal (~ matters), profane (~ literature)
Kirchenfest	religious (or church) festival, feast (e.g. Christmas*, Easter, Whitsun)
Weihnachtsabend	Christmas* Eve
Silvester	New Year's Eve
Kirchenjahr	ecclesiastical year
Kult, Verehrung	worship
verehren	to worship
Ritus	rite
feierlich	solemn
Zeremonie	ceremony
Gottesdienst	(divine) service
Messe	mass*
Predigt	sermon
predigen	to preach
Kirchenlied	hymn*
Gesangbuch	hymn-book

Psalm	psalm*	bekehren	to convert
Taufe	baptism	Ungläubiger	infidel
taufen	to baptize*, to christen*		

24. Weltall und Erde

das Abendmahl	the Lord's Supper		
Kultstätte	place of worship	Welt	world (are there any other ~s besides ours? round the ~ in 80 days; the New W~; to know the ~; all the ~ knows; to get on in the ~)
Heiligtum	sanctuary		
Pilger	pilgrim		
heilig	holy (the Holy Ghost, the Holy Land), sacred (a temple ~ to Jupiter), saint (St Peter)		
		Weltall	universe
Kirche	church	Welt(en)raum	space
Altar	altar	Raumfahrer	astronaut, space-man+
Kanzel	pulpit*		
Kreuz	cross	Raumfahrt, -flug	space flight, space travel
Glocke	bell		
läuten	to ring	Raumschiff	spaceship
Kapelle	chapel	Raumfähre	space shuttle
weihen	to consecrate	Kosmos	cosmos
segnen	to bless (God ~ you)	kosmische Strahlen	cosmic rays
Segen	blessing		
Frömmigkeit	piety, devotion	Natur	nature
fromm	pious, devout	die Naturkräfte	natural forces, the forces of nature
beten	to pray		
Gebet	prayer*	die Geheimnisse	the secrets (or mysteries) of nature
knien, nieder~	to kneel (down)		
Fanatiker	fanatic	~erscheinung	(physical) phenomenon+
Sünde, sündigen	(to) sin		
Sünder	sinner	Naturgesetz	natural law, law of nature
in Versuchung führen	to lead into temptation		
		natürlich	natural (in a ~ state; ~ ability)
der Versuchung widerstehen	to resist temptation		
		Himmel	sky; heaven
bereuen	to repent	Himmelskörper	celestial body
bekennen, beichten	to confess	Firmament	firmament
		Horizont	horizon*
Bekenntnis	confession	Komet	comet
vergeben	to forgive	Kopf, Kern	nucleus*+
Vergebung	forgiveness	Schweif	tail
Skepsis	scepticism (US sk-)	Meteor, Sternschnuppe	meteor*, shooting star
Skeptiker, Zweifler	sceptic* (US sk-)		
Aberglaube	superstition	Meteorit	meteorite
abergläubisch	superstitious	Milchstraße	Milky Way, galaxy
Zauberer	magician, (in Märchen) sorcerer	Mond	moon (new ~; full ~)
Hexe	witch		
Heide, heidnisch	heathen, pagan	zunehmend	waxing

abnehmend Mondsichel, Halbmond	waning crescent
Satellit, Trabant	satellite
Mondfinsternis	lunar eclipse*
Planet	planet
Planetenbahn	orbit
Planetensystem	planetary system
s. um die Sonne drehen	to revolve round the sun
Erdsatellit	(earth) satellite
auf e-e Umlaufbahn bringen	to (launch into) orbit
Mehrstufenrakete	multi-stage rocket
Trägerrakete	carrier rocket
Abschußbasis	rocket base, launching site
bemannter Flug	manned flight
Schwerelosigkeit	weightlessness
weiche Landung	soft landing
Mondlandung	lunar landing
Sonne	sun
aufgehen	to rise
untergehen	to set
Sonnenaufgang	sunrise
Sonnenuntergang	sunset
Sonnenfinsternis	eclipse* of the sun, solar eclipse
Sonnenfleck	sun-spot
Sonnenstrahl	sunbeam, *(astron.)* sun-ray
Sonnensystem	solar system
Stern	star
Fixstern	fixed star
Sternwarte	observatory
beobachten	to observe
Polarstern	Pole Star
Sternbild	constellation
der Wagen, der Große Bär	the Plough, the Great Bear, US Big Dipper
der Kleine Bär	Little Bear, *bes* US Little Dipper
Orion	Orion*
Erde	earth
irdisch	earthly
Lufthülle	atmosphere
Erdkugel, Erdball, Globus	globe
Achse	axis+
sich um seine eigene Achse drehen	to rotate about one's own axis
Halbkugel	hemisphere
Erdteil	continent
Festland	mainland, continent
das europäische F. (im Gegens. zu den British Isles)	the Continent
die vier Himmelsgegenden	the four cardinal points (east, west, north, south)
geogr. Breite und Länge	latitude and longitude*
Äquator	equator
südl./nördl. Polarkreis	antarctic/arctic circle
Nordpol	North Pole
Südpol	South Pole
die Erdoberfläche	the surface of the earth (*or* the earth's s.)
Landkarte	map
Atlas	atlas
Landschaft	landscape, scenery (a most picturesque mountain sc.)
Gegend	region
Abhang	slope; hillside
Berg	hill, *(hoch, spitz)* mountain
Hügel	small hill, hillock
Bergkette	chain of mountains, m. chain, m. range
Bergrücken	ridge (of a m.)
Gipfel	summit (of a m.), top (of a hill)
steil	steep
Hang	slope
500 Fuß über dem Meeresspiegel	500 feet above sea-level
Boden	ground, *(Acker~)* soil; *(Unterste)* bottom (of the sea)
Bucht	bay, *(kleine ~)* cove
Golf, Meerbusen	gulf
Damm	dam
Staudamm	dam, barrage*

Deich (am Meer)	dike	Sumpf	swamp, marsh
Ebbe und Flut	ebb and flow, low tide and high tide	Tal	valley
die Gezeiten	the tides	Schlucht	gorge, ravine*
Ebene	plain	Teich	pond
Hochebene	plateau*+	Tümpel, Wasserlache, Pfütze	pool, puddle
Eisberg	iceberg	stehendes Wasser	stagnant water
dahintreiben	to float, to drift	Überschwemmung, Flut	inundation, flood
Erdbeben	earthquake	überschwemmen	to flood, to submerge
Erdrutsch	*bes* BE landslip, landslide	Ufer	bank (of a river)
Fels	vgl. Stein	Meeres~	shore
Fluß	s. Wasser	Meeresküste	coast
Gletscher	glacier*	flacher Strand	beach
Heide	heath, *(torfig)* moor	Steilufer	bluff
Höhle	cave	Umwelt	environment
Insel	island	Umgebung	surroundings
Halbinsel	peninsula	umweltfeindlich	ecologically harmful, polluting
Kanal	canal, *(Flußlauf, Meerenge)* channel	umweltfreundlich	environmentally beneficial, non-polluting
Schleuse	lock		
Land	country, *(Gegens. Meer)* land	Umweltpolitik	ecological policy
~enge	isthmus	Umweltschutz	environmental protection
Meer, die See	sea	Umweltverschmutzung	pollution
Weltmeer	ocean		
an der See	at the seaside	Wiederverwertung	recycling
Brandung, Woge usw.	s. Kap. 13.3. (S. 71)	Vorgebirge, Kap	cape, promontory*, headland
Meerenge	strait(s)	Vulkan	volcano+
Moor	peat-bog	Krater	crater
Torf	peat (to cut ~)	Ausbruch	eruption
Paß	mountain pass	erloschen	extinct
Quelle	spring, source	untätig	dormant
See (Binnen~)	lake	tätig	active
Stausee	reservoir*	Wald	s. Kap. 16. (S. 79)
Stein	stone	Lichtung	clearing, glade
Fels	rock	Unterholz	undergrowth
Klippe	cliff	Wasser	water
Sand	sand	Wasserfall	waterfall
Steppe	steppe	Fluß	river
Strömung	current, *(Gegen~)* eddy	Nebenfluß	tributary*
		Strom, großer Fluß	large river
Strudel	whirlpool, *(klein)* eddy	Mündung	mouth
		fließen	to flow
		Bach	brook, US creek

Wasserscheide	watershed, divide	Wetterkarte	weather chart, weather map
Wildnis	wilderness*	Wettervorhersage	weather forecast
Wüste	desert*	Wetteramt	meteorological* office, US weather bureau*+
Oase	oasis*+		

25. Wetter und Klima

	Meteorologie — meteorology*
Luft	air
Atmosphäre	atmosphere
Luftdruck	atmospheric pressure
Barometer	barometer, glass (what does the glass say?)
Temperatur	temperature
Thermometer	thermometer
Skala	scale
Grad	degree
Gefrierpunkt	freezing-point
Siedepunkt	boiling-point
Celsius	centigrade (30° centigrade = 86° Fahrenheit*)
Wetter	weather
schön	fine, beautiful, fair
prächtig	glorious
schlecht	bad
garstig	nasty, foul, BE dirty
stürmisch	rough, stormy
unbeständig	unsettled
veränderlich	changeable
neblig	foggy
kühl	cool
ziemlich kalt, frostig	chilly
bitterkalt	bitterly cold
heiß	hot
schwül	close, sultry
e. trüber Tag	a gloomy day
heiterer (trüber) Himmel	serene (dull) sky
bedeckt	overcast
bewölkt	clouded
es hellt sich auf	it's clearing up
jetzt scheint die Sonne	the sun is shining
Wetterbeobachtung	meteorological* observation

Meteorologie	meteorology*
Eis	ice
Eiszapfen	icicle
Feuchtigkeit	moisture, humidity
feucht	moist, (unangenehm ~) damp
naß	wet
Frost	frost
Glatteis	black ice, *bes* BE glazed frost, *bes* US glaze
plötzliches Frostwetter, Kältewelle	sudden spell of frost, cold snap
Rauhreif	hoarfrost
Gewitter	thunderstorm
heftig	violent
Donner	thunder
Blitz(strahl)	(flash of) lightning
es blitzt und donnert	it's lightening and thundering
der Blitz hat in e-n Baum eingeschlagen	lightning has struck a tree
unter e-m Baum Schutz suchen, sich unterstellen	to (take) shelter under a tree
Blitzableiter	lightning-conductor
Hagel(wetter)	hail(storm)
Hagelkorn	hailstone
Hoch	high
Tief	low
Kälte, kalt	cold
Nebel	fog
neblig	foggy
Dunstschleier	haze
dunstig	hazy
feuchter Dunst	mist
Regen	rain
Regenbogen	rainbow*
Niederschlag	precipitation, fall
es gießt in Strömen	it is pouring* with rain

es hat sich für heute eingeregnet	the rain seems to have set in for the day
Regentropfen	raindrop
Regenschauer	rainfall, shower
Reguß	drench(er), violent shower
Platzregen	downpour
starker Regen	heavy rain
strömender Regen	pouring* rain
Nieseln, Sprühregen	drizzling rain, drizzle
Wolkenbruch	cloudburst
Regentag	rainy day
Schnee	snow (snowball; snowfall; snowflake)
Schneemann	snow man*
schmelzen	to melt
Lawine	avalanche*
Tau	dew (dew is falling)
Tauwetter	thaw (a ~ has set in)
es taut	it is thawing
Matsch	slush
Trockenheit	dryness (of the air)
regenlose Zeit, Dürre	drought*
Wärme	warmth
warm, wärmen	(to) warm
Hitze	heat
sengende Hitze, Gluthitze	scorching heat
Hitzewelle	heat-wave
Hundstage	dog-days
Schatten	shade, (~ nbild) shadow
Wind	wind
Windstille	calm
Windstoß	gust (of wind), blast
Wirbelwind	whirlwind
Brise (leichter, mäßig starker W.)	breeze (a soft ~)
Föhn	foehn
Bö	gust, (Regenbö) squall
steife Brise, stürmischer Wind (bes. auf See)	gale
Sturm (auf See)	strong gale
starker Sturm, Unwetter	storm
Schneesturm	snow-storm, (starker) blizzard
Wirbelsturm	whirlwind
Orkan	hurricane
blasen, wehen	to blow
heulen	to howl
pfeifen	to whistle
wüten	to rage
nachlassen, sich legen	to drop, to abate
Luftzug	draught*, US draft*
Wolke	cloud
ziehen	to drift
s. bewölken	to cloud over
wolkig, bewölkt	cloudy
Klima	climate (healthy, mild, rough, unwholesome)
kalte, gemäßigte, heiße Zone	frigid zone, temperate z., torrid z.
die Tropen	the tropics
tropisch	tropical

26. Tiere und Pflanzen

Ordnung	order
Familie	family
Gattung	genus*+
Art	species*+
Abart	variety
Rasse	race; breed, stock
reinrassig (Tier)	thoroughbred, of pure breed

26.1. Tiere

Tier	animal; beast
männl., Männchen	male
weiblich, Weibchen	female
a) **Wirbeltiere**	vertebrates
Haustiere	domestic animals
zahm, zähmen	(to) tame
Esel	donkey*, (bes. fig.) ass
Geflügel	poultry
Ente	duck
Gans	goose+

Hahn	cock, rooster	Zicklein	kid
Henne, Huhn	hen, *(jung)* chicken	Säugetiere	mammals
Küken	chick	Raubtier	beast of prey
Pfau	peacock (peahen)	das Junge	the cub
Taube	pigeon, dove	Nagetier	rodent
Truthahn	turkey (-cock, -hen)	nagen	to gnaw*
Hund	dog	Biber	beaver
Hündin	female ~, bitch	Eichhörnchen	squirrel
junger H., Hündchen	puppy	**Fledermaus**	bat
wachsam	watchful	**Fuchs**	fox
bissig	snappy, snappish	**Gemse**	chamois*+
beißen	to bite	**Hamster**	hamster
Dackel	dachshund*	**Hase**	hare
Jagdhund	hound	**Igel**	hedgehog
deutscher Schäferhund	BE Alsatian, US German shepherd	Stachel	spine
Windhund	greyhound	**Marder**	marten
Bulldogge	bulldog	**Maulwurf**	mole (~-hill)
Pudel	poodle	**Maus**	mouse+
Boxer	boxer	Wühlmaus	vole
Terrier	terrier (fox t., Scotch t.)	**Nerz**	mink (~ coat)
Kaninchen	rabbit	**Ratte**	rat
Katze	cat	**Rotwild**	(red) deer+
Kuh	cow	Hirsch	stag
Ochse	ox+	Hirschkuh	hind
Bulle, Stier	bull	Reh	roe
Haut	hide	Rehbock	buck
Kalb	calf+	Renntier, Ren	reindeer*
Pferd	horse	Geweih	antlers
Mähne	mane	**Wiesel**	weasel
Zugpferd	draught* (US draft) horse	**Wildschwein**	wild boar
Hengst	stallion	**Affe**	monkey
Stute	mare	Menschenaffe	ape
Schaf	sheep+	**Antilope**	antelope
Schafherde	flock of sheep	**Bär**	bear
Fell	skin	Eisbär	polar bear
Wolle	wool	**Büffel**	buffalo+ (water ~; bison+)
Lamm	lamb	**Elefant**	elephant
Widder	ram	Stoßzahn	tusk
Hammel	wether	Rüssel	trunk
Schwein	pig, *bes* US hog	Elfenbein	ivory
Eber	boar	**Giraffe**	giraffe*
Sau	sow	**Hyäne**	hyena*
Ferkel	piglet	**Kamel**	camel
Ziege	goat		

Höcker	hump
Löwe	lion
Löwin	lioness
Nilpferd	hippo(potamus)+
Tiger	tiger
Tigerin	tigress
Wolf	wolf+
Seehund, Robbe	seal
Walroß	walrus
Wal	whale
Zebra	zebra*
Vogel	bird
Feder	feather
Flügel	wing
Schnabel	bill, *(stark, gekrümmt, bes. von Raubvögeln)* beak
Schwanz	tail
Nest	nest
fliegen	to fly
flattern	to flutter
Eier legen	to lay eggs
Schale	shell
brüten	to brood
ausbrüten	to hatch
Zugvögel	birds of passage, migratory birds
Raubvogel	bird of prey
Adler	eagle
Amsel	blackbird
Bachstelze	wagtail
Elster	magpie
Eule	owl
Falke	falcon*
Fasan	pheasant
Fink	finch
Buchfink	chaffinch
Geier	vulture
Habicht	hawk
Krähe	crow
Kranich	crane
Kuckuck	cuckoo
Lerche	lark
Feldlerche	skylark
Meise	titmouse*
Möwe	gull
Nachtigall	nightingale
Rabe	raven
Rebhuhn	partridge
Reiher	heron
Rotkehlchen	robin
Rotschwänzchen	redstart
Schnepfe	snipe+
Schwalbe	swallow
Hausschwalbe	martin
Schwan	swan
Specht	woodpecker
Sperling, Spatz	sparrow
Star	starling
Storch	stork
Zaunkönig	wren
exotische Vögel	exotic birds
Kanarienvogel	canary*
Käfig	cage
Papagei	parrot
Sittich	parakeet
Grassittich	budgerigar*, *coll.* budgie
Strauß	ostrich
Reptilien, Kriechtiere	reptiles
kriechen	to crawl, to creep
Blindschleiche	slow-worm
Eidechse	lizard
Krokodil	crocodile
Schlange	snake
Giftschlange	poisonous snake
Kreuzotter	adder, common viper
sich zusammenrollen	to coil o. s. (up)
Schildkröte, Landschildkröte	tortoise*
Seeschildkröte	turtle
Amphibien	amphibians
Frosch	frog
Kröte	toad
Fisch	fish
Flosse	fin

Gräte	fishbone	Stechmücke	mosquito*+, BE gnat*
Schuppe	scale	Moskito	(tropical) mosquito*+
schwimmen	to swim		
Süßwasserfisch	freshwater fish		
Aal	eel	**Laus**	louse+
Forelle	trout+	**Floh**	flea
Hecht	pike+	**Libelle, Wasserjungfer**	dragonfly
Karpfen	carp+		
Lachs	salmon*+	**Made**	maggot (maggoty cheese)
Hering	herring		
Räucher~	kipper	**Wanze**	bug, *bes* US bedbug
Makrele	mackerel+	**Ungeziefer**	pests, vermin+
Kabeljau	cod+, codfish	**Krebs**	crab
Lebertran	cod-liver oil	Flußkrebs	*bes* BE crayfish, *bes* US crawfish
Schellfisch	haddock+	Hummer	lobster
Scholle	plaice+	**Muschel**	shellfish+
Steinbutt	turbot+	Schale	shell
Hai(fisch)	shark	Perle	pearl
		Auster	oyster
b) Wirbellose Tiere	**invertebrates**	**Schnecke**	snail, *(ohne Haus)* slug
Insekt, Kerbtier	insect, US *coll.* bug	Schneckenhaus	(snail-)shell
Flügel	wing	**Spinne**	spider
Fühler	antenna+, feeler	Spinnengewebe	cobweb
Larve	larva+	Faden	thread
Raupe	caterpillar	spinnen	to spin
Ameise	ant	**Wurm**	worm
Ameisenhaufen	ant-hill		
Biene	bee	**c) Tierstimmen**	**voices of animals**
Stich, Stachel	sting	**bellen**	to bark
stechen	to sting	**blöken**	to bleat
Honig(wabe)	honey(-comb)	**brüllen (Kuh)**	to low, *(Löwe)* to roar
Wachs	wax		
Wespe	wasp	**brummen (Bär)**	to growl, *(Käfer)* to drone
Hornisse	hornet		
Hummel	bumble-bee		
Grille, Heimchen	cricket	**fauchen (Katze)**	to spit
Heuschrecke (Laub-)	locust	**gackern**	to cackle
Grashüpfer	grasshopper	**grunzen**	to grunt
Käfer	beetle	**gurren (Taube)**	to coo
Maikäfer	cockchafer	**heulen (Hund, Wolf)**	to howl
Schmetterling	butterfly	**knurren (Hund)**	to growl, to snarl
Motte	moth	**krächzen**	to croak, *(Krähe)* to caw
Seidenraupe	silkworm		
Fliege	fly	**krähen**	to crow
Mücke	gnat*		

kreischen (Raubvögel, Papagei)	to scream	Schale	*(Nuß)* shell, *(Obst)* skin, peel, *(Kartoffel)* peel
miauen	to miaow	**Baum**	tree
pfeifen	to whistle	Laubbaum	hardwood, deciduous tree
piepsen (Maus)	to squeak, *(Vogel)* to cheep	Nadelbaum	softwood, coniferous tree
quaken	to croak	Nadel	needle
quieken (Schwein)	to squeak	Stamm	trunk
schlagen (Nachtigall)	to sing, to warble	gefällter Baum, Holzklotz	log
schnattern (Gans)	to cackle	Ast	bough*
summen (Biene)	to hum, *(Fliege)* to buzz	Zweig	branch, *(klein)* twig
wiehern	to neigh	Rinde	bark
winseln (Hund)	to whine	Laub	foliage
zirpen	to chirp	Holz	wood
zischen (Schlange, Gans)	to hiss	**Ahorn**	maple
zwitschern	to twitter	Birke	birch
		Buche	beech

26.2. Pflanzen

Eiche	oak
Fichte	spruce
Platane	plane
Pflanze	plant
Tanne	fir(-tree)
Samen	seed
Zapfen	cone
Samenkorn	grain of seed
Kastanie	chestnut*(-tree)
Keim	germ
Lärche	larch
Wurzel	root
Linde	lime(-tree)
Blumenzwiebel	bulb
Pappel	poplar
Stengel, Stiel	stalk, stem
Trauerweide	weeping willow
Saft	sap, juice*
Ulme	elm
Blatt	leaf+
Mahagoni	mahogany*
Knospe	bud
Strauch, Busch	shrub, bush*
Blüte	flower, *(von Blumen)* bloom, *(von Bäumen, Sträuchern)* blossom (the apple-trees are in blossom, the tulips are in bloom now)
Rosenstrauch	rose-bush
	Beerenstrauch	fruit-bush
	Zierstrauch	ornamental shrub
	Flieder	lilac*
	Holunder	elder
	Stechpalme	holly
	Wacholder	juniper
	Kraut	herb
blühen	to flower, *(Bäume)* to blossom, *(Blumen)* to bloom	Gräser	grasses
	Unkraut	weed
	Distel	thistle*
Frucht	fruit	stachlig	prickly
eßbar	edible	**Getreidearten**	cereals*, crops (winter, summer crops)
giftig	poisonous		
Kern	kernel		
Stein	stone	Getreide	corn *(in Engl. bes. = Weizen)*, US grain
Hülse	husk		

Gerste	barley
Hafer	oats
Mais	BE maize, US (Indian) corn
Roggen	rye
Weizen	wheat
Klee	clover
Tabak	tobacco
Gemüsepflanzen	vegetable plants
Blumenkohl	cauliflower
Bohne	bean
Erbse	pea (sugar*-pea)
Grün-, Braunkohl	kale
Gurke	cucumber*
Kohl	cabbage (white c., red c.)
Kohlrabi	kohlrabi
Kopfsalat	lettuce*
Kürbis	pumpkin
Linse	lentil
Porree, Lauch	leek
Radieschen	radish
Rettich	large radish
Meerrettich	horse-radish
Rosenkohl	Brussels sprouts
Rübe (weiße)	turnip
gelbe R., Möhre	carrot
rote R., rote Bete	red beet, *bes* BE beetroot
Zuckerrübe	sugar*-beet
Sellerie(blätter)	celery, *(Knolle)* celeriac*
Spargel	asparagus
Spinat	spinach*
Tomate	tomato*+
Wirsing	savoy
Zwiebel	onion*
Kartoffel	potato+
Frucht, Obst	fruit
reif	ripe
Apfel	apple (fall ~, cooking ~, dessert* ~)
Aprikose	apricot
Birne	pear*
Kirsche	cherry (sweet ~, sour ~)
Nuß	nut
Haselnuß	hazelnut
Walnuß	walnut
Pfirsich	peach
Pflaume	(clingstone) plum
Zwetschge	plum
Mirabelle	yellow plum
Backpflaume	prune
Reineclaude	greengage
Obstbäume	fruit-trees (apple-tree, pear-tree, cherry-tree)
Beere	berry
Brombeere	blackberry, *bes* BE bramble
Erdbeere	strawberry
Heidelbeere	BE bilberry, US blueberry
Himbeere	raspberry*
Johannisbeere	currant (red, white, black ~)
Stachelbeere	gooseberry*
Blume	flower
Blumenstrauß	bunch of flowers, bouquet*
Duft	perfume, fragrance, scent
duftend	fragrant
verwelken	to fade, to wither
Butterblume	buttercup
Enzian	gentian
Fingerhut	foxglove
Gänseblümchen	daisy
Glockenblume	bellflower, harebell
Kornblume	cornflower
Lilie	lily
Löwenzahn	dandelion*
Maiglöckchen	lily of the valley
Mohn	poppy
gelbe Narzisse	daffodil
Nelke	carnation, pink
Pfingstrose	peony*
Primel	primrose, cowslip
Rittersporn	larkspur
Rose	rose
Dorn	thorn
Schneeglöckchen	snowdrop
Sonnenblume	sunflower
Stiefmütterchen	pansy
Tulpe	tulip
Veilchen	violet
Vergißmeinnicht	forget-me-not

Kletter- oder Schlingpflanze	climber, vine	(chemische, physikal.) Eigenschaft	(chemical, physical) property
Efeu	ivy	organisch	organic
immergrün	evergreen	anorganisch	inorganic
Hopfen	hop	fester Zustand	solid state
Weinstock, Rebe	(grape)vine	flüssig	liquid
Weintraube	grape	gasförmig	gaseous*
Schilf(rohr)	reed	**Atom**	atom
Binse(n)	rush	der Aufbau des Atoms	the structure of the atom
Schmarotzer	parasite		
Mistel	mistletoe*	Atomkern	atomic nucleus*+
Blütenpflanzen	phanerogams	Kernspaltung	nuclear fission
blütenlose Pflanzen	cryptogams	Kernkraftwerk	s. Kap. 12. (S. 67)
Farn	fern	Atomzertrümmerung	splitting of the atom
Moos	moss	Kettenreaktion	chain reaction
Pilz	fungus*+	(Atom-)Energie freisetzen	to release (atomic) energy
Eßpilz, Champignon	mushroom		
Pfifferling	chanterelle*	Aussendung von Strahlen	emission of rays
Steinpilz	(edible) boletus*+	aussenden	to emit
Giftpilz	toadstool	Strahlung	radiation
exotische Pflanzen und Früchte	exotic plants and fruits	**Molekül**	molecule*
Ananas(frucht)	pineapple	**Grundstoffe (chemische ~)**	(chemical) elements
Banane	banana*	Aluminium	aluminium*, US aluminum*
Baumwollstaude	cotton plant		
Dattel	date	Kohlenstoff	carbon
Erdnuß	peanut, BE groundnut	Chlor	chlorine*
		Kobalt	cobalt*
Grapefruit, Pampelmuse	grapefruit	Kupfer	copper
		Gold	gold
Kaffeebohne	coffee bean	Wasserstoff	hydrogen*
Orange, Apfelsine	orange	Eisen	iron*
Palme	palmtree	Blei	lead*
Reis	rice	Quecksilber	mercury
Teestrauch	tea-plant	Nickel	nickel
Zitrone	lemon*	Stickstoff	nitrogen*
Zuckerrohr	sugar* cane	Sauerstoff	oxygen*
		Phosphor	phosphorus
		Platin	platinum*

27. Die anorganische Natur

		Kalium	potassium
das **Mineralreich**	the mineral kingdom	Radium	radium
Bodenschätze	mineral resources	Silber	silver
Stoff	substance	Natrium	sodium
Zusammensetzung	composition	Schwefel	sulphur*, US sulfur
Bestandteile (e-s Stoffes)	constituents (*or* components) (of a substance)	Zinn	tin
		Wolfram	tungsten
		Uran	uranium

117

Zink	zinc
(chem.) Verbindung	compound (water is a ~ of oxygen and hydrogen)
(chem.) Formel	formula+
chemischer Vorgang	chemical process
Umformung	transformation
Legierung	alloy
Messing	brass
legieren	to alloy
Mischung	mixture
Synthese	synthesis+
synthetisch, künstlich hergestellt	synthetic (~rubber)
Gift	poison, *(Tier~)* venom
Salz	salt
Säure	acid
Metall	metal
Rost	rust
rostig	rusty
rostfrei	rustproof
Erz	ore (iron* ~, silver ~)
Edelstein	precious stone
Diamant	diamond
Rubin	ruby
Smaragd	emerald
Saphir	sapphire*
Aquamarin	aquamarine*
Topas	topaz*
Türkis	turquoise*
Amethyst	amethyst
Kalkstein	limestone
Kreide	chalk
Marmor	marble
Ton	clay
Lehm	loam
Porzellanerde	porcelain* clay
Wasser	water (pure, hard, soft, heavy ~)
Erdöl, Mineralöl	petroleum, mineral oil
Ölfeld	oilfield
Ölquelle	oil well
Ölleitung	pipeline
bohren nach...	to bore for
auf Öl stoßen	to strike oil
raffinieren	to refine
Kohle	coal
Kohlenbergwerk	coal-mine, BE colliery
Kohlenflöz	coal-seam
Braunkohle	brown coal
Steinkohle	hard coal
Teer	tar
Pech	pitch

28. Raum und Form; Beschaffenheit

Beschaffenheit	quality, property; *(Aufbau)* structure
Ausdehnung	extent
sich ausdehnen	to extend
Länge	length
Breite	breadth, width*
Höhe	height
Tiefe	depth
Entfernung	distance
Fläche(ninhalt)	area
Form, Gestalt	form, shape
Größe, Format	size
Linie	line
gerade	straight
krumm	curved
parallel	parallel
punktiert	dotted
gedacht	imaginary
Zickzacklinie	zigzag line
e-e Linie ziehen	to draw a line
das äußerste Ende	the extreme end
am entgegengesetzten Ende	at the opposite end
Mitte	middle
Mittelpunkt	centre, mean (the golden mean)
Oberfläche (e-s Körpers)	surface
Platz, Ort, Stelle	place; spot
Punkt (im geometr. Sinn)	point
Querschnitt	cross-section

Rand	edge (of a table, a forest, a lake), *(Gefäß)* brim (of a cup, glass; full to the ~), *(etwas Rundes)* rim (of a cup, spectacles), *(Papier)* margin (don't write in the ~)
Raum	room (to make ~ for s-o; the table takes up too much ~); space (time and ~; separated by a ~ of 5 feet)
Rauminhalt	volume (of a box)
Seite	side
Streifen	stripe (the zebra's ~s; a grey ~ on the sleeve), strip (a ~ of paper, cloth, metal, land)
Umriß	outline, contour
Fläche (geometr.)	plane
geometrische Figur	geometrical figure*
Dreieck	triangle
gleichseitig	equilateral
rechtwinklig	right-angled
konstruieren	to construct
Rechteck	rectangle
Quadrat	square
Viereck	quadrangle
Winkel	angle
rechter Winkel	right angle
spitz	acute
stumpf	obtuse
Grad	degree
Kreis	circle
Halbkreis	semi-circle
beschreiben	to describe
Kreisausschnitt	sector
Kreisumfang	circumference, periphery
Durchmesser	diameter
Ellipse	ellipse (elliptic)
Körper, fester ~ (geometr., physikal.)	solid
Kegel	cone
kegelförmig	cone-shaped
Kugel	sphere
kugelförmig	spherical
Pyramide	pyramid
Würfel	cube
würfelförmig	cubic
Zylinder	cylinder (cylindrical)
ähnlich, ~ gestaltet	similar, shaped alike
gleich	equal
ungleich	unequal
kongruent, deckungsgleich	congruent
regelmäßig	regular
unregelmäßig	irregular
wohlgebaut, ebenmäßig	well-proportioned
mißgestaltet	mis-shapen, deformed
symmetrisch	symmetrical
groß	big (toe, game; ~ man, the Big Three; ~ business)
flächengroß, umfangreich	large (building; ~ family, sum)
hervorragend	great (man, artist, achievement)
großartig	grand
hoch	tall (man)
klein	small (room, town, sum), *(not big)* little (toe, child, girl, a pretty ~ house, a nice ~ room), *(not tall)* short (man)
riesig	huge, gigantic
unermeßlich, ungeheuer	immense
winzig	tiny, minute*
breit	broad (street, ribbon, margin; 3 feet ~), *(bes. von Öffnung)* wide (street, ribbon, margin; 3 feet ~; ~ wound*, opening, view)

geräumig	spacious	
eng, schmal	narrow (street, staircase), close (sit ~ together, ~ friend), tight (jacket, shoes)	
lang	long	
kurz	short (distance, time, speech), brief (interview, discourse, reply)	
hoch	high	
niedrig	low	
dick	thick	
dünn	thin	
hart	hard	
weich	soft	
starr	rigid	
biegsam	flexible (~ wire)	
elastisch	elastic	
fest (nicht flüssig, locker, hohl)	solid	
flüssig	liquid	
locker, lose	loose	
hohl	hollow	
voll	full	
leer	empty	
eben	level (ground), flat (surface, ground)	
ebenes Land	flat country	
flach	flat	
uneben	uneven	
glatt	smooth	
rauh	rough	
rund	round	
kreisförmig	circular	
viereckig	square	
spitz(ig)	pointed (roof, gable, arch)	
keilförmig	wedge- *or* V-shaped	
scharf	sharp (edge, outline)	
stumpf	blunt	
senkrecht	vertical, perpendicular	
waagrecht	horizontal, level	
schräg, schief	oblique, diagonal; slant(ing) (roof), askew (the tie is ~, the blinds hang ~)	

schiefe Ebene	inclined plane

29. Mengenangaben und Maße

Teil	part, *(Teilstück)* portion, *(Anteil)* share (of the profits; the lion's ~)
Teilchen	particle
Stück	piece
Bruchstück	fragment
Bruchteil	fraction
ein bißchen	a bit (not a ~ of bread; wait a ~)
Gruppe	group
Bindeglied	link
das Ganze	the whole
ganz	all (England, not for ~ the world, ~ day long), *(ungeteilt, vollständig)* whole (the ~ world, the ~ of England, the ~ truth), *(umfassend)* entire (confidence, affection, happiness), *(gesamt)* total (amount, number, output)
unversehrt	intact
vollständig	complete
unvollständig	incomplete
allgemein	common (error; ~ly used), general (rule, elections; he spoke in ~ terms), universal (place, remedy)
teilweise	partial (a ~ eclipse* of the sun)
halb	half
bestehen aus	to consist of, to be composed of
Menge	quantity, *(mehr als genug)* plenty (of time, money), a great number of (books, pupils)
viel	much, a lot of
ziemlich viel	a good deal of (money, etc.)

sehr viel	a great deal of	Null	zero+, (~ zeichen) zero+, cipher, (~ punkt) zero+
viele	many		
ziemlich viele	a good many		
sehr viele	a great many	Zehner und Einer	tens and units
wenig	little (money, time; to have ~ patience; he knew ~)	zählen	to count
		zahlreich	numerous
		unzählig	innumerable
wenige	few	Nummer, numerieren	(to) number
ein Paar	pair (of shoes, gloves, eyes, horses; a happy ~), (nicht zusammengehörig) couple (bought a ~ of eggs, pigeons)		
		zusammenzählen, addieren	to add
		abziehen, subtrahieren	to subtract
		vervielfachen, multiplizieren	to multiply
Dutzend	dozen		
20 Stück	a score (of...)	teilen, dividieren	to divide
e-e Reihe, Folge, Serie	a series+ (of events, misfortunes, letters, lectures)	doppelt, verdoppeln	(to) double
		Summe	sum (a large ~ of money)
e. Haufen	a heap (of sand, coal, rubbish)		
		Gesamtbetrag	the total
aufgeschichteter H., Stapel	pile (of books, of bricks, etc.)	rechnen	s. Kap. 3.1. (S. 22)
		er kann gut r.	he is good at figures*
die Hauptmasse	the bulk (the ~ of the population)	**Maß**	measure
		Längenmaß	linear measure
der Rest	rest (two articles are interesting, the ~ are dull; for the ~ of his life); (bes math) remainder (the ~ of his life, of the books; 10−8: the ~ is 2); remains (~ of Pompeii); remnants (a sale of ~); balance (~ to be paid within 2 weeks); residue (water leaves a ~ of lime)	Flächenmaß	square measure
		Raummaß	cubic measure, measure of volume
		Hohlmaß	measure of capacity
		Flüssigkeitsmaß	liquid measure
		Trockenmaß	dry measure
		Maßeinheit	unit (e.g. ~ of length, of time)
		Normalmaß	standard (measure)
		e-e genaue Messung	an exact measurement
		messen	to measure (a piece of ground; this room ~s 30 feet across)
Zahl	number		
Grundzahl	cardinal n.		
Ordnungszahl	ordinal n.	Skala, Gradeinteilung	scale, graduation
gerade Zahl	even n.		
ungerade Zahl	odd n.	Maßstab	yardstick, criterion*+, (auf Karten) scale
ganze Zahl	whole n.		
Bruchzahl	fractional n.		
Bruch	fraction	Gewicht	weight
Ziffer	figure*	Inhalt	contents
arabische Ziffer	Arabic numeral	enthalten	to contain
römische Ziffer	Roman numeral	Fassungsvermögen	capacity
		Zoll	inch (= 2,54 cm)

Fuß	foot (= 12 inches, = 30,48 cm)
Yard	yard (= 3 feet, = 91,44 cm)
Meile	mile (= 1760 yards, = 1,6 km)
Quadratzoll	square inch (= 6,45 qcm)
Quadratfuß	square foot (= 144 sq. in., = 929 qcm)
Kubikzoll	cubic inch (= 16,39 ccm)
Kubikfuß	cubic foot (= 1728 cu. in., = 0,028 cbm)
Viertelpinte	gill* (= BE 0,14 l, US 0,12 l)
Pinte	pint* (= 4 gills, BE = 0,57 l, US = 0,47 l)
Quart	quart (= 2 pints, BE = 1,14 l, US = 0,95 l)
Gallone	gallon (= 4 quarts, BE = 4,55 l, US = 3,79 l)
Unze	ounce (= 28,35 g)
engl. Pfund	pound (= 16 ounces, = 453,59 g)
Zentner	hundredweight+ (BE = 112 pounds, = 50,8 kg; US = 100 pounds, = 45,34 kg)
britische Tonne	long ton (= 2240 pounds, = 1016 kg)
amerikan. Tonne	short ton (= 2000 pounds, = 907,19 kg)
(metrische) Tonne (= 1000 kg)	metric ton(ne)
Stein (Körpergewicht)	stone+ (= 14 pounds, = 6,35 kg)
Handelsgewicht	avoirdupois* weight
Feingewicht	troy weight
Geschwindigkeit	speed
Höchst~	top~
mit e-r ~ von...	at the rate of (50 miles an hour)

30. Die Zeit

Zeit	time
im Laufe der ~	in (the) course of t.
vergehen	to pass
früh(zeitig)	early (at an ~ hour)
spät	late
sich verspäten	to be (too) late
Zeitabschnitt	period
Stadium	stage
Zeitalter	age (the Stone Age; the ~ of Enlightenment)
Ära, Zeitrechnung	era* (the Christian* ~ ; an ~ of progress)
Epoche	epoch*
vorgeschichtlich	prehistoric
Steinzeit	Stone Age
Altertum, Antike	antiquity
Mittelalter	the Middle Ages
mittelalterlich	medieval*
Aufklärung	(Age of) Enlightenment
Zeitgenosse	contemporary
Zeitraum	space of time, period
bestimmte, begrenzte Frist	term (the president is elected for a ~ of four years)
Dauer	duration
Zwischenraum, Pause	interval, break
Zwischenzeit	meantime
Unterbrechung	interruption
Verzögerung	delay
dauern	to last
dauernd	lasting (~impressions), permanent (a ~institution)
dauerhaft	durable
immerwährend	everlasting (joy)
ewig	eternal
Ewigkeit	eternity
fortwährend, fortgesetzt	continuous (noise, labour), *(immer wiederkehrend)* continual (noise, supply of goods, interruptions)

(be)ständig	constant	**Jahreszeit**	season
stetig	steady (increase)	Frühling	spring
unaufhörlich	perpetual, incessant, ceaseless	Sommer	summer
		Herbst	autumn, US fall
ununterbrochen	uninterrupted	Winter	winter
zeitweilig	temporary (relief, possession)	**Monat**	month
		monatlich	monthly
flüchtig, vorübergehend, kurzfristig	transient (gleam of hope), passing (joys)	**Woche**	week
vergänglich	transitory (life is ~)	wöchentlich	weekly
momentan (nur einen Augenblick dauernd)	momentary (confusion of thought)	**Tag**	day
		täglich	daily
		Morgen	morning (in the ~)
plötzlich	sudden (~ change)	Vormittag	morning (late in the ~)
augenblicklich, sofortig	instantaneous, immediate (~ effect; this is for ~ use)	Mittag	noon (at ~), midday
		Nachmittag	afternoon* (in the ~)
gleichzeitig	simultaneous		
allmählich	gradual (improvement)	Abend	evening (in the ~)
		Nacht	night (in the ~)
Gegenwart	the present (time)	Mitternacht	midnight (at ~)
gegenwärtig	present	Tagesanbruch	daybreak
Vergangenheit	the past	bei Anbruch der Nacht	at nightfall
vergangen	past		
kürzlich (geschehen)	recent (events)	Dämmerung	*(Morgen~)* dawn, *(Abend~)* dusk
früher	former (in ~ times; my ~ occupation)	Zwielicht	twilight
		Dunkelheit	darkness
seit unvordenklichen Zeiten	from time immemorial	**Stunde**	hour
		e-e Viertelstunde	a quarter of an hour
Zukunft	the future	Minute	minute*
die unmittelbare Zukunft	the immediate future	Sekunde	second
zukünftig	future	**Augenblick**	moment (the decisive ~, the finest ~ of her life), *(fast nicht wahrnehmbar)* instant (it passed in an ~; not an ~ too soon)
Nachwelt	posterity		
Kalender	calendar		
Datum	date		
das genaue Datum	the exact date		
Feiertag	holiday		
Glücks-, Festtag	red-letter day		
Jahr	year	**Uhrzeit: Wieviel Uhr ist es?**	What time is it? What is the time?
Schaltjahr	leap-year		
Jahrzehnt	decade*	Sonnenuhr	sundial
Jahrhundert	century	Uhr	s. Kap. 8.2., 7. (S. 55/50)
Jahrtausend	millennium+		

Anhang

1. Aussprache

abdomen [ˈæbdəmən, bes. US æbˈdəʊmən]
ache [eɪk]
accumulate [əˈkjuːmjʊleɪt]
accuracy [ˈækjʊrəsɪ]
admirable [ˈædmərəbl]
address [əˈdres, bes. US a. ˈædres]
addressee [ædreˈsiː]
advertise [ˈædvətaɪz]
advertisement [ədˈvɜːtɪz-, US ædvərˈtaɪzmənt]
aerial [ˈeərɪəl]
afternoon [ɑːftəˈnuːn]
agenda [əˈdʒendə]
alien [ˈeɪlɪən]
allege [əˈledʒ]
altimeter [ˈæltɪmiːtə]
alto [ˈæltəʊ]
aluminium [æljʊˈmɪnɪəm], US aluminum [əˈluːmənəm]
amateur [ˈæmətə, -tʃʊə]
amortize [əˈmɔːtaɪz, US ˈæmərtaɪz]
anaesthesia [ænɪsˈθiːzɪə, US -ˈθiːʒə]
anaesthetic [ænɪsˈθetɪk]
anchor [ˈæŋkə]
anxiety [æŋˈzaɪətɪ]
apoplexy [ˈæpəpleksɪ]
apostle [əˈpɒsl]
apostrophe [əˈpɒstrəfɪ]
appendicitis [əpendɪˈsaɪtɪs]
appropriate [əˈprəʊprɪɪt]
aquamarine [ækwəməˈriːn]
aquaplane [ˈækwəpleɪn]
archangel [ˈɑːkeɪndʒl]
archives [ˈɑːkaɪvz]
arithmetic [əˈrɪθmətɪk]
artiste [ɑːˈtiːst]
asylum [əˈsaɪləm]
atmosphere [ˈætməsfɪə]

atmospheric [ætməsˈferɪk]
attaché [əˈtæʃeɪ, US ætəˈʃeɪ]
attorney [əˈtɜːnɪ]
avalanche [ˈævəlɑːnʃ, US -lænʃ]
avoirdupois [ævədəˈpɔɪz]
axis [ˈæksɪs]
ballet [ˈbæleɪ]
banana [bəˈnɑːnə, US bəˈnænə]
baptize [bæpˈtaɪz]
baroque [bəˈrɒk, bes. US bəˈrəʊk]
barrage [ˈbæraːʒ, bes. US bəˈrɑːʒ]
bass [beɪs]
bayonet [ˈbeɪənɪt]
beret [ˈbereɪ, US bəˈreɪ]
biology [baɪˈɒlədʒɪ]
biscuit [ˈbɪskɪt]
blouse [blaʊz]
boletus [bəˈliːtəs]
bomber [ˈbɒmə]
bough [baʊ]
bow (Bogen) [bəʊ]
bow (Schiffsbug; Verbeugung) [baʊ]; to bow [baʊ]
bowl [bəʊl]
breeches [ˈbrɪtʃɪz, US ˈbriː-]
brigadier [brɪgəˈdɪə]
briquette [brɪˈket]
brooch [brəʊtʃ]
budgerigar [ˈbʌdʒɪrɪˈgɑː]
buoy [bɔɪ, US bɔɪ, ˈbuːɪ]
bureau [ˈbjʊərəʊ]
burial [ˈberɪəl]
bury [ˈberɪ]
bush [bʊʃ]
bushel [ˈbʊʃl]
business [ˈbɪznɪs]
businessman [ˈbɪznɪsmæn]
busy [ˈbɪzɪ]
butcher [ˈbʊtʃə]

caecum [ˈsiːkəm]
café [ˈkæfeɪ, US kæfeɪˈ]
cafeteria [kæfɪˈtɪərɪə]
callisthenics [kælɪsˈθenɪks]
canary [kəˈneərɪ]
canoe [kəˈnuː]
caprice [kəˈpriːs]
capriciousness [kəˈprɪʃəsnɪs]
capsize [kæpˈsaɪz, US ˈkæpsaɪz]
caravan [ˈkærəvæn]
casual [ˈkæʒʊəl, ˈkæʒwəl]
catarrh [kəˈtɑː]
catastrophe [kəˈtæstrəfɪ]
cease [siːs]
celeriac [sɪˈlerɪæk]
cello [ˈtʃeləʊ]
cemetery [ˈsemɪtrɪ, US ˈsemətərɪ]
cereals [ˈsɪərɪəlz, US ˈsɪrɪəlz]
cha-cha [ˈtʃɑːtʃɑː]
chamber [ˈtʃeɪmbə]
chamois (Gemse) [ˈʃæmwɑː, US mst. ˈʃæmɪ]; (Leder) [ˈʃæmɪ]
champagne [ʃæmˈpeɪn]
chanterelle [tʃɑːntəˈrel, tʃæn-, US ʃæntəˈrel]
chassis [ˈʃæsɪ]
chemist [ˈkemɪst]
cheque [tʃek]
chestnut [ˈtʃesnʌt]
chlorine [ˈklɔːriːn]
choir [kwaɪə]
chord [kɔːd]
chorus [ˈkɔːrəs]
Christ [kraɪst]
christen [ˈkrɪsn]
Christian [ˈkrɪstʃən]
Christmas [ˈkrɪsməs]
circuit [ˈsɜːkɪt]
clarinet [klærɪˈnet]
cleanliness [ˈklenlɪnɪs]
cleanse [klenz]
clerk [klɑːk, US klɜːrk]

124

cloth [klɒθ]
clothes [kləʊðz]
cobalt ['kəʊbɔːlt, BE a.
 kəʊ'bɔːlt]
cocoa ['kəʊkəʊ]
coerce [kəʊ'ɜːs]
colonel ['kɜːnəl]
comb [kəʊm]
combat ['kɒmbət, 'kʌm-,
 bes. US kəm'bæt]
comment ['kɒment]
compass ['kʌmpəs]
complaisant
 [kəm'pleɪzənt, bes. US
 kəm'pleɪsənt]
composure [kəm'pəʊʒə]
compote ['kɒmpəʊt]
comrade ['kɒmrɪd, US
 'kɒmræd]
conceit/ed [kən'siːt/ɪd]
conciliatory [kən'sɪlɪətərɪ,
 US -'sɪljətɔːrɪ]
conjurer ['kʌndʒərə]
conquer ['kɒŋkə]
conqueror ['kɒŋkərə]
conquest ['kɒŋkwest]
conscientious
 [kɒnʃɪ'enʃəs]
constable ['kʌnstəbl]
constituency
 [kən'stɪtjʊənsɪ]
cough [kɒf, bes. US kɔːf]
courage ['kʌrɪdʒ, US
 'kɜːr-]
courageous [kə'reɪdʒəs]
court [kɔːt]
courtesy ['kɜːtɪsɪ]
crepe [kreɪp]
criterion [kraɪ'tɪərɪən]
cucumber ['kjuːkʌmbə]
cuisine [kwɪ'ziːn]
cupboard ['kʌbəd]
cushion ['kʊʃɪn]

dachshund ['dækshʊnd]
dandelion ['dændɪlaɪən]
deaf [def]
debt [det]
decade ['dekeɪd]
decrepit [dɪ'krepɪt]

Derby ['dɑːbɪ, US
 'dɜːrbɪ], US derby
 (steifer Hut)['dɜːrbɪ]
desert (wüst, Wüste)
 ['dezət]
desert (Verdienst)[dɪ'zɜːt]
to desert [dɪ'zɜːt]
dessert [dɪ'zɜːt]
detour ['diːtʊə, US a.
 dɪ'tʊər]
devil [devl]
diabetes [daɪə'biːtiːz]
diabetic [daɪə'betɪk]
dialogue ['daɪəlɒg]
diameter [daɪ'æmɪtə]
differentiate
 [dɪfə'renʃɪeɪt]
digest [dɪ'dʒest]
dilettante [dɪlɪ'tæntɪ]
diocese ['daɪəsɪs, -siːs]
diphtheria [dɪf'θɪərɪə]
diplomat ['dɪpləmæt]
disciple [dɪ'saɪpl]
disease [dɪ'ziːz]
donkey ['dɒŋkɪ]
double-bass ['dʌbl-'beɪs]
doubt [daʊt]
dough [dəʊ]
draught [drɑːft, US dræft]
drought [draʊt]

eclipse [ɪ'klɪps]
efficacious [efɪ'keɪʃəs]
either ['aɪðə, US 'iːðər]
emigré ['emɪgreɪ, US
 emɪ'greɪ]
encyclopaedia
 [ensaɪklə'piːdɪə]
entrepreneur
 [ɒntrəprə'nɜː]
epoch ['iːpɒk, US 'epək]
equality [ɪ'kwɒlɪtɪ]
era ['ɪərə]
espionage ['espɪənɑːʒ]
exchequer [ɪks'tʃekə]

facile ['fæsaɪl, US 'fæsəl]
Fahrenheit ['færənhaɪt]
falcon ['fɔːlkən, US
 'fælkən]

farina [fə'raɪnə, US
 fə'riːnə]
fatigue [fə'tiːg]
fiancé(e) [fɪ'ɒnseɪ, US
 fiːɑːn'seɪ]
fibre ['faɪbə]
figure ['fɪgə, US fɪgjər]
folk [fəʊk]
forehead ['fɒrɪd]
frontier ['frʌntjə, US
 frʌn'tɪər]
fungus ['fʌŋgəs]
furrier ['fʌrɪə, US 'fɜːrɪər]

gabardine [gæbə'diːn,
 bes. US 'gæbədiːn]
gaol (= jail) [dʒeɪl]
garage ['gærɑːʒ, 'gærɪdʒ,
 US gə'rɑːʒ]
gaseous ['gæsɪəs]
gateau [gɑː'təʊ]
genus ['dʒiːnəs]
giant ['dʒaɪənt]
giddy ['gɪdɪ]
gill (Maß)[dʒɪl]
giraffe [dʒɪ'rɑːf, US
 dʒə'ræf]
gist [dʒɪst]
glacier ['glæsjə, US
 'gleɪʃər]
gnat [næt]
gnaw [nɔː]
gooseberry ['gʊzbərɪ, US
 'guːsberɪ]
guarantee [gærən'tiː]
guinea ['gɪnɪ]
guitar [gɪ'tɑː]
gymnasium
 [dʒɪm'neɪzjəm]
gymnast ['dʒɪmnæst]

hangar ['hæŋə]
haughtiness ['hɔːtɪnɪs]
headache ['hedeɪk]
heir [eə]
hero ['hɪərəʊ]
heroine ['herəʊɪn]
heroism ['herəʊɪzm]
horizon [hə'raɪzn]

125

housewife *(Hausfrau)*
['haʊswaɪf]
hover ['hɒvə, US 'hʌvər]
hydrogen ['haɪdrədʒən]
hyena [haɪ'i:nə]
hymn [hɪm]

incomparable
[ɪn'kɒmpərəbl]
inexorable [ɪn'eksərəbl]
ingenious [ɪn'dʒi:njəs]
ingenuous [ɪn'dʒenjʊəs]
injure ['ɪndʒə]
interrogate [ɪn'terəgeɪt]
intestines [ɪn'testɪnz]
intimacy ['ɪntɪməsɪ]
inventory ['ɪnvəntrɪ, US
'ɪnvəntɔ:rɪ]
iron ['aɪən]
irony ['aɪərənɪ]
irreconcilable
[ɪ'rekənsaɪləbl]
irreparable [ɪ'repərəbl]
issue ['ɪʃu:]

javelin ['dʒævlɪn]
jeopardy ['dʒepədɪ]
juice [dʒu:s]

kitchenette [kɪtʃɪ'net]
knowledge ['nɒlɪdʒ]

laboratory [lə'bɒrətərɪ,
bes. US 'læbrətɔ:rɪ]
lament [lə'ment]
lead *(Blei)*[led]
learned *(adj.)*['lə:nɪd]
leisure ['leʒə, US 'li:ʒər]
lemon ['lemən]
lettuce ['letɪs]
lever ['li:və, US 'levər]
lieutenant [BE lef'tenənt,
US lu:'tenənt]
lilac ['laɪlək]
linen ['lɪnɪn]
liqueur [lɪ'kjʊə, US
lɪ'kə:r]
liquid ['lɪkwɪd]
loggia ['lɒdʒə]
longitude ['lɒndʒɪtju:d]

long-winded ['lɒŋ'wɪndɪd]

machine [mə'ʃi:n]
mahogany [mə'hɒgənɪ]
major ['meɪdʒə]
mankind [mæn'kaɪnd]
manoeuvre, US
maneuver [mə'nu:və]
margarine [mɑ:dʒə'ri:n,
bes. US 'mɑ:rdʒərɪ(:)n]
mass *(Messe)*[mæs, BE *a.*
mɑ:s]
matinée ['mætɪneɪ, US
mætə'neɪ]
mayor [meə, US 'meɪər]
medieval [medɪ'i:vəl, *bes.*
US mi:dɪ-]
menu ['menju:]
meteor ['mi:tjə]
meteorological
[mi:tjərə'lɒdʒɪkəl]
meteorology
[mi:tjə'rɒlədʒɪ]
microphone
['maɪkrəfəʊn]
mimeograph
['mɪmɪəgrɑ:f, US -græf]
minute *(winzig)*
[maɪ'nju:t]; *(Minute)*
['mɪnɪt]
mischief ['mɪstʃɪf]
missile ['mɪsaɪl, US 'mɪsəl]
mistletoe ['mɪsltəʊ]
molecule ['mɒlɪkju:l]
monotonous
[mə'nɒtənəs]
moral ['mɒrəl]
mortgage ['mɔ:gɪdʒ]
mosquito [məs'ki:təʊ]
motif [məʊ'ti:f]
moustache [məs'tɑ:ʃ], US
mustache ['mʌstæʃ]
muscle [mʌsl]

naive [nɑ:'i:v]
naked ['neɪkɪd]
nausea ['nɔ:sɪə, US 'nɔ:ʃə]
navel ['neɪvəl]
NCO ['en'si:'əʊ]
necklace ['neklɪs]

née [neɪ]
ne'er-do-well ['neəduwel]
neither ['naɪðə, US
'ni:ðər]
neologism [nɪ'ɒlədʒɪzm]
nephew ['nevju:, US
'nefju:]
neurology [njʊə'rɒlədʒɪ]
nicety ['naɪsɪtɪ]
niece [ni:s]
nitrogen ['naɪtrədʒən]
nucleus ['nju:klɪəs]

oasis [əʊ'eɪsɪs]
oblique [ə'bli:k]
obstetrics [ɒb'stetrɪks]
occurrence [ə'kʌrəns, US
ə'kɜ:rəns]
oesophagus [i:'sɒfəgəs]
omelet(te) ['ɒmlɪt]
onion ['ʌnjən]
opaque [əʊ'peɪk]
ophthalmology
[ɒfθæl'mɒlədʒɪ]
ophthalmologist
[ɒfθæl'mɒlədʒɪst]
orator ['ɒrətə]
orchestra ['ɔ:kɪstrə]
original [ə'rɪdʒənəl]
Orion [ə'raɪən]
orthopaedics
[ɔ:θəʊ'pi:dɪks]
oven [ʌvən]
oxygen ['ɒksɪdʒən]

paediatrics [pi:dɪ'ætrɪks]
paediatrician
[pi:dɪə'trɪʃən]
palate ['pælɪt]
parachute ['pærəʃu:t]
parenthesis [pə'renθɪsɪs]
parliament ['pɑ:ləmənt]
pear [peə]
pekingese [pi:kɪŋ'i:z]
peony ['pɪənɪ]
personnel [pɜ:sə'nel]
physique [fɪ'zi:k]
piano [pɪ'ænəʊ]
pianist ['pɪənɪst, US
pɪ'ænɪst]

piquant [ˈpiːkənt]
plague [pleɪg]
plait [plæt, US pleɪt]
plateau [ˈplætəʊ, US plæˈtəʊ]
platinum [ˈplætɪnəm]
plebiscite [ˈplebɪsɪt, bes. US -saɪt]
plumber [ˈplʌmə]
pneumonia [njʊˈməʊnjə]
poll [pəʊl]
porcelain [ˈpɔːslɪn, US ˈpɔːrsələn]
portmanteau [pɔːtˈmæntəʊ]
Poste Restante [ˈpəʊst ˈrestɑːnt, US resˈtɑːnt]
pour [pɔː]
P. O. W. [ˈpiː ˈəʊ ˈdʌbljuː]
prayer [preə]
preface [ˈprefɪs]
Premier [ˈpremɪə, US prɪˈmɪər]
prestige [presˈtiːʒ]
procedure [prəˈsiːdʒə]
promontory [ˈprɒməntərɪ, US -tɔːrɪ]
pronunciation [prənʌnsɪˈeɪʃən]
prophecy [ˈprɒfɪsɪ]
prophesy [ˈprɒfɪsaɪ]
psalm [sɑːm]
psychology [saɪˈkɒlədʒɪ]
pulpit [ˈpʊlpɪt]

quay [kiː]
questionnaire [kwestʃəˈneə]
queue [kjuː]

rachitis [ræˈkaɪtɪs]
radar [ˈreɪdɑː]
rainbow [ˈreɪnbəʊ]
raspberry [ˈrɑːzbərɪ, US ˈræzberɪ]
rather [ˈrɑːðə, US ˈræðər]
ravine [rəˈviːn]
realm [relm]
receipt [rɪˈsiːt]
recipe [ˈresɪpɪ]

recollect [rekəˈlekt]
recommend/ation [rekəˈmend, rekəmenˈdeɪʃən]
recompense [ˈrekəmpens]
reconcile [ˈrekənsaɪl]
reconciliation [rekənsɪlɪˈeɪʃən]
regiment [ˈredʒɪmənt]
Renaissance [rəˈneɪsəns, bes. US renəˈsɑːns]
repartee [repɑːˈtiː, US repərˈtiː]
reservoir [ˈrezəvwɑː]
righteous [ˈraɪtʃəs]
rococo [rəˈkəʊkəʊ]
rugged [ˈrʌgɪd]

salmon [ˈsæmən]
sandwich [ˈsænwɪdʒ, US -wɪtʃ]
sapphire [ˈsæfaɪə]
saucepan [ˈsɔːspən, US -pæn]
sausage [ˈsɒsɪdʒ, US ˈsɔːsɪdʒ]
scarce [skeəs]
scarlatina [skɑːləˈtiːnə]
scenario [sɪˈnɑːrɪəʊ, US sɪˈnɛərɪəʊ]
sceptic [ˈskeptɪk]
schedule [ˈʃedjuːl, US ˈskedʒʊl]
scheme [skiːm]
sciatica [saɪˈætɪkə]
sculpture [ˈskʌlptʃə]
scythe [saɪð]
semolina [seməˈliːnə]
sew [səʊ]
sewer(age) [ˈsjʊər(ɪdʒ)]
shove [ʃʌv]
sieve [sɪv]
sign [saɪn]
signal [ˈsɪgnəl]
signature [ˈsɪgnɪtʃə]
ski [skiː]
skier [skɪə]
soccer [ˈsɒkə]
slovenly [ˈslʌvənlɪ]
somersault [ˈsʌməsɔːlt]

soprano [səˈprɑːnəʊ, US səˈprænəʊ]
souvenir [suːvəˈnɪə, ˈsuːvənɪə]
species [ˈspiːʃiːz]
speedometer [spiːˈdɒmɪtə]
spinach [ˈspɪnɪdʒ, US -ɪtʃ]
sponge [spʌndʒ]
stingy [ˈstɪndʒɪ]
stomach [ˈstʌmək]
strafe [strɑːf, US streɪf]
stratagem [ˈstrætədʒəm]
strophe [ˈstrəʊfɪ]
studio [ˈstjuːdɪəʊ]
subtle [sʌtl]
suet [sjʊɪt]
sugar [ˈʃʊgə]
suggest [səˈdʒest, US səgˈdʒest]
suicide [ˈsjʊɪsaɪd]
sulphur [ˈsʌlfə]
sundae [ˈsʌndɪ]
superficiality [sjuːpəfɪʃɪˈælɪtɪ]
swear [sweə]
sweat [swet]
sweater [ˈswetə]

tablecloth [ˈteɪblklɒθ]
technique [tekˈniːk]
tenement [ˈtenɪmənt]
tenor [ˈtenə]
thistle [θɪsl]
thorough [ˈθʌrə, US ˈθɜːrəʊ]
thoroughfare [ˈθʌrəfeə, US ˈθɜːrəfeər]
thyroid [ˈθaɪrɔɪd]
tissue [ˈtɪʃuː]
tomato [təˈmɑːtəʊ, US -ˈmeɪtəʊ]
tomb [tuːm]
toothache [ˈtuːθeɪk]
topaz [ˈtəʊpæz]
tortoise [ˈtɔːtəs]
trachea [trəˈkiːə, US ˈtreɪkɪə]
tributary [ˈtrɪbjʊtərɪ, US -terɪ]

127

tributary ['trɪbjʊtərɪ, US -terɪ]
trousseau ['truːsəʊ, US truːˈsəʊ]
turquoise ['tɜːkwɔɪz, US -kɔɪz, -kwɔɪz]
tuxedo [tʌkˈsiːdəʊ]
tyrant ['taɪərənt]
tyranny ['tɪrənɪ]

vague [veɪg]
valise [vəˈliːz, US vəˈliːs]
vase [vɑːz, US veɪs]
vaudeville ['vɔːdəvɪl, 'vəʊ-, US 'vɔːdvɪl, 'vəʊ-]
vehicle ['viːɪkl]

venison [venzn, US 'venəzən]
veterinary ['vetərɪnərɪ, US -rənerɪ]
vinegar ['vɪnɪgə]
vineyard ['vɪnjəd]
violin [vaɪəˈlɪn]
violoncello [vaɪələnˈtʃeləʊ]
visa(ed) ['viːzə(d)]

waistcoat ['weɪskəʊt]
weapon ['wepən]
weary ['wɪərɪ]
whooping-cough ['huːpɪŋkɒf, US -kɔːf]
wicked ['wɪkɪd]

width [wɪdθ]
wilderness ['wɪldənɪs]
wound *(Wunde)* [wuːnd]
wretched ['retʃɪd]

xylophone ['zaɪləfəʊn]

yacht [jɒt]
yolk [jəʊk]

zeal [ziːl]
zealous ['zeləs]
zebra ['ziːbrə]
zoology [zəʊˈɒlədʒɪ]
zwieback ['zwiːbæk, 'tsviːbɑːk, US 'zwaɪbæk]

2. Unregelmäßige Plurale

Alle Zusammensetzungen mit *-man, -woman* bilden den Plural wie *man* und *woman*.

aircraft, aircraft
alto, altos
antenna [ænˈtenə] *(Fühler, Antenne)*
antennae [ænˈteniː], in der Bedeutung *Antenne* auch antennas
apparatus, apparatus *oder bes.* BE apparatuses
appendix [əˈpendɪks] *(Blinddarm)* appendixes [əˈpendɪksɪz], *(Anhang)* appendices [əˈpendɪsiːz]
axis, axes ['æksiːz]

bacillus [bəˈsɪləs], bacilli [bəˈsɪlaɪ]
bacterium [bækˈtɪərɪəm], bacteria [bækˈtɪərɪə]
boletus, boletuses
bison, bison
buffalo, buffalo *oder* buffaloes
bureau, bureaux ['bjʊərəʊz], US *mst.* bureaus

caecum [siːkəm], caeca ['siːkə]
calf, calves
cargo, cargoes, US *a.* cargos
carp, carp
cello ['tʃeləʊ], cellos
chassis ['ʃæsɪ], chassis ['ʃæsɪz]
circus, circuses
cod, cod
court martial, courts martial
craft *(Schiff, Flugzeug)*, craft
crisis, crises ['kraɪsiːz]
criterion [kraɪˈtɪərɪən], criteria [kraɪˈtɪərɪə] (US *öfter* criterions)
curriculum, curriculums *oder* curricula

deer, deer
diagnosis [daɪəgˈnəʊsɪs], diagnoses [daɪəgˈnəʊsiːz]
dice, dice

echo, echoes

formula ['fɔːmjʊlə] *(math., wiss.)* formulae ['fɔːmjʊliː], *sonst* formulas
fungus ['fʌŋgəs], fungi ['fʌŋgaɪ, 'fʌndʒaɪ], funguses

gateau, gateaux [gɑːˈtəʊz]
genus ['dʒiːnəs], genera ['dʒenərə]
goose, geese
gymnasium, gymnasiums

haddock, haddock
hero, heroes
hippo, hippos
hippopotamus, hippopotamuses, *a.* hippopotami [hɪpəˈpɒtəmaɪ]
hundredweight, hundredweight

index *(Register)* indexes

['ɪndeksɪz], *(math. Index)* indices ['ɪndɪsiːz]

knife, knives

larva [ˈlɑːvə], larvae [ˈlɑːviː]
larynx [ˈlærɪŋks], larynxes [ˈlærɪŋksɪz]
leaf, leaves
libretto, librettos *oder* libretti [lɪˈbretiː]
louse, lice

mackerel, mackerel
man, men
midwife, midwives
millennium, millenniums (*a.* millennia)
mosquito, mosquitoes
mouse, mice

nebula [ˈnebjʊlə], nebulae [ˈnebjʊliː], US *mst.* nebulas
nucleus [ˈnjuːklɪəs], nuclei [ˈnjuːklɪaɪ] (US *a.* nucleuses

oasis, oases [əʊˈeɪsiːz]
oath, oaths [əʊðz]
oesophagus [iːˈsɒfəgəs], oesophagi [iːˈsɒfəgaɪ, iːˈsɒfədʒaɪ]

ox, oxen

parenthesis [pəˈrenθɪsɪs], parentheses [pəˈrenθɪsiːz]
pelvis, pelves [ˈpelviːz] (*a.* pelvises)
phenomenon [fɪˈnɒmɪnən], phenomena [fɪˈnɒmɪnə], US *a.* phenomenons
pike, pike
pincenez [ˈpænsneɪ]
pincenez [ˈpænsneɪz]
plaice, plaice
plateau, plateaus *oder* plateaux [ˈplætəʊz]
potato, potatoes

salmon, salmon
sanatorium, sanatoriums *oder* sanatoria
scarf, scarfs *oder* scarves
scenario, scenarios
series, series [ˈsɪəriːz]
sheep, sheep
shelf, shelves
shellfish, shellfish
sinus [ˈsaɪnəs], sinuses [ˈsaɪnəsɪz]
snipe, snipe
soprano, sopranos
species, species [ˈspiːʃiːz]
stadium, stadiums *oder* stadia

stimulus [ˈstɪmjʊləs], stimuli [ˈstɪmjʊlaɪ]
stone *(Gewicht)*, stone
studio, studios
syllabus [ˈsɪləbəs], syllabuses (*a.* syllabi [ˈsɪləbaɪ])
synthesis [ˈsɪnθɪsɪs], syntheses [ˈsɪnθɪsiːz]

tango, tangos
tibia, tibiae [ˈtɪbiiː]
titmouse, titmice
tomato, tomatoes
torpedo, torpedoes
tooth, teeth
trachea [trəˈkiːə], tracheae [trəˈkiːiː]
trout, trout
truth, truths [truːðz]
turbot, turbot

vermin, vermin
violoncello, violoncellos [vaɪələnˈtʃeləʊz]
virus, viruses
volcano, volcanoes
wharf, wharfs, *bes.* US wharves
wife, wives
wolf, wolves
woman, women [ˈwɪmɪn]
wreath, wreaths [riːðz]

zero, zeros, US *a.* zeroes

Schlußbemerkung

Die Aneignung des englischen Wortschatzes (vor allem in den Grundlagen) wird dem Lernenden deutscher Muttersprache durch die Verwandtschaft der beiden Sprachen erleichtert. Nicht wenige englische Wörter indogermanisch-germanischer Herkunft, die mannigfachen Bereichen des Alltags angehören, decken sich in Form und Bedeutung noch fast ganz mit den entsprechenden deutschen Wörtern (father, son, widow; house, home, bed; name; friend, guest; arm, finger, hand, elbow, shoulder, breast, lip, nose, rib, lungs, foot, hair, blood; hunger, thirst; milk, bread, salt; ox, cow, hen; fox, wolf, bear, roebuck, mouse, stork, swan, finch, starling, bee, wasp, worm; nest; field, bush, garden, grass, hay, straw, flax; hat, shoe; hoof; fire, ashes; baker, miller, smith; water, fish, ship; thing; axe, hammer, net, saddle, shovel; gold, sand, stone, glass, leather, wool; sun, moon; summer, winter; north, west, east; wind, weather, snow, frost; day, yesterday, night, year; world; work; word; book; long, broad, deep, thick, thin; hard, stiff, sharp, loud; blue, brown, green; cold, warm, mild, bitter, sour, ripe, fresh; blind, naked; open, full, half; good, better, best, free, young; alone; begin, help, send, sleep, dream, sing, bite, wash, drink, think, thank, sit, forbid, forget, I can; born; my, we; and, here, often, more; six, seven, ten, hundred, thousand u. a.). Bei einer großen Anzahl anderer Wörter germanischer Herkunft ist die Ähnlichkeit nicht ganz so sinnfällig, aber immer noch groß genug, um dem Gedächtnis eine Stütze bieten zu können. Auch viele Wörter aus dem Lehnwortgut (z. B. wine, oil, butter, radish, plum, pepper, rice, pound, copper, kettle, cat, cook, market, school, forest, coast, anchor, mass, cost, fine) und natürlich auch viele neuere Fremdwörter stehen unseren Wortformen sehr nahe.

Der Lernende darf aber nicht übersehen, daß die äußere Ähnlichkeit auch Gefahren in sich birgt und für ihn zu einer Fehlerquelle werden kann. In vielen Fällen deckt sich die Bedeutung eines englischen Wortes entweder nur zum Teil mit der des ihm etymologisch entsprechenden und äußerlich ganz ähnlichen deutschen Wortes bzw. Fremdwortes oder sie ist völlig von ihr verschieden, z. B. man, wife, bride, flesh, meal (dt. *Mehl*), harvest (dt. *Herbst*), hound, hall, stool, pipe, street, stream, bottom, boat, rudder, ghost; bring, do, make, go, ride, drive, wander, warn; marmalade, toast, comfort, compass, control, intelligence, minister, paragraph, process, residence, rent, sensation, to adopt, to realize, to protest; wall, dish, clock, hose, warehouse, deer, shellfish, freshwater, meaning, mood (= *Stimmung, Laune*; vgl. dt. *Mut*), dumb, keen, plump, true; become, behold, overhear, rise, starve, outspoken, also; billet, blame, caution, concern, concurrence, discretion, fabric, gymnasium, map, stadium, actual, brave, consequent, eventual, famous, fatal, genial, gracious, sensible.

Aber auch vom Englischen her gesehen gilt es, sich vor Verwechslungen bei ähnlichen oder ähnlich klingenden Wörtern zu hüten. Nur einige Beispiele seien genannt: artist *(Künstler, bes. Maler)*, artiste* (professional singer, dancer, etc.); ceremonial *[als Adj.] (nicht v. Personen; zeremoniell, feierlich:* a ~ costume), ceremonious (*v. Personen und deren Verhalten; zeremoniös, steif:* ~ people, a ~ bow*); comic *komisch, komödiantisch (a* ~ *opera, a* ~ *paper [Witzblatt])*, comical *komisch, drollig* (a ~ incident, a ~ expression); complacent *(mit sich u. anderen zufrieden)*, complaisant* *(gefällig, willfährig; nachgiebig)*; contemptible *(verächtlich* = *verachtenswert)*, contemptuous (*verächtlich* = *verachtungsvoll:* ~ air; to speak ~ ly of ...); definite *(fest begrenzt, klar umrissen; genau, eindeutig:* a ~ offer, a ~ answer, ~ terms), definitive *(endgültig, unabänderlich:* a ~ offer, a ~ answer, ~terms); delightful *(köstlich, entzückend, wundervoll:* a ~ companion, a ~ evening, a ~ prospect), delicious *(köstlich für Geschmack od. Geruch:* a ~ fruit: *auch:* he has a ~ sense of humour); economic *([volks]wirtschaftlich:* ~ questions, ~ geography, ~ help for

underdeveloped countries), economical *(sparsam)*; elemental (*die Naturgewalten betreffend:* ~power *[elementare Gewalt],* ~ passion), elementary *(grundlegend:* ~ arithmetic *[elementare Ar.],* ~*school [Grundschule];* historical (*das übliche Wort für »geschichtlich«:* ~events, a ~ novel; it is of purely ~ interest), historic (*denkwürdig, geschichtlich merkwürdig:* a ~ debate, a ~ building); human *(menschlich)*, humane *(menschenfreundlich, human)*; imaginable (*denkbar:* the greatest difficulty ~, the only way ~), imaginary (*nur in der Einbildung bestehend, nur vorgestellt, gedacht, eingebildet:* an ~ illness, an ~ line), imaginative *(voll Einbildungskraft, phantasiereich)*; industrial *(industriell, gewerblich)*, industrious *(fleißig)*; ingenious* *(erfinderisch, sinnreich:* an ~ mechanic, an ~ contrivance; *Subst.:* ingenuity *Erfindungsgabe, Scharfsinn)*, ingenuous* *(offenherzig, ungekünstelt:* an ~ young man, an ~ declaration; *Subst.:* ingenuousness); intense *(sehr stark, heftig:* ~ heat, ~emotion, an ~ly cold night), intensive *(konzentriert, angestrengt:* an ~ bombardment, ~study, ~cultivation [of ground] = *intensive [Gegensatz: extensive] Bodenbewirtschaftung)*; judicial *([meist] gerichtlich, richterlich;* ~murder *Justizmord)*, judicious *(verständig, einsichtsvoll)*; legislation *(Gesetzgebung)*, legislature *(gesetzgebende Körperschaft od. Gewalt)*; luxuriant *(üppig im Wachstum* [vgl. exuberant]: ~vegetation, imagination, style [*blütenreicher Stil]*), luxurious (*voll Luxus, luxuriös, schwelgerisch, üppig:* ~palaces, a ~ meal, to lead a ~life); masterful (*herrisch:* ~ manners), masterly (*meisterlich, meisterhaft:* ~ work, a ~ speech, a ~ game); momentary *(augenblicklich, momentan, vorübergehend)*, momentous *(gewichtig, bedeutsam)*; official *(amtlich)*, officious *(übertrieben diensteifrig; offiziös:* an ~ communication); regretful *(Bedauern fühlend od. zeigend)*, regrettable (*bedauerlich:* a ~ misunderstanding); rightful (*rechtmäßig:* the ~ heir), righteous (*rechtschaffen:* a ~ man); sensible (*wahrnehmbar:* ~ phenomena, a ~ difference; *vernünftig:* a ~ man; that is very ~ of him), sensitive (*empfindlich:* a ~ skin, a ~ mind, to be very ~ to heat); sensual (*sinnlich:* ~pleasures, appetite), sensuous *(sinnenfreudig [Mensch, Stil, Dichtung]; nicht in herabsetzendem Sinn)*; spiritual (*geistig [nicht materiell];* geistlich *[nicht weltlich]:* the Lords S~ [*im* House of Lords]); spirituous (*geistig* = alkoholisch: ~ liquors); triumphal *(nicht v. Personen:* ~ arch, ~car), triumphant *(triumphierend, siegreich, glänzend:* a ~ look, a ~ voice; he was ~ at last; it was a ~ success); vacancy *(die Leere; freie, unbesetzte Stelle)*, vacation *(Ferien)*; woollen (*aus Wolle hergestellt:* ~stockings), woolly (*wollig = mit Wolle od. wollähnlichem Haar bedeckt; wollähnlich:* the ~ flock, a ~ head, ~hair; *unklar, verschwommen im Denken u. im Ausdruck). Weitere solche Wörter sind z. B.* affect, effect; base, basis; continual, continuous; council, counsel; deprecate, depreciate; derisive, derisory; distinct, distinctive; effective, efficient, efficacious, effectual; fateful, fatal; inflammable, inflammatory; moral, morale, morality; perspicacity, perspicuity; policy, politics; principal, principle; purport, purpose; recourse, resource, resort; respectable, respectful; reverend, reverent(ial); shade, shadow; use, usage. Die meisten der hier genannten Wörter sind auch für viele, die Englisch als Muttersprache sprechen, eine Quelle des Irrtums.
Für den Lernenden besteht auch sonst des öfteren die Gefahr einer Falschdeutung: vgl. z. B. axe *(Axt)*, axis *(Achse, geometr. u. polit.)*, axle *(Radachse)*; golf *(Golfspiel)*, gulf *(Golf =* *Meerbusen, Abgrund)*; helm *(Steuer eines Schiffs)*, helmet *(Helm)*; physician *(Arzt)*, physicist *(Physiker)*; physics *(Physik)*, physique *(Körperbau)*; police *Polizei; aber Police, Versicherungsschein =* (insurance) policy; postmark = *Poststempel; aber Briefmarke =* (postage-)stamp; provision = *Fürsorge, Vorrat,* aber: *Provision, Vergütung =* commission *(auch = Kommission, Ausschuß)*; typist (*Maschinenschreiber[in]; vgl.* shorthand typist), typewriter *(Schreibmaschine)*; undertaker = *Leichenbestatter* (*Unternehmer =* entrepreneur*, businessman*); self-conscious = *befangen, gehemmt; selbstbewußt =* self-confident, self-reliant.
Schließlich ist noch bei gewissen Wörtern eine (teilweise durch die englische Aussprache

bedingte) von der unsrigen abweichende Schreibung zu beachten, z. B. address, battalion, committee, crystal, flannel, gallery, gallop, gramophone, herring, interval, marmalade, mattress, metal, model, parliament, personnel, platform, purse, rhyme, telegram, violet; eccentric; quartz, waltz.

Literaturangaben

The Concise Oxford Dictionary of Current English. Adapted by H. W. Fowler and F. G. Fowler from the Oxford Dictionary. Fourth edition revised by E. McIntosh. OUP, Oxford 1951; 7th edition 1982.
A. S. Hornby, A Learner's Dictionary of Current English. OUP, Oxford 1948; 4th edition 1989.
Webster's Seventh New Collegiate Dictionary, G. & C. Merriam Company, Springfield 1963.
Jess Stein, The Random House Dictionary of the English Language, Random House, New York 1973.
Webster's Dictionary of Synonyms, G. & C. Merriam Co., Springfield 1973.
The Pocket Oxford German Dictionary, 2nd edition, OUP, Oxford 1962.
Harrap's Standard German & English Dictionary, George G. Harrap & Co., London 1963-1974.
The English Duden, Bibliographisches Institut Mannheim and George G. Harrap & Co., London 1960.
The American College Dictionary. Edited by Clarence L. Barnhart. Random House, New York 1958.
A General Service List of English Words. Compiled and edited by Michael West. London 1953.
A. Reum, A Dictionary of English Style. (Max Hueber Verlag, München 1960).
H. Galinsky, Die Sprache des Amerikaners. Band II, S. 7-44. (Langenscheidt, Berlin 1958).
An English Pronouncing Dictionary by Daniel Jones. 14th edition. J. M. Dent & Sons, London 1977.
J. Windsor Lewis, A Concise Pronouncing Dictionary of British and American English, OUP, London 1972.
V. H. Collins, The Choice of Words, Longmans, Green & Co., London 1953.
H. W. Fowler, A Dictionary of Modern English Usage. OUP, Oxford 1965.
Hans Wilhelm Klein-Wolf Friederich, Englische Synonymik. 4. Aufl., Max Hueber Verlag, München 1975.
Wolf Friederich, Bertelsmann Wörterbuch, Englisch-Deutsch, Deutsch-Englisch, Gütersloh 1981.
Wolf Friederich, Systematischer englischer Wortschatz (Schriftenreihe des Sprachen- und Dolmetscher-Instituts München): Art / Postal Service, Telecommunication, Newspapers / The Weather and the Sky / Family, Household, Food / Education / Human Body, Medicine. Studentenwerk München Lehrmitteldienst München, 1971/75.
Wolf Friederich — Günther Haensch — Edeltraud Lawatsch, Taschenwörterbuch des Fremdenverkehrs, Deutsch-englisch, englisch-deutsch, Max Hueber Verlag, München 1970.
Breitsprecher-Terrell, Collins German-English, English-German Dictionary (= Klett Globalwörterbuch), Collins, London 1983.